HOW WE SHALL
BRING ABOUT
THE REVOLUTION

HOW WE SHALL BRING ABOUT THE REVOLUTION

Syndicalism and the Co-operative Commonwealth

EMILE PATAUD and EMILE POUGET

Foreword by Tom Mann
Preface by Peter Kropotkin

Translated from the French by
Charlotte and Frederic Charles

New Introduction by Geoff Brown

PLUTO  PRESS
London • Winchester, Mass

This edition first published 1990 by Pluto Press
345 Archway Road, London N6 5AA
and 8 Winchester Place, Winchester MA 01890, USA

First published in France in 1909 as
Comment nous ferons la révolution

First published in the UK in English in 1913 as
Syndicalism and the Co-operative Commonwealth

Introduction copyright © 1990 Geoff Brown

British Library Cataloguing in Publication Data
Pataud, Emile
   How we shall bring about the revolution:
   syndicalism and the co-operative commonwealth.
   1. Syndicalism
   I. Title II. Pouget, Emile III. Comment nous ferons la révolu-
tion. *English* 335′.82
   ISBN 1–85305–017–2

Pataud, Emile, b. 1870.
      [Comment nous ferons la révolution. English]
      How we shall bring about the revolution: syndicalism and
   the co-operative commonwealth/Emile Pataud and Emile
   Pouget; foreword by Tom Mann; preface by Peter
   Kropotkin; translated from the French by Charlotte and
   Frederick Charles ; new introduction by Geoff Brown.
         p.   cm.—(Libertarian critique)
      Translation of: Comment nous ferons la révolution.
      ISBN 1–85305–017–2
      1. Syndicalism.   2. Anarchism.   3. Socialism.
   4. Communism.   5. Revolutions and socialism.   I. Pouget,
   Emile, 1860–1931.   II. Title.   III. Series.
   HD6477.P4513   1990
   335′.82—dc20   89–26579
                                                         CIP

Printed in Great Britain by Billing and Sons Ltd, Worcester

CONTENTS.

Drawings by Will Dyson.

INTRODUCTION

GEOFF BROWN

How We Shall Bring About the Revolution, first published in France in 1909 under the title *Comment nous ferons la révolution*, was translated into English by Frederic and Charlotte Charles and published, effectively by them, in Oxford in 1913 as *Syndicalism and the Co-operative Commonwealth* (the latter term was commonly used in the labour movement to denote a socialist society). It is a spirited account of how two French revolutionary syndicalists saw both the processes by which the revolution might come about and how the subsequent, transformed society might organise itself. It is an exposition, in imaginative form, of the doctrines, practices, and aspirations of the French revolutionary syndicalist movement in its most radical period, written, respectively, by one of its leading militants and one of its most outstanding and creative propagandists. With its foreword by Tom Mann, the major advocate in Britain of a version of syndicalism which seemed at the time to threaten the stability of British society and the state; its preface by the internationally renowned theoretician of anarchist communism, Peter Kropotkin; and with the direct connection of at least one of its translators with William Morris and the Socialist League, it illustrates both the international nature of the anarchist and syndicalist movement and something of the continuities inside an important libertarian strand in the British socialist movement between the 1880s and the First World War.

Fred and Charlotte Charles were a husband and wife team who had had a long history of activity in the libertarian socialist movement. A good deal is known about Fred, though little about Charlotte, except that she was once a schoolteacher in Norwich. Fred Charles's full name was F. C. Slaughter and he had been a leading member of the very active Norwich branch of the Socialist League in the 1880s, quickly moving further than the anti-parliamentary position of Morris towards one of fully-fledged anarchism. The arrival of Kropotkin in England in

1886 and the subsequent formation of the Freedom group, according to E. P. Thompson, helped to turn the League even more firmly in an anarchist direction. By 1888 Charles was a key member of a declared anarchist group in the League leadership, one increasingly at odds with the non-anarchist but still anti-parliamentary leftist group amongst whom Morris was numbered.[1] The Socialist League eventually broke up under these pressures, but the anarchists thrived in provincial towns like Leeds, Sheffield, Norwich and Walsall. The anarchist David Nicoll was now the editor of *Commonweal* in place of Morris. The beliefs of the anarchist tendency are amply summarised by Nicoll's assertion in the issue of 23 May 1891 that: 'Individual assaults on the system will lead to riots, riots to revolts, revolts to insurrection, insurrection to revolution.'[2]

From now on appeals to 'propaganda by the deed' became common among the anarchist-communists as they now called themselves. Fred Charles spent the early part of the 1890s in Sheffield where the movement was particularly active, and edited a paper *The Sheffield Anarchist*, set up with help from a French 'comrade', Coulon. After its failure, Charles moved to Walsall, where in February 1892 he was arrested, along with others, for planning to make a bomb. These were the years of anarchist bomb plots and assassination attempts throughout Europe and especially in France. It transpired that Coulon was a police spy and *agent provocateur*. Charles was sentenced on flimsy and circumstantial evidence to ten years' hard labour, of which he was to serve seven and a half years. One of the people most involved in the campaign to get Charles's sentence reduced was his former Sheffield comrade, Edward Carpenter: poet, songwriter, homosexual, socialist advocate of the 'simpler life' and of new relations between men and women. Carpenter had given Charles a character reference at his trial, and in his autobiography wrote of him as 'one of the most devoted of workers. No surrender or sacrifice for the "Cause" was too great for him; and as to his own earnings (as clerk) or possessions, he practically gave them all away to tramps or the unemployed.'[3]

Carpenter visited Charles in Portland Gaol in October 1896 to inform him that William Morris had died. Charles was greatly distressed by the news.[4] Six years previously, in 1890, Morris had produced his own utopian *News from Nowhere*, a work with which this book has parallels, not least in its use of the general strike as the ultimate means by which the 'Change' would come.[5] (It can be seen that the 1913 English edition of *How We Shall Bring About the Revolution* carried quotations from both Carpenter and William Morris on the frontispiece.) By that time syndicalist agitation and the threat of a General Strike had become a major issue for the British Labour Movement – and for the British state.

Fred Charles was released from gaol in 1899, at a time when the anarchist movement itself was very much in decline. According to a recent historian of British anarchism, Charles then 'went quietly back to Norwich where he married'.[6] By the time the book was published the Charleses were living in Oxford and contributing vigorously to many of the 'rebel' movements associated with the contemporary 'Labour Unrest'. They made their translation at a time when industrial militancy was at a high point. Trade union membership rose from about 2.5 million in 1909 to over 4 million in 1914. About 10 million days were 'lost' due to stoppages in each of the years 1910, 1911, 1913 and 1914. In 1912, largely because of the national miners' strike, the figure was nearly 41 million. There were major nationwide strikes in 1911 amongst dockers, seamen and railwayworkers; in 1913 there were large strikes, in effect organising drives, of less skilled workers in metal working and other low-paid industries; a major dispute of building workers took place early in 1914. There were frequent outbreaks of strike violence, often associated with the interventions of police and troops – there were some deaths and many injuries. Dublin, London, Liverpool, Manchester and Hull were all scenes of major industrial conflict and dramatic incident. The government's chief conciliator wrote of Hull in 1911 that he heard a town councillor remark 'that he had been in Paris during the Commune and he had never seen anything like this ... he had not known there were such people in Hull – women with hair streaming and half nude, reeling through the streets, smashing and destroying.' A well-known journalist of the day wrote of Liverpool, during the same transport workers' strike of 1911, that 'There was a general strike in Liverpool to which I was sent. It was as near to a revolution as anything I had seen in England.' Smaller industrial centres also seemed to 'explode' into action, with often previously unorganised workers engaging in struggles on behalf of themselves – and in sympathy with others. Workers in the china clay industry in Cornwall, the women chain and pipe makers of the Midlands, furniture makers in the Chilterns and many other groups entered the fray. As well as substantial accessions to membership of trade unions and displays of industrial militancy, there were also some important structural changes in the trade union movement, such as the formation of the National Transport Workers' Federation in 1910; the formation by amalgamation of the National Union of Railwaymen in 1912, and the formation of the Triple Alliance, a solidarity pact, between the miners, the transport workers and the railwaymen in 1914.[7]

All of these trends seemed to bear witness to the influence of syndicalism, which some ill-informed commentators denounced as an entirely alien importation from France. The writer of the foreword to this book, Tom Mann, was the person most associated with syndicalism in Britain. His enormous energy, combined with his outstanding talent as a labour organiser and orator, was remarked upon by many. An economist in conversation with R.H. Tawney about the causes of the labour unrest spoke of the influence of Tom Mann: 'His personality can hold a crowd of 5,000 labourers and make them act as one.' In 1910 Mann had launched his campaign of what he called Industrial Syndicalism, in part as a result of a visit to France to see the leaders of the revolutionary syndicalist movement there on his return from an eight and a half year stay in Australia and New Zealand. At a conference on industrial syndicalism held in Manchester in November 1910 he had stated his organisational priorities: 'It is a big order we are here for: nothing less than an endeavour to revolutionise the trade unions, to make unionism, from a movement of two millions ... into a movement that will take in every worker.'[8]

By 1913 when *Syndicalism and the Co-operative Commonwealth* appeared there was evidently much truth in Mann's rather elliptical remark in his foreword that, 'Industrial Solidarity and Direct Action methods are being increasingly resorted to here in Britain.' While Mann welcomed that fact, Sir George Askwith, the government's overworked conciliator, saw it from the opposite perspective. He felt that things could only get worse.

He told an audience, 'That the present unrest will cease I do not believe for a moment; it will increase, and probably increase with greater force.'[9]

Also by 1913 the militant trade union movement had created many new institutions to assist in the process of raising the class–consciousness of workers and to equip itself with people capable of (to use Mann's words) taking 'responsibility in the control of all industrial affairs'. The *Daily Herald* had emerged as a non-sectarian labour daily paper, successfully combining all the 'rebel' causes of the day, with the League created to support the paper's becoming an important local focus of militant labour activity. Mann was a frequent speaker on its platforms and the Charleses were active in its Oxford branch. It was the *Daily Herald's* famous cartoonist, Will Dyson, who contributed the drawings to *Syndicalism and the Co-operative Commonwealth*. The first, 'The Doubting Atlas', expresses very well the syndicalist – whether French or British – belief that the objective power of labour in society was such that were it ever to be realised, opposition from the ruling class and the state would amount to very little. Fred Charles had also been heavily involved in the movement for independent working–class education after the Ruskin College strike of 1909. Representing Oxford Cooperative Society, he was a member of the committee set up to run the new labour college, and he also acted as tutor in industrial and political history during the eighteen or so months the college remained in Oxford before it moved to London.[10] This was the context into which this book was published in England in 1913.

*   *   *

Who were the authors of this book? Emile Pataud was born in Paris in 1870 and was for some years one of French revolutionary syndicalism's leading and most colourful militants. An electrician by trade, he came to prominence as a result of his efforts in organising the electricians of Paris, bringing together the various electricians' unions in the city in May 1907. He was soon instrumental in organising some particularly dramatic workers' actions, notably a general strike of electricians in the same year. In 1908 he published his *Manuel du parfait électricien* which, according to a report in the police archives, should have been called the 'Manual of the Perfect Saboteur Electrician'. He practised what he preached. During the general strike of building workers in 1908, on the evening of the notorious Villeneuve-Saint-Georges affair when the cavalry charged a crowd of strikers and demonstrators, killing seven and wounding nearly 200, Pataud brought about a general stoppage of electricity supply in Paris for two hours.[11] He quickly became one of the key leaders of the strike wave that the revolutionary syndicalist group at the head of the *Confédération Générale du Travail* had attempted to encourage, starting with the miners' strike of 1906. The electricians' strike of 1907 was followed most notably by those of building workers in 1908, public employees in 1909, and railwaymen in 1910. The Clemenceau government, which included several former socialists (Millerand, Briand and Viviani) took an entirely repressive approach to the strike wave. Forty thousand soldiers were deployed during the miners' strike; military engineers were called in to get electricity supplies going during the electricians' strike; strikes in the vineyards around Narbonne led to clashes with troops; a strike at Raou-l'Etape was put down by the military with one striker being killed and 32 wounded; there were clashes between police and troops and strikers at Draveil-Vignoux and Villeneuve-Saint-Georges during the builders' strike. Over a period of two years 19 workers had died and the CGT estimated (denouncing the government as assassins and talking of massacres) 700 were injured.[12] In 1909, during the strike of public employees, a strike in which Pataud was, as *The Times* put it, 'certainly the firebrand', he expressed vividly, but in rather oratorical terms, the working-class hatred of the state and the belief in revolutionary action which the CGT was attempting to engender. He told a mass meeting that there was not a single member of the CGT who was not in revolt and ready to overthrow the regime, and so rotten was it that it could be toppled at any moment.

Pataud became especially well known in the Paris area for his spectacular and audacious actions as well as words, as rioting and high drama often became a feature of incidents he organised. There was, for instance, a riot at the Auteuil races in June 1909 as a result of his deployment of CGT building workers, some of

them armed with revolvers, to help get union recognition for the
stable lads. The building workers, under his direction, held up the
horses on the way to the racecourse. The delay to the races that
this caused sparked off a riot amongst the crowd.[13] The following
month, during a banquet at the Hotel Continental, he cut the
lights, forcing the hotel's management to accept the demands of
the workers in their establishment. He was subsequently tried for
extorting the agreement, but was found not guilty. In December
1909 he repeated his industrial sabotage during a gala given at the
Opéra for the King of Portugal. On this occasion, however, he
was clearly less optimistic about escaping incarceration, for early
in 1910 he fled to Belgium and retired from the movement.

Emile Pouget (1860–1931) was one of the three or four major
figures of French revolutionary syndicalism: a remarkable radical
journalist and pamphleteer, an exceptionally able and dedicated
militant, a brilliant articulator and populariser of revolutionary
ideas. At the age of 14 he had produced a republican newspaper
at his *lycée*. When his stepfather died, however, when Pouget was
15, he was forced to end his formal education in order to earn his
living and he became a shop assistant in Paris. He became a
regular attender at public meetings, associating himself with the
plethora of advanced groups which in the 1880s were at last
beginning to emerge after the tragic defeat of the Commune. It
was not long before he committed himself wholeheartedly to
revolutionary propaganda, initially on behalf of a rather idealistic
anarchism. By this time he had already begun his involvement
with collective forms of organisation, and had organised the first
union of shopworkers in Paris.[14] He involved himself, typically
for anarchists in the early 1880s, with agitation amongst the more
depressed elements of society, particularly the unemployed in
Paris.

In 1883, after a demonstration of the unemployed was broken
up by the police, Pouget led about 500 of the demonstrators
towards the Boulevard Saint-Germain. On the way a baker's
shop was looted (the crowd acting on the direct action principle
that if you are hungry, take bread). Both Pouget and Louise
Michel, the commune veteran, were arrested, tried and sentenced
– Pouget to eight years. He served only three years of his
sentence. The amnesty under which he was released resulted

from public opinion's being outraged by the explicitly anti-anarchist and rather trumped-up trial they received. The large-scale trial of anarchists in Lyons, when a total of 68 people were tried – Kropotkin being one of three condemned to five years' imprisonment – had also been widely condemned.[15]

Pouget's 'passion for journalism' (as his friend and comrade Paul Delesalle described it) began in earnest shortly afterwards. In February 1889 the first number of his famous journal, *Le Père Peinard*, appeared. Written in a highly popular manner, using slang and the language of the street (readers were referred to as '*les bons bougres*'), it had a massive impact. George Woodcock states that 'it represented a new direction in anarchist journalism'; it was 'humorous, unpredictable, scurrilous, irascible' and that it 'reflects more eloquently than any ... the spirit of the period of propaganda by the deed'.[16] Intermittently through the 1880s and seemingly in earnest in the early 1890s, anarchist activity became associated (indelibly perhaps in the popular mind) with terrorism, assassination attempts and bomb plots – Ravachol, Vaillant and Henri being the most well known names. The assassination of President Carnot in June 1894 was, for the French state, the last straw. It invoked an infamous set of measures (*les lois scélérates*), which had shortly before been put on the statute book, and which basically made any support for any sort of anarchist propaganda illegal.

After *Le Père Peinard* was forced to close down in February 1894, Pouget fled to England, and from his London address of 23 King Edward Street, Islington, he published a further eight issues. In France the government set up another badly handled 'show trial' of anarchists and burglars (the Trial of the Thirty), with the anarchists being on this occasion acquitted. Pouget was tried in his absence. This trial essentially brought to a close the terrorist epoch.[17]

By May 1895, Pouget had returned to France under the terms of a general amnesty, and was publishing a new paper, *La Sociale*, which lasted until he began a new series of *Le Père Peinard* in October 1896. A new theme had already emerged in Pouget's writings during his exile in London, one which anticipated and encouraged a sea-change in anarchist opinion and activity. In an issue of *Le Père Peinard* for early October 1894 he had already outlined the new tactic of working inside the unions (*syndicats*) where revolutionary-minded workers were organising themselves. This new feeling may have been encouraged by Pouget's observations of the relative strength of the British trade union movement, especially the unions of less skilled workers – often led by socialists such as Tom Mann – which had sprung into existence in the explosion of the 'New Unionism' in 1889–91 and which survived into the mid 1890s in spite of a concerted counter-offensive by the employers.[18] In the *Almanach du Père Peinard* of 1897 Pouget returned to the same theme, attacking the isolationism of some anarchists, saying with some irony, 'I am an anarchist; I want to spread my ideas: I already have the bistro; I want something better.'[19] That something better was the trade union movement. He continued by arguing that 'if there is one place into which the anarchists must get themselves, it is clearly the trade union movement.'[20]

Pouget was thus a key figure in the creation of revolutionary syndicalism, and one whose career allows us amply to explore its dimensions.

During the subsequent anarchist 'takeover' of the trade unions, anarchists such as Ferdinand Pelloutier and Paul Delesalle infiltrated the *Bourse du Travail* movement, turning it into a network of militant, worker-controlled labour exchanges and centres of revolutionary education. Others had already begun to work inside the *Fédération Nationale des Syndicats* and managed to unseat the electoralist Marxist supporters of Jules Guesde, with the help of socialists of a more revolutionary stance such as the Blanquists and the supporters of Jean Allemane. By 1895 the *Fédération* had become the *Confédération Générale du Travail*, committed to the general strike to transform society in the working-class interest, though it was not until 1902 that the *Bourses* merged with the CGT. The former Blanquist, Victor Griffuelhes, became secretary general; the *Bourses* section was run by Georges Yvetot and Paul Delesalle; and Emile Pouget became assistant secretary of the CGT and head of the section of national (union) federations.[21]

Pouget had already made his mark inside the *Confédération*. At the Congress of Toulouse in 1897 he gave the report on boycott and sabotage, enshrining two important elements in the

canon of tactics available to militant workers.[22] The Toulouse
Congress also committed the CGT, in principle, to the production of a weekly paper. Considerable financial difficulties had to
be overcome but Pouget, greatly helped by Pelloutier (who died
young in 1901), saw to it that the first number of *La Voix du
Peuple* appeared on 1 December 1900. He took very seriously his
responsibilities as editor of the paper, making it reflective of the
aspirations of revolutionary workers and dedicated to articulating
and energising their struggle. In his obituary notice for Pouget,
written in 1931, Delesalle pointed out that it was clear from
looking at the CGT Congress reports between 1896 and 1907 just
how influential Pouget was. He wrote: 'His reports, his interventions and especially his effective work in the body of the
commissions are the most certain proofs of what he gave to
syndicalism.'[23] Delesalle recalled additionally that it was Pouget
who did a good deal of the drafting of the motion which
produced the famous Charter of Amiens, whereby the CGT
asserted its revolutionary, non-political stance.[24]

Although the Charter was formally based on the principle of
the separation of the trade union and the socialist movements and
the belief in the principle that the individual member was at
liberty 'to take part, outside of his union, in whatever forms of
action correspond to his philosophical or political views', Pouget
frequently used *La Voix du Peuple* as a forum for anti-socialist
propaganda and called for abstention in elections.[25] Syndicalism
was not a rival to socialism. The trade union movement was
sufficient to itself. The party was not only unnecessary for the
emancipation of the proletariat, it was a positive hindrance to it.
In his articles, speeches and pamphlets Pouget articulated the
revolutionary syndicalist position, developing 'theory' out of the
day-to-day activity of the workers in struggle. The list of titles of
his pamphlets reveals his constant preoccupation with the task of
explanation and consciousness raising: *Le Parti du Travail* (1905),
Les Bases du Syndicalisme (1906), *Le Syndicat* (1907), *La Confédération du Travail* (1908), *Le Sabotage* (1910). *L'Action Directe*
(1910), and in 1914 an attack on the scientific management
methods of F. W. Taylor entitled *L'Organisation du Surmenage*
(literally the organisation of overwork). Pouget constantly elaborated revolutionary syndicalist doctrine, seeking above all to

convey a sense of what was possible when labour realised its own sheer power. For him and the other leading figures, syndicalism was not an artificial set of doctrines imposed on the working class, rather it sprang from it. In *Les Bases du Syndicalisme* he described it as the *'interprétation clairvoyant'* of the experience of the labour movement. Strikes, for example, were a natural form of workers' struggle – it was up to workers to use them to best effect. They were a preparation for the revolution, a vital training ground on which a sort of revolutionary drill was practised and which provided a preview of the tactics that would be necessary on the great day itself.[26]

At the Amiens Congress, moving the Charter, Griffuelhes had spoken of the twin tasks of revolutionary syndicalism. 'In the work of everyday demand', he said, 'Syndicalism pursues the coordination of working-class efforts and the increase of the well-being of labour by the realisation of immediate improvements ... but this task is only one side of the work of Syndicalism; it prepares entire emancipation, which can only be realised by capitalist expropriation.' According to the Charter itself, 'The trade union, which is today a fighting organisation, will in the future be an organisation for production and distribution and the basis of social reorganisation.'[27] The general strike was to be both the means of revolutionary change and the revolution itself. Negatively, it meant the total suspension of work; positively the seizure of the means of production.[28] Such was the potential power of labour, that once it was realised – on the day that all workers folded their arms – neither the employers nor the state would prevail against them. Were troops to be used against the general strike, they would be likely to succumb to anti-militarist propaganda, but if they did not there would simply not be enough of them to protect the installations of capitalism and the state against the entire striking proletariat.

In his years of office at the CGT, Pouget was by no means a desk-bound theoretician. According to Eduard Dolléans, the major historian of the working-class movement in France, he used his position to act as the animator of the direct action campaigns mounted by the CGT.[29] After the affair of Villeneuve-Saint-Georges, for instance, he involved himself both in activities on the streets and in the editorial office – producing three issues of *La Voix du Peuple* in the same week.[30] Such was the government's fear of the effectiveness of Pouget, Griffuelhes and Yvetot, that they were detained in prison between 1 August and 31 October 1908. On his release Pouget wrote what was to be his last article in *La Voix du Peuple* on 8 November 1908. For reasons which have never been adequately explained, both Griffuelhes and Pouget subsequently dropped out of activity at the head of the CGT. A police report in September 1909 incorrectly suggested that Pouget had almost entirely re-established his influence in the CGT: 'It is him, more than ever, who is the official negotiator of this organisation and the inspirer of its action,' the report stated.[31] Though in many respects this had been the case between 1901 and 1908, Pouget had retreated to the sidelines to produce his own daily paper, *La Révolution*, in February and March 1909. After its failure he wrote regularly for Gustave Hervé's *La Guerre Sociale*, but parted company with it after Hervé's conversion to extreme patriotism on the outbreak of war. Pouget effectively retired from the movement, dying at Lozère in 1931.[32]

*   *   *

What are we to make of this book? Bob Holton, the author of the best modern account of British syndicalism, clearly urges us to take it seriously when he writes of 'the dramatic scenario of revolutionary conflict presented by the French syndicalists Pataud and Pouget in their important work *Comment nous ferons la révolution*.[33] Yet Professor F. F. Ridley in his *Revolutionary Syndicalism in France* (1970) refers to the book as 'pure fantasy'.[34] A contemporary but rather sectarian British syndicalist, reviewing the book in *The Syndicalist* in January 1914, wrote that its 'practical value is very slight, there is a fine slap-dash vigour about the story and the ideas. It is all so magnificently successful ... there is a little boycotting, a little sabotage, a little rioting, and the Capitalist State reels, falls and smashes into pieces. And, out of the chaos, brisk, happy, and new, steps the Syndicalist Republic ... It is so fascinatingly easy.'

There is clearly some justice in these last remarks – the obstacles are always overcome, problems always solved by extra feats of agitation and the production of more solidarity and revolutionary determination. But this, after all, is the story of a great victory, the greatest victory achievable by a working class conscious of its power and determined to emancipate itself from the oppressions of capitalism, of Church and of state. Its purpose was clearly inspirational – to get across, as Kropotkin puts it in his preface, echoing Proudhon, 'the general idea of the revolution'. It is also an expository book, a summary of the many points of tactics and strategy that syndicalists such as Pouget had extracted from the practice of militant labour movements. Many incidents in the book are clearly based on things that happened: the incident with which the book opens and from which the revolution unfolds has clear similarities with the Villeneuve Saint-Georges affair, and the incidents involving the disruption of electricity supply are pure Pataud. It also incorporates the lessons that the CGT felt it had learnt from the experience of struggles: to give just one example, the estimate of the powerlessness of the government simultaneously to replace the work of strikers on the railways and to protect other capitalist property and state institutions throughout France (see Chapter VI) is very similar to the calculations made by the railway workers' leader, Guérard.[35] The descriptions of people in struggle solving problems in class conscious ways are clearly based on the many occasions on which such things happened. There was ample contemporary experience in the French labour movement that consciousness did at times 'explode' in the ways depicted in the book, and there is much evidence of this phenomenon in other places and at other times: Britain 1910–14, Spain 1936, *les événements* in France of May and June 1968, spring readily to mind.[36]

Nevertheless, there are obviously times when in reading this book one has to suspend disbelief. It is, after all, a work of fiction and a pessimism, emanating from one's knowledge of the many facts of failure of revolutions in the real world, comes to the fore. While truth is often stranger than fiction, in this way fiction based partly on truth and partly on hope seems considerably stranger still. This book, however, is the story of a successful revolution: there is, therefore, in its very form no place for defeat. One can still cavil at the ease with which it all happens in Pataud and Pouget's book and join with Kropotkin when he writes in his preface that the authors 'have considerably attenuated the resistance that the Social Revolution will probably meet with on its way'. The chapters on 'The Revolt of the Army', 'The Death Throes of Reaction' and 'Foreign Complications' are particularly weak in this respect. But as unsatisfactory as these sections are, it has to be said in the authors' defence that they did at least raise the issues. Problems of counter-revolution, coup d'etat, and sabotage by the police force or armed services have, as the author of a recent and most perceptive study has reminded us, to be taken very seriously by those interested in the prospects for real socialist change.[37]

How We Shall Bring About the Revolution, naturally enough, given its provenance, has no time for any parliamentarianism. The course of the revolution is steered safely away from that direction, and from municipalism too. While, for the most part, the outcomes of the syndicalist revolution are the conventional ones of late nineteenth and early twentieth century socialism – better housing, public transport, education and improved social conditions generally – the authors stress that they were communally rather than municipally provided. The *syndicats* were, throughout society, the basis for the organisation of production and the delivery of services, with co-operatives also having a greatly enhanced role. Workers' control of production is the central feature of the new society. In the workshops scientific management has replaced sabotage now that producers' and consumers' interests are identical. Statistical information is collected by the CGT and production co-ordinated through it. Interestingly, workers in luxury industries such as jewellery making and 'useless' ones like weapons production are redeployed to alternative employment and socially useful production.

A large programme of education is established on what at first seems like a non-sexist basis; but the system of higher education includes 'special colleges where women's occupations were taught, and where they could prepare themselves for such social work as they wished to take up' (p. 183). This revolution is very much a man's affair: women have little to do with either its creation or with the subsequent organisation of the new society. True, there is Chapter XXX on 'The Freeing of Woman', but there is clearly much more to that agenda than the inauguration of communal meal preparation and the installation of machines to clean clothes, boots and houses. The views of our syndicalist utopians are, of course, neither worse nor different than those of many of their other socialist contemporaries.

The main virtues of this book clearly lie in its discussion of means rather than ends; in effect in its celebration of the sheer power of labour to transform society without having recourse to what the authors regarded as the snares and delusions of parliamentary and municipal politics. Those who reject the non-parliamentary view should, of course, be extremely wary of the perpetual and persistent naivety of those who assert, against all the evidence, that the arrival of socialism by parliamentary means is unproblematic. Paul Delesalle, in his obituary article for Pouget, pointed out that Jules Guesde, the Marxist leader of French socialism, used to declaim: 'Send into Parliament, you working class, half of the deputies plus one and the Revolution will not be far from being accomplished.' To this Pouget and his comrades would reply: 'Group yourselves in your workers' organisations, in your unions and take possession of your workshops.'[38] The superior wisdom of the latter sentiment was clearly what led Lenin and the Bolsheviks to give such a high priority in the early days of the Communist International to securing the support of those from the revolutionary syndicalist tradition such as Tom Mann and Jack Tanner in England, Pierre Monatte and Alfred Rosmer in France and W.D. Haywood and W.Z. Foster in the United States. For Pataud and Pouget and the revolutionary syndicalists, the Marxism of their day was, as E.J. Hobsbawm has put it, 'the ideology of parties which used it as an excuse for not trying to make the revolution.'[39]

Although the peaceful and parliamentary transition to socialism was put on the agenda of theoretical possibilities, at least in the British case, as long ago as 1872 by Marx, the latter never neglected to draw attention to the high likelihood of a 'pro-slavery' rebellion by the ruling class. Although the experiences of Labour governments in the 1920s and early 1930s led those such as Stafford Cripps, G.R.Mitchison, R.H. Tawney, Harold Laski and G.D.H. Cole to examine the 'Can Socialism Come By Constitutional Means?' question, the arguments they put on the political agenda have been commonly forgotten about or brushed

aside in fits of usually misplaced electoral triumphalism.[40] Forty
years previously William Morris in his *News from Nowhere*
(1890) had predicted many of these problems and anticipated
Pataud and Pouget, though Morris's utopian novel is, without
doubt, a much better written and more subtly nuanced book than
this one. Morris cannot be accused of naivety about the possibility
of the arrival of socialism by electoral means: he straightforwardly
rejected it. Nor was he any more welcoming of the possibility of
the administration of socialism through parliament: his Chapter
13, 'Concerning Politics', consists of a mere ten lines and is the
shortest in the book. Morris, though, would have shared Kropotkin's criticism of Pataud and Pouget for underestimating the
tenacity of ruling class and state resistance to revolution. *News
from Nowhere* has a very long perspective – the revolution has
not happened, for instance, by the time that Morris gets his tale
to 1952, a year which is portrayed as a particularly bad one for
the working class. In his section on 'How the Change Came' (the
general strike is here too a moment of great importance) he
indicated the great destructive power of the counter-revolution.
He wrote that 'the party of order' 'fought with great bitterness,
and cared little what they did, so long as they injured the enemies
who had destroyed the sweets of life for them.'[41]

There has been a very substantial discussion amongst socialist
intellectuals about the status of *News from Nowhere*, and a good
deal of that debate has been gone through in E.P. Thompson's
postscript to his 1976 edition of his book on Morris. The debate
has been about, in very crude terms, whether or not Morris's
book is a work of Marxism; the doubts having been raised
because of the firm rejection of utopian socialism by Marx and
Engels. To explore the point about whether works like those of
Morris and Pataud and Pouget are books which assist the revolutionary movement – for that is what the argument ought to be
about, not about whether they pass a test of textual scrutiny
against a sort of holy scripture – it is interesting, and at first sight
may seem ironic, to note that it was precisely its rejection of
utopianism which led the contemporary French socialist intellectual, Georges Sorel, to argue in 1906 that French revolutionary
syndicalism was 'on the true Marxian track'. [42] It was Sorel,
friend of Pelloutier, Marxist scholar and keen observer of syn-

dicalism, who wrote of the great transition in the French labour movement for which Pouget was so much responsible that: 'Historians will see one day in this entry of the anarchists into the unions one of the greatest events that has been produced in our time.' He regarded revolutionary syndicalism as the salvation of revolutionary ideas and the revolutionary movement, it being responsible for arresting 'a threatened deviation to middle class ideas'.[43] Sorel wrote that 'too much stress' could not be put on Marx's rejection of 'all attempts to determine the conditions of a future society'.[44] But Pataud and Pouget's book is more about the articulation of one of Sorel's central ideas, the importance of myth in social movements, than a conventional 'shopping list' utopia of desirable measures which would be enacted in the days after the morrow of the revolution. Its stresses are elsewhere: they are on the means by which the revolution will come about and about the means by which the revolution would not get diverted by the old forms of administration of life, or in other words, the avoidance of the degradation of the revolution. In an explanatory letter about his *Reflections on Violence*, Sorel spelt out the idea which informed everything he wrote: 'that men who are participating in a great social movement always picture their coming action as a battle in which their cause is certain to triumph. These constructions ... I propose to call myths: the syndicalist 'general strike' and Marx's catastrophic revolution are such myths.'[45]

For Sorel myths were not things of fantasy or unreality that could not be achieved, rather they were, as Larry Portis puts it, 'the expressions of a will to act on reality so as to change it'.[46] The general strike was, in Sorel's words, 'the myth within which all of socialism is contained; that is, it involves a complex of images capable of naturally evoking all the feelings which are raised in the struggle of the socialist movement against contemporary society'.[47] On this test Pataud and Pouget's book is no worthless utopia, but rather a rallying cry of support for the most potent call to revolutionary change. Neither *News from Nowhere* or *How We Shall Bring About the Revolution* fall into the category of what Marx and Engels in *The Communist Manifesto* called 'fantastic pictures of future society, painted at a time when the proletariat is still in a very undeveloped state and has but a fantastic conception of its own position.' Both books seek to make people aware of their power and their ability to change things fundamentally. Their purpose is, as Miguel Abensour puts it of Morris's book, 'the education of desire'; the instilling into people of a general sense of redefining the impossible as the possible: to 'teach desire to desire, to desire better, to desire more, and above all to desire in a different way.'[48]

Revolutionary propagandists have clearly always felt the need to answer the two big questions of how a transforming socialism will come about and how, in general terms, life will be both different and better under it. Many of the expressive forms of socialist agitation and propaganda – be it in speech, song, leaflet, paper, pamphlet, book, picture, banner, badge or even sermon – have been devoted to an exposition and articulation of these themes. For class consciousness to develop, people surely have to think it possible to change things. There have, therefore, at least to be imaginings, if examples and models are not available. In the twentieth century there have, of course, been the models provided by the revolutions which brought the arrival of states of 'actually existing socialism', models which, for all but a few people, have clearly lost most of their inspirational force as time has passed and the harsh realities have emerged. For others, even Labour governments in Britain, or at least those of 1945–51, provided a beacon of hope. For those who share the wish of Tracy Chapman in her song 'Revolution' that 'People gonna rise up and take what's theirs', *How We Shall Bring About the Revolution* with all its limitations, offers ideas and hope. We may be living in 'New Times', but the potential of labour to transform society and to end oppression is far from exhausted. In this task, there is still enormous scope for direct action, which Emile Pouget in 1912 defined as follows:

> action by the working class, drawing on its own strength, acting independently and through its own organisation, relying on the help of no intermediary, expecting nothing from men or forces outside itself, creating its own conditions of struggle, its own means of resistance and aggression, bringing into everyday life the formula 'the emancipation of the proletariat is the task of the proletariat itself.'[49]

Geoff Brown
December 1989

Notes

1. E.P. Thompson, *William Morris: Romantic to Revolutionary* (London, 1977 edn) pp. 505–8.
2. Quoted in John Quail, *The Slow Burning Fuse: the lost history of the British Anarchists* (London, 1978) p. 97.
3. Edward Carpenter, *My Days and Dreams* (London, 3rd edn, 1918) p. 132. For the Walsall anarchists see J.Quail, *Slow Burning Fuse*, Chapter 6.
4. E.P. Thompson, *William Morris*, p. 637.
5. See Chapter 17, 'How the Change Came' in *News from Nowhere*, in A. Briggs (ed) *William Morris: Selected Writings and Designs* (Harmondsworth, 1968 edn) esp. pp. 288ff.
6. See J. Quail, *Slow Burning Fuse*, Chapter 11, and esp. p. 218.
7. I have attempted to convey this picture of the 'Labour Unrest' in considerably greater detail in my introduction to *The Industrial Syndicalist, 1910–1912* (reprinted by Spokesman Books, Nottingham, 1974), pp. 5–25. Of a very large literature, I like best David Rubinstein, 'Trade Unions, Politicians and Public Opinion, 1906–1914', Chapter 3 of *Trade Unions in British Politics*, eds B. Pimlott and C. Cook (London, 1982).
8. Tom Mann in *The Industrial Syndicalist*, December 1910.
9. Lord Askwith, *Industrial Problems and Disputes* (London, 1920), p. 349.
10. On the Daily Herald League see R.J. Holton, 'Daily Herald v. Daily Citizen, 1912–15', in *International Review of Social History*, 1974. On the Central Labour College, see W.W. Craik, *The Central Labour College* (London 1964) p. 82 and pp. 90–1 and also J. Quail, *Slow Burning Fuse*, pp. 229–30 where he tells of Charles' involvement in a building workers' co-operative in Oxford of over 100 members, and of his retirement in the 1930s to the anarchist colony, Whiteways.
11. On Pataud, see Christian Gras, *Alfred Rosmer et le mouvement révolutionnaire international* (Paris, 1971), p. 46, note 41. On Villeneuve-Saint-Georges, see Robert Brécy, *Le Mouvement Syndical en France, 1871–1921* (Paris 1963), p. 68.
12. See F.F. Ridley, *Revolutionary Syndicalism in France* (Cambridge 1970), p. 59.
13. F.F. Ridley, *Revolutionary Syndicalism in France*, p. 115.
14. On Pouget's life generally, see Paul Delesalle, 'La Vie Militante d'Emile Pouget' in Daniel Guérin (ed), *Ni Dieu, Ni Maître, anthologie historique du mouvement anarchiste* (Lausanne, n.d.), pp. 424–9.

15. George Woodcock, *Anarchism*, (Harmondsworth, 1963 edn) pp. 284–5. On the Lyons trial, see pp. 193–4.
16. Woodcock, *Anarchism* p. 280. There is a chapter on Le Père Peinard in Richard D. Sonn, *Anarchism and Cultural Politics in Fin de Siècle France* (Nebraska University Press, 1989). Camille Pissarro and his son Lucien provided many illustrations, and much support, often financial, for the paper: see R.E. Shikes and P. Harper, *Pissarro: his life and work* (London, 1980), Chapter 18.
17. Woodcock, *Anarchism*, pp. 294–5.
18. See Robert Brécy, *Le Mouvement Syndical en France*, p. xii and pp. 134–5.
19. Quoted in F.F. Ridley, *Revolutionary Syndicalism in France*, p. 260.
20. Quoted in R. Brécy, *Le Mouvement Syndical en France*, p. xii.
21. See G. Woodcock, *Anarchism*, pp. 300–1 and D. Guérin, *Anarchism: From Theory to Practice* (New York, 1970), pp. 77–8.
22. I have tried to outline this development in Chapter 1, 'Emile Pouget and the C.G.T.' in G. Brown, *Sabotage: a study in industrial conflict* (Nottingham, 1977), and subsequent chapters deal with the international migration of sabotage as a labour movement tactic.
23. P. Delesalle, 'La Vie Militante d'Emile Pouget', p. 428.
24. On the Charter of Amiens, see Val. R. Lorwin, *The French Labour Movement* (Cambridge, Mass., 1954), p. 31.
25. F.F. Ridley, *Revolutionary Syndicalism in France*, p. 90.
26. This is very fully dealt with by F.F. Ridley, *Revolutionary Syndicalism in France*, p. 105.
27. Griffuelhes' speech, quoted by G.D.H. Cole, *The World of Labour* (London, 1920 edn), pp. 77–8.
28. On syndicalist tactics see F.F. Ridley, *Revolutionary Syndicalism in France*, pp. 147–8 and p. 149.
29. E. Dolléans, *Histoire du Mouvement Ouvrer* (Paris, 1936–1939) Vol. 2, p. 119.
30. See R. Brécy, *Le Mouvement Syndical en France*, p. 139.
31. Quoted in R. Brécy, *Le Mouvement Syndical en France*, p. 72, note 2.
32. R. Brécy, *Le Mouvement Syndical en France*, p. 139, note 1 and p. 141, note 1.
33. Bob Holton, *British Syndicalism*, 1900–1914 (London, 1976), p. 267.
34. F.F. Ridley, *Revolutionary Syndicalism in France*, p. 112.
35. See Val. R. Lorwin, *The French Labour Movement*, p. 32.

36. For an academic discussion of this see Michael Mann, *Consciousness and Action Among the Western Working Class* (London 1973), esp. chapter 6, 'The Explosion of Consciousness'.

37. Geoff Hodgson, *Socialism and Parliamentary Democracy* (Nottingham, 1977), p. 19.

38. P. Delesalle, 'La Vie Militante d'Emile Pouget', p. 426.

39. E.J. Hobsbawm, *The Age of Empire, 1875–1914* (London, 1989 edn), p. 134. For a stimulating general discussion, see E.J. Hobsbawm, 'Bolshevism and the Anarchists', Chapter 7 of his *Revolutionaries* (London, 1977). I have tried to deal with some of the British side of this in 'Tom Mann and Jack Tanner and International Revolutionary Syndicalism, 1910–1922' in *Bulletin of the Society for the Study of Labour History*, Autumn 1973.

40. On this discussion, see Ralph Miliband, *Parliamentary Socialism* (London, 1973 edn), pp. 196–200.

41. See Morris, *News From Nowhere* in A. Briggs (ed), *William Morris: Selected Writings and Designs*, p. 297.

42. Georges Sorel, *Reflections on Violence* (trans. T.E. Hulme and J. Roth) (New York, 1967 edn), p. 141.

43. G. Sorel, 'Letter to Daniel Halévy', introduction to G. Sorel, *Reflections on Violence*, p. 56.

44. G. Sorel, *Reflections on Violence*, p. 141.

45. G. Sorel, 'Letter to Daniel Halévy', pp. 41–2.

46. Larry Portis, *Georges Sorel*, (London 1980), p. 57.

47. G. Sorel, from *Reflections on Violence*, quoted by Portis, *Georges Sorel*, p. 58.

48. Quoted in E.P. Thompson, 'Postcript: 1976' in *William Morris* (London, 1977 edn), p. 791.

49. Emile Pouget, in *L'Encyclopédie du mouvement syndicaliste*, eds V. Griffuelhes and L. Jouhaux (Paris, 1912).

Go right on. Have good faith yet. . . .
EDWARD CARPENTER. — "Towards Democracy."

These are they who dream the impossible dream—and it comes true;
Who hear the silent prayers, who accept the trampling millions, as the earth dreaming accepts the interminable feet of her children;
Who dream the dream which all men always declare futile;
Who dream the hour which is not yet on earth—
And lo! it strikes.
EDWARD CARPENTER.—"Towards Democracy."

There amidst the world new-builded shall our earthly deeds abide,
Though our names be all forgotten, and the tale of how we died.
Life or death then, who shall heed it, what we gain or what we lose?
Fair flies life amid the struggle, and the Cause for each shall choose.
WILLIAM MORRIS.—"All For The Cause."

THE DOUBTING ATLAS.

FOREWORD.

It is with very great pleasure I write a few words to arrest the attention of fellow workers and direct them to this valuable forecast of the Revolution by our French comrades Pataud and Pouget. The remarkable change that has taken place in recent years in the revolutionary movement has received its chief inspiration and stimulus from France.

The reliance upon the State, or the confidence that the machinery of the State could be democratised and used by the workers to achieve the Social Revolution or that the State could be used for such a purpose even if it were "captured" by votes, is no longer entertained by whole-hearted Revolutionaries.

In political Socialist ranks, as well as among the reactionaries, the most frequent of all questions is, "How are you going to do it without the State?" This book gives a clear and well-thought out account of how the writers think it may happen in France: and whilst it cannot be that these precise lines will be followed, all the present day developments compel acquiescence in the main lines of the forecast.

Many will be specially interested in Chapter 7, where definite action is described to actually achieve the change.

In this and subsequent chapters it will be seen how great an importance is attached to the Trade Unions. It is the Unions that step in, and in the most natural manner assume the responsibilities of provisioning, cloth-ing, and housing the people. The General Federation, in conjunction with the Trades Councils (translated as Labour Exchanges) and the National and Local Unions, become the directing and controlling agencies supervising the carrying on of all necessary services. It is precisely here that the workers of Britain stand in need of the greatest lesson: that the Unions themselves must at once prepare to accept or take responsibility in the control of all industrial affairs.

Of corresponding importance is it to notice how many times the Authors refer to the great value of the Co-operative Societies. In industry and in agriculture, artizan and peasant alike find the change made easy where Co-operation is known, the lesson to us is, that *all* workers should, without delay be identified with the Co-operative movement, Distributive and Productive.

A hundred objections can be raised no doubt as to the value of the army to the Capitalist class, the difficulties of the workers assuming entire Control, the break up of Parliamentary institutions, the readiness of the agricultural labourers to resort to Direct Action methods, and the Co-operative cultivation of the soil, etc., etc.

That the book is splendidly suggestive, thought provoking and guiding I think all will admit who read it.

With greetings and congratulations to our French Comrades, I earnestly advise all I can reach to read this book, to which it is pleasing to find our grand old comrade Kropotkin has written a preface.

Industrial Solidarity and Direct Action methods are being increasingly resorted to here in Britain, and this most interesting and enlightening forecast of the Revolution is sure to help on the movement that will precede the actual Revolution.

TOM MANN.

Manchester, 1913.

PREFACE.

It is often said that plans ought not to be drawn up for a future society.

All such plans we are told, are of the nature of romances, and they have the disadvantage, that some day they may hamper the creative force of a people in Revolution.

There may be some truth in this. Doubtless a certain number of reasoning theorists were influenced in this way by Cabets "Voyage en Icarie." But all sociological works that have made any deep impression have done this.

On the other hand, it is necessary to have a clear idea of the actual concrete results that our Communist, Collectivist, or other aspirations, might have on society. For this purpose we must picture to ourselves these various institutions at work.

Where do we want to get to by means of the Revolution? We need to know this. There must therefore be books which will enable the mass of the people to form for themselves a more or less exact idea of what it is that they desire to see realized in a near future.

It has always happened that a concrete idea preceeds its realization. For instance, would the modern progress in aviation have been made if during the last fifty years a certain number of French physicists and engineers had not placed before themselves in a concrete fashion this aim——this "romance" if you will. "The conquest of the air by a machine heavier than air."

It is only necessary to accustom oneself never to attach more importance to a book, to a treatise of any kind, than such a book or treatise—however good it may be—has in reality.

A book is not a gospel to be taken in its entirety or to be left alone. It is a suggestion, a proposal—nothing more. It is for us to reflect, to see what it contains that is good, and to reject whatever we find erroneous in it.

With this reservation then, we need—side by side with statements that tell us what past Revolutions have gained—sketches that will show in their main lines what the coming Revolution proposes to realize.

And when people who plume themselves on being "practical," (because they are nothing of the kind, since they work to put a drag on progress), say to us: "All these sorts of things are romances, Utopias," we have only to ask them whether they too have not their Utopias?

In truth, all of them, whoever they may be, have their own, a Utopia opposed to progress. Napoleon Ist. had his, that of a political and military World Empire; the General of the Jesuits has his Utopia, of an Empire based on superstition and religious submission. The good bourgeois sighs for a strong Government, protecting as the song says " Ceux qui mettent des queues aux Zeros." Briand has his Utopia, Millerand has his, Lepine himself has one—that of knocking people on the head for the benefit of the bourgeois.

This means that it is impossible, in fact, for a man to influence in any way the development of his epoch without having a more or less definite idea of what he wishes to see developing in society.

Only, it is necessary, when reading a social "Utopia," never to forget that the author does not offer us anything unchangeable, anything decreed in advance, like those plans of campaign drawn up by the German general staffs during the wars of 1793-1809, which were always upset by the spirit of the peoples, who were sympathetic to the sans-culottes.

The idea—"the general idea of the Revolution," as Proudhon said — that is what is needed ; and not revolutionary recipes.

Now it is this *general idea* that Pataud and Pouget seek to develope in their book.

It is evident, when a book of this kind is written, that the author is obliged to give some precise details of

events. But these details—the reader will readily per-
ceive—are only given in order to materialize the ideas,
to avoid floating about in vague abstractions.

Whether the encounter between the rebels of a near
future and the defenders of a past which is dying takes
place in front of the statue by Dalou, or elsewhere;
whether the first encounter decides the victory or not—
matters little.

That which does matter is, that we should try to
gain a clear idea of the *general tendency* to be impressed
on the Revolution.

Will it be Bourgeois Individualism and the exploitation of man by man, only mitigated by a few laws? Will
it be State Socialism that we shall seek to establish?
Will it be Bureaucratic Centralization in the State, in the
Commune, in the "Confédération du Travail" and the
Trade Unions that we shall establish by our votes, or will
it be Independence and the Free Federation of groups
of Producers and Consumers, formed through affinities
of trade or of needs?   Will it be Centralization—the
hierarchical scale of Goverments—or will it be the definite abolition of the Government of man by man that
we shall exert ourselves to realize?   These are the questions that the book of Pataud and Pouget places before
us, and which it invites us to discuss—no longer in an
abstract way, but in a concrete way, by starting from
facts themselves, from the actual needs of society.

Without doubt, life is infinitely more complicated
than anything that can be foreseen. It contains more
of the unexpected than any romance; we have just seen
this during the last attempt at Revolution in Russia. But
the *general aspect* of the coming society is already taking
shape. What is germinating can already be seen; it is
only necessary to observe it.   The whole force of the
desire for equality, for justice, for independence, for free
association, which is manifesting itself in society, can
already be felt. And these social data enable us to fore-
see with sufficient accuracy where we are going—provided
we study *what is really happening*, instead of discussing

about what this or that one would *like to believe is hap-pening*.

It was guided by these ideas that I endeavoured, some thirty years ago, to sketch a Communal Utopia in "The Conquest of Bread."

Pataud and Pouget write to-day a *Syndicalist Utopia*. They show us how the Trade Unions, groups formed for combat against Capital, could transform themselves, in a time of Revolution, into groups for production; how they could work, each within its own proper sphere, at the re-organisation of production and the *social* distribution of its products, without waiting for orders coming from above. They tell, in a very attractive way, how the groups, Industrial, Communal, and Co-operative, could undertake the functions which up to the present have been appropriated by the State (and local governing bodies; such as Town and County Councils, etc. Tr.) how the Trade Unions could draw up the necessary statistics and communicate them to one another, without waiting for the intervention of the officialism of Statistical Committees; how they could make expropriation a reality—and so on.

True, it is not Anarchism that they picture for us. But the organisation of which they tell has already the advantage of being no longer based on a hierarchy of officials, as has been advocated up to the present by State Socialists. In this book of Pataud's and Pouget's can be felt, on the contrary, the life-giving breath of Anarchism in their conceptions of the future, especially in the pages devoted to Production and Exchange. And what they say on this subject should be seriously considered by every worker who loves Freedom, Justice, and Equality, as well as by everyone anxious to avoid the sanguinary struggles of a coming Revolution.

It is probable that Pataud and Pouget still pay too heavy a tribute to the past. That is inevitable in works of this kind. Their Trade Union Congress which discusses if the children, the sick, and the aged are to be made a charge on the community, concerns itself, in our

opinion, with questions that will be settled on the spot;
and when they decide that no Union, no social service,
shall be able "to separate itself from the community"
they decide a question that the local life, alone, is in a
position to solve.   As to the "Confederal Committee,"
it borrows a great deal too much from the Government
that it has just overthrown.

Well, these great questions are precisely matters for
discussion.   The authors have stated them for us;   they
have called our attention to a tendency;   it is for us to
reflect about it—before the Revolution calls upon us to
act!—And whoever is inspired by the *spirit* of this book
of Pataud's and Pouget's, will already be in a position to
decide about these questions with a certain independence
of judgment.   Very probably, they will decide that centralisation is useless, and will at once be able to suggest
means for avoiding it.

In this book, what also commends itself to the attention of the reader is the spirit, which runs through the
whole book, of tolerance for diverse tendencies, different
from those of the authors—a spirit of tolerance and of
good nature, quite characteristic of the mental state of
the French working-class population, which contrasts so
strongly with the love of regulation, of general laws,
which still remains so ingrained in those nations which
have not had the revolutionary experience of the French
nation.

The tendency to conciliation is also seen in a new
idea of the authors, who propose to combine Communism
for all objects of *first necessity,* with a book of "labour
notes," delivered to each member of society, for articles
of luxury.   This idea, which recalls Bellamy's idea in
"Looking Backwards," is well worth discussion.

Finally, the same toleration is also found in their
other proposal for expropriation and exploitation of the
large landed estates by Unions of Agricultural Workers
on one side, and on the other side, the maintenance of the
small and medium sized farms, which would continue to
be worked by their actual occupiers.

Faithful to this principle of toleration, the authors attach also, and with much reason, a fundamental importance to the *propaganda by example* instead of placing their hope in the vote, the law and the guillotine for the obstinate.

One would have liked, however, to have seen them apply this principle more widely to the prison population. One stroke of boldness, like Pinel's, after having served as an example somewhere, will one day remove all doubts from this subject.

The sole reproach that I shall allow myself to address to the authors—an observation rather than a reproach — is that they have considerably attenuated the resistance that the Social Revolution will probably meet with on its way.   The check of the attempt at Revolution in Russia has shown us all the danger that may follow from an illusion of this kind.

Certainly, there will be no need to dread this resistance, if between now and then the *revolutionary spirit* —the courage to demolish institutions—spreads in the country districts, at the same time as the *spirit of revolt.* Then the success of the Revolution will be assured.   Unfortunately, one cannot be sure that it will be so.   How many excellent rebels do we not know ourselves, endowed with a personal courage that could be relied upon in all cases, and yet lacking the courage of the revolutionary spirit?

It is to be feared this is the case with whole regions. And it is there above all that it is necessary to direct the efforts of all those who—like the authors of this book—conceive the Revolution, not as a reign of Terror and a cutting off of human heads, but as a cutting down of the State and Capitalist forest.

For a parliamentary party, which expects success from artificial electoral majorities—and for Jacobins who still count on the terror inspired by punitive expeditions —backward regions may be a negligeable quantity.

These forget—or rather they have never known— what bleeding wounds the Midi and the Vendée were in

1793. But for us who know that either the people will make the Revolution, or the Revolution will never be made — the intellectual conquest of future Vendées presents itself as an imperious duty.

And if we give ourselves to this work, we shall soon find in what directions Socialist ideas, as they have been preached up to now, remain incomplete. We shall easily discover what represents the still unconscious ideal for these districts, and we shall know then what must be done to gain the whole of agricultural France for the Revolution.

This book of Pataud's and Pouget's makes us think about all these things, and that is why it should be spread abroad everywhere, read everywhere, discussed everywhere.

The better we understand what we want—and the fewer the obstacles the Revolution meets with on its way ; the fewer struggles it will have to sustain, and the fewer victims it will cost.

27 February, 1911.   PETER KROPOTKIN.

TO THE READERS OF THIS BOOK.

At baptism, our book changed its name. This was the fault of our publisher, who, in presenting its title page to the printer's ink—the baptismal font for books—shamelessly committed an act of sabotage.

Not being of a morose disposition, we bear him no ill-will on this account, and we plead his cause with you; like us, you will grant our publisher a free pardon.

And yet, the sabotage is obvious!

In place of the anachronistic title which appears on the title page, there should have blazed forth, in three lines.

"HOW
WE BROUGHT ABOUT
THE REVOLUTION."

Such was the title, this book of ours should have borne.

For, you all know it, the Revolution is over!—Capitalism is dead.

For long, Death dogged the steps of the old society. The death pangs were severe. The beast would not die. And yet, the devil knows how sick it was! Finally, its last hour sounded.

The event had been discounted for so long, that the working class, who awaited the inheritance, were not taken unawares. That was because, in the first place, a work of gestation and reflection had been going on amongst them, which, when the psychological moment arrived, enabled them to triumph over difficulties; little by little, they had acquired social capacity, had become qualified to manage their own affairs, without intermediaries, or figure-heads.

They made their own the phrase that Sieyès applied, at the end of the 18th century, to the Third Es-
tate, and tired of being nothing, they wanted to be
everything.

Standing in opposition to the wealthier class, they
proclaimed a state of permanent insurrection, and prepared themselves to take its place. In the fissures of
capitalism they lodged the seeds of new institutions. Inspired by the idea of a General Strike, they made themselves familiar with the work of expropriation which they
declared was necessary and inevitable.

As long ago as 1902, The Confédération Générale
du Travail had issued a series of questions which showed
what the Workers meant to do.

It directed the attention of Trade Unions to what
they would have to do in the case of a triumphant
General Strike. It asked them to consider how they
would proceed to transform themselves from societies
for combat into societies for production? How they
would accomplish the taking possession of the machinery
of production. What were their ideas as to how factories
and workshops should be re-organised? What part did
they consider the Trade Union Federation and Labour
Exchanges should play in a re-organised society? On
what basis did they anticipate the distribution of goods
would take place.

This was the whole social problem put in questions.

This inquiry, however, was not the only symptom
which showed what were the subjects which more and
more absorbed the attention of the working class. The
" What's to be done on the morrow of the General
Strike ? " became an obsession, it sank into people's minds,
where it crystallized and took form.

And that was why, when the great revolutionary
storm burst, the masses of the people were not ignorant
and not helpless. That was why, after having fought,
after having overthrown, they knew how to rebuild.

It was a time of magnificent enthusiasm. The
coldest, the most indifferent were stirred and fired.

Ah! What great and glorious days of tumult and fever! Tragic they were to live through—delightful they are to recall.

.What this Revolution was—the greatest and most far reaching that has yet been brought about—we are going to tell.

We are going to call up and live over again this grand and tremendous time. We are going to be present at the birth of a world.

EMILE PATAUD.
EMILE POUGET.

Syndicalism and the Co-operative Commonwealth.

CHAPTER I.

THE BREAK UP OF THE ICE.

During a Sunday afternoon in the spring of the year 19—, thousands of strikers in the building trade met at the Saint Paul Riding School. The crowd, packed together in the hall, already very much excited by the long strike, electrified by the speeches, irritated by trampling about on sawdust and mouldy dung, became exasperated and noisy.

Storms were in the air. The growling of anger was like the noise of distant thunder, a storm ready to burst into flame.

For a full fortnight work had been suspended, and the whole of the Union was on strike.

The workers resisting stubbornly, meant to win; and the masters, sure of the support of the Government, refused to make the least concession.

The meeting came to an end.

The departure of the people was hampered by the usual police measures. The ease with which the narrow street, where the Riding School was situated, could be barred, enabled the police cordons to be made more compact. And, by an excess of precaution, the crowd was only allowed to filter through with an irritating slowness, which hindered the emptying of the hall.

The crowd became irritated at the way in which it was pent up. Like an element under too great pressure, it expanded suddenly, and, with a fierce rush, broke up the police barriers. In spite of their strength, the police belonging to the central brigades were driven back, and the crowd dispersed more rapidly.

The police officers, angry at the check to their arrangements, ordered a rally, and threw their men on the rear of the human wave which noisily flowed away through the Rue Saint Antoine.

The strikers faced round when attacked, and in a short time the scuffle degenerated into a skirmish; some tables and chairs taken from the pavement before the cafés, some planks, an overturned tramcar, and a barricade began to appear. The workmen's resistance was keen, they fought furiously.

Whilst these events were happening in the Rue Saint Antoine, a column of strikers marched in an oblique direction through the Rue de Rivoli, and towards the chief boulevards.

As neither the few scattered policemen, nor the few parties of soldiers guarding deserted sheds, or camping here and there, were in a position to bar their way, they arrived there without difficulty.

The boulevards were encumbered by the usual mob of promenaders, as well as by the loungers seated outside cafés. The demonstration caused surprise, uproar, and consternation amongst this throng, and carrying some of them along with them, they descended like a torrent, swollen by inquisitive people and young folk, towards the Madeleine.

The prefect of police, as soon as he was informed of this, ordered some bodies of police to be sent against the demonstrators. In order to arrive quickly, they were packed into the underground railway, and got out at the Place de l'Opéra.

These bodies of police, increased by the soldiers who were guarding work sheds on the square and in the neighbourhood, were sent to encounter the strikers.

The collision occurred near the Vaudeville. The police at once drew their swords and rushed upon the demonstrators. The latter, indignant and enraged, stood their ground. They defended themselves as well as they could, using as arms whatever they found to their hands.

But what an unequal fight!—Before long, shots rang out. Where did the first shots come from?—From the police? —From the strikers?—No one knew! Anyhow, the police service revolvers made more victims than the pistols of the demonstrators.

These still held their ground, and the fight only increased their courage. What would be · the end of it? Although badly armed, the crowd was formidable on account of its rage and vehemence. But the police officers, not wishing that their men should have to retreat, called on the troops.

The soldiers, rendered still more irresponsible by the excitement of the fight, by the blows received, obeyed like automata. In accordance with the orders given, they brought their guns to their shoulders—they fired.

There was a frightful recoil amongst the crowd, it was as though a scythe had passed through them. Cries of pain mingled with shouts of rage and curses. Besides the wounded, of whom there were many on the workmen's side, there were also some dead.

The cavalry, sent for in all haste, came to the rescue. They rushed on to the boulevards from the adjacent streets, and succeeded in breaking up the demonstration. But the crowd, although cut up into fragments, did not disperse. Groups driven outside the great artery coagulated afresh, and marched towards the faubourgs; they then went to the public halls, where, during the evening, meetings were held. On the way, their shouts showed their indignation, and spread everywhere the news of the massacre.

After the great fusillade there had been for a short moment a distressing lull. The demonstrators collected the wounded, and carried them to the neighbouring chemists' shops. As to the dead, their bodies, fiercely guarded by their comrades, had been laid upon automobiles, and in a mournful procession transported to the offices of the Builders' Federation. There, in a room hastily transformed into a mortuary chamber, the dead bodies of these unfortunate men were laid.

The tragedy of this day, so suddenly raised to the diapason of the social war, did not burst forth from a sky without clouds. The air was already heavy with ill-will and anger. It was a troubled, anxious time to live in. This nervousness and general uneasiness caused a foreboding that small incidents might expand into events of increasing gravity.

A long and severe winter had emphasized the causes for anxiety. There had been bitter suffering around the workman's hearth; to the season's trials were added the resentment due to high prices, which could not be explained by the shortness of supplies. The people put this to the account of the monopolists.

Thus, from the beginning of the spring, the industrial unrest increased. It might have been said that under the sun's smiles, although the sun had little warmth as yet, the toilers were seized with the need for action, the necessity for stretching their muscles, for trying their strength, in order to assure themselves that the hardships of the winter had not weakened their opposition.

The antagonism between workers and masters had, moreover, arrived at such a pitch that it might have been supposed the tension had reached its maximum. In both camps they considered themselves to be in a state of permanent war, interrupted by armistices which only brought into the relations between masters and men ameliorations which did not last long.

On both sides they were strongly organised for the struggle. In opposition to the workmen's Unions and their Trade Federations, which were united by the Confédération du Travail, the capitalists had in many branches of industry formed Trusts, or at least associations for protection and defence against strikes. Thus, as soon as a stoppage of work threatened their security, the masters replied by a lock-out, thrusting outside the factories or workshops indiscriminately all the workers who belonged to that Trade.

These methods of defence adopted by the employers, had on many occassions caused grevious reverberations

amongst the ranks of the workers, spreading misery far
and wide, and for a time breaking up the Unions concerned. As these crises had only been momentary and
partial, the sufferings they brought in their train had not
passed beyond a restricted area. As a whole, the working class only felt the full effect of these measures
through its sense of solidarity; therefore, far from lessening the virulence of its demands, they had strengthened
and accentuated them.

Their effect had therefore been diametrically opposite to that which the masters had expected; they
had not depressed the enthusiasts, but they had thrown
the most wavering, the most indolent, the least combative amongst the proletarians within the Trade Union
orbit.

There happened then, what happens during times
of revolutionary ferment; the attempts made to check
the growth of the subversive movement turned to its
advantage.

In this case, the most obvious result of the repressive efforts of the capitalists was to make the breach
between them and the working class deeper and wider.
Things had come to such a pass, that periods of calm
were now rare.

When the crisis was lessened in one Union, it became
envenomed in another. Strikes followed strikes; lock-
outs were replied to by boycotts; sabotage was employed with ruinous intensity.

This happened to such an extent, that there were
manufacturers and commercial people who came to regard
their privileged position as a not very enviable one,
and even doubted its being tenable.

From the political point of view the horizon was
not less cloudy than from the economic point of view.
The Republic had lost the attraction it formerly had.
It had disappointed all hopes. Instead of becoming, what
under the Empire it was dreamed it would become, a
social régime, the outline of a new world, it was what

the structure of society rendered inevitable, a Government looking after the affairs of the possessing class, of the bourgeoisie, like its predecessors.

Various parties had attained to power one after the other without any improvement being experienced by the people, or their seeing any visible progress. Men who seemed reactionists had joined with opponents who stood as reformers, and had even prided themselves on their Socialism. But these latter, who in opposition had battled for great principles—for truth, for justice--once hoisted into power, and become the stronger, proved to be no better than the others.

And these things completed the ruin of popular illusions; it suddenly dawned on even the most prejudiced, that Parliamentarism had morbid germs at its heart, which dissolved good-will, and corrupted consciences.

To crown all, the vices of Governmentalism showed themselves more crudely than ever. Fraud, the trade in influence, the plunder of the public treasury, trickery, rascalities, constant scandals. The Ministries were offices where the least dishonest trade carried on was that in decorations, which only injured the pockets of vain men.

All this mud, all this disgrace, which arose inevitably from the State system, did not flow any blacker or more fetid than under previous systems. But the critical sense of the people had developed, their clearness of sight had grown, and they felt repulsion for that which formerly left them indifferent. Thus their disgust and hatred did not cause them to lose the perception of realities; it did not turn their looks backward, they did not count on getting any advantage from a return to antiquated forms of Government. If they were saturated with scepticism, and submitted to Parliamentarism, as to a disease of which one does not know the method of cure, they knew at least that none of the political specifics would be an effective remedy.

This maturity of reason, this growth of consciousness which more and more gained ground amongst the people, did not illuminate them so far as fully to light up their road. They foresaw that the new life, as a whole, was beyond Parliamentarism. They caught glimpses of its germs in the economic Federalism which the Trade Unions preached. They felt a social force developing within themselves which would eliminate the declining military, governmental, and capitalist forces. But these were only vague aspirations. To give them form, the quickening of the revolutionary spirit was necessary.

Towards the working class, who were becoming more and more vigorous and strong, and constantly developing in consciousness, the Government adopted sometimes a friendly and sometimes an antagonistic manner. But neither mad repression, and furious persecution, nor mild corruption, and the distribution of favours, weakened them. The mass of the people were sustained by such a strong will, they had drunk so deeply of the spirit of revolt, that nothing depressed them. There was within them a force driving them forward that baffled all reactionary schemes, and made those oppressive measures miscarry that seemed the best thought out; whilst, on the other hand, the misery of the people, their blunders, and even their faults contributed to the success of their cause.

This phenomenon, which had often been observed before, was about to show itself still more as events worked themselves out.

The Trade Union organisations, the centre of popular hopes, were the permanent danger that the authorities sought to break down, either by a frontal attack, or by hypocritically undermining them. Neither proved effective.

When the Government became amiable and conciliatory, and endeavoured to cajole the workers, they, far from allowing themselves to be caught, took advantage of these circumstances to accentuate their action.

In the same way, they did not allow themselves to be beaten down when, changing tactics, the Government returned to the brutal manner, and on the smallest dispute, mobilised the army, making it camp on one strike field after another, and multiplying the number of tragic incidents.

In the one case, as in the other, the working class became more warlike. They took possession of the streets, and familiarised themselves with the tactics of resistance. They learned how to stand their ground before bodies of police, and how to deal with the troops marched against them.

Being successively pampered and reprimanded, they learned to hold the Government in profound contempt, they felt nothing but hatred for it, and they became less passive day by day.

This was the reason why the interrupted exit from the meeting at Saint Paul's Riding School had so rapidly developed into a conflict, into a riot.

For a fortnight the builders' strike had kept Paris in effervescence. It began by a slight dispute with the workmen at one shed; their comrades in various other departments threw down their tools on an appeal being made to their sense of solidarity, and soon the whole yard was on strike, on behalf of this handful of wronged workers. The masters, intoxicated by the knowledge of their strong coalition, instead of seeking to limit the area of the conflict, thought it would be good policy to envonom it, and, spreading from one section to another, the strike had affected the whole trade.

Other strikes had broken out simultaneously, both in Paris and the provinces, increasing the unrest, and very much exciting the minds of the people.

In Paris alone the nearest approximate statistics gave a hundred thousand workers in various trades as being engaged in disputes.

In the provinces, although spread over wider districts, the agitation was not on that account less keen, and a characteristic symptom was, that the unrest was not confined to the industrial centres, but the agricultural districts were also contaminated. Everywhere, on the least occasion, troubles and collisions between labour and capital grew into violent conflicts, into strikes showing an always growing bitterness.

In this highly charged atmosphere, where hatred against the masters and the Government alternately smouldered and burst forth, the news of the fray around Saint Paul's Riding School, and the drama which afterwards stained the pavement of the chief boulevards with workmen's blood, spread with the spontaneity of an electric spark.

There was at first stupefaction, consternation. Then fists were clenched, anger blazed forth. The mass of the people distressed, indignant, were intensely agitated, and the excitement reached a climax.

The storm burst.

This massacre—not more murderous than many preceding ones—precipitated and created a revolutionary situation.

CHAPTER II.

THE MORROW OF THE MASSACRE.

On Monday morning, Paris had the feverish aspect of momentous days. A red sun's rays struggled through the low grey clouds. The wind blew in gusts, bringing from the east a tingling cold. It seemed as if the weather reflected the people's state of mind. Amongst them rolled dark and tumultuous thoughts, that the rising wind of anger made one forebode were big with revolt.

Since daybreak the crowd from the faubourgs had streamed along less dense than usual. The carriages of the underground railway, the motor busses, the tramways were less packed.

The workers, who from force of habit had left their homes to go to work, eagerly read their daily papers, bought at the kiosk, fresh from the rotary presses, still damp, and bringing with them the heavy odour of printer's ink. Painful presentiments, and a vague anxiety were in the air, which made heavy hearts and frowning brows. There were short conversations, punctuated by rough comments at the expense of the Government.

The dominant note was pessimist. "Things are going to take an ugly turn," the cautious ones said. Here and there sudden and impetuous movements, furious words, shook the sheeplike torpor.

It was the pliable, the resigned, the docile workmen who had gone to work. But to-day, gusts of anger, fused into violent exclamations passed over even these.

At the factories, in the workshops, the staffs were incomplete. And, what was more, the workers present did not bring to the work their usual zeal, their actions showed the uneasiness and anxiety that oppressed them.

The night before, in the various assemblies which
met during the evening, meetings, social gatherings, and
entertainments, the events of the day were discussed by
orators made eloquent by their indignation.

Members of the strike committee had visited these
assemblies one after the other. To render their speeches
dramatic, they painted the death scene of the victims,
they described the grief of their relatives, they told of
the dread and despair of the widows and children, and
expressing the wrath with which they overflowed, they
ended by urging that proletarian solidarity should mani-
fest itself by a total stoppage of work. It should be
suspended at once, without waiting for the Trade Union
organisations to give the signal.

The word of command spread by spontaneous waves,
by tacit agreement. That explains why, on Monday
morning, there was already an important current in favour
of a strike, and the resumption of work was very partial.

Soon the streets were filled by an excitable crowd
in search of news, some going towards the street where
the offices of the Confédération Générale du Travail were
situated, and some towards the Labour Exchange,* but
having, as the central point of attraction the theatre of
the butchery, the corner of the great boulevards where
the victims fell.

All day long the people made pilgrimages to this
spot. The human stream descended from the heights,
a great crowd, deeply moved, but without cries being
heard other than those of the newspaper sellers offering
the latest editions. When eddies were formed in the
crowd, when groups gathered together, they were immediately broken up by the police, with their traditional
"Move on," an order given with an unusual compunction;

* "Bourses du Travail." These receive a subsidy from the Government and combine the functions of our English Trade Councils and
Labour Exchanges—in France the Labour Exchanges are organised by
the Unions—and form centres for all kinds of Trade Union activities. Tr.

it was obeyed sullenly, restively. It seemed as though the crowd had awakened from a long torpor, they looked upon the police as objects of horror, but without as yet having sufficient energy for resistance.

During the night, bunches of flowers were brought and these accumulated in pyramids on the spots stained with blood. The authorities, fearing to increase the popular excitement, had left them alone, limiting themselves to making the police measures more stringent, and reinforcing the military guards at the worksheds and the crossways.

The Trade Union Councils, and the committees of Trade Federations, and of the Confédération Générale du Travail held an urgency meeting. The decision anticipated from their deliberations was in course of being carried out; the Strike of Solidarity.

It was agreed to call upon the workers of all trades to suspend work, and to continue the strike until the Government undertook to prosecute the murderers, and to find out those who were really responsible, not alone the arms that had struck, but the head that had commanded.

The declaration of the strike soon becoming known, it spread with such rapidity, that, although it was only decided it should commence on the morrow, the stoppage of work extended very largely during the course of the afternoon. Processions of demonstrators were formed, who going to the workshops and the factories, announced that a strike was decided on, and shamed those who were undecided, and who sulked at leaving their work, into joining the strike. In most cases long objurgations were needless; the works were cleared out without much bother.

Whilst the minds of the people began to ferment, the events which stirred them glided over the epidermis of the Parliamentarians, the demand for an interpellation handed in by the Socialist deputies in the Chamber was coldly received by the ministerialists and reactionists, who formed a "bloc" against the Trade Unions. The ministers refused to furnish explanations, and demanded that they should be supported without debate; later, when calm was re-established, they would reply to their critics. Besides with the optimism and blindness which on the eve of Revolutions has always characterized Governments, they announced that there was no need to take things too seriously, that in a few days order would reign supreme. By a show of hands, a compact majority approved of their attitude.

The people, far from expecting anything useful from Parliament, rightly considered it as their enemy. They replied by contempt and sarcastic taunts about its indifference. They were not indignant at its attitude, they no longer hoped for anything from it, and they knew how to mark this by their lack of eagerness to march on the Palais-Bourbon (Houses of Parliament).

The Place de la Concorde, where, during the troublous times at the end of the 19th century when anxiety was still felt about the decisions of the Chamber a human wave broke in foam, was now nothing more than a centre for separating and returning home.

The multitude, which overflowed the boulevards, coming there from sympathy, or simple curiosity, to see the theatre of the massacre, was swept along towards the Madeleine and the Place de la Concorde.

It came there driven and not attracted!

The crowd ebbed around the Obelisk, and the fountains which form a girdle to it, held a moment by the magic of the spectacle which offered itself to their view: the sun, plunging behind the Arc de Triomphe, illuminated the avenue, setting on fire the still blackish branches of the trees. The enchantment of this sight held the people spellbound, and their eyes were not turned aside by the legislative palace, whose overwhelming mass, plunged in shade, looked like a funeral monument; it seemed to be entering into the night, to be a dead thing, to belong already to the past.

The day ended without any very serious incidents. A day of expectation, during which the adversaries observed each other, but did not collide. Scuffles only broke out at certain points. These were caused by the clumsiness of the police, who, not appreciating the extent to which the habitual docility of the crowd had diminished, and thinking they could jostle them about as usual, had the imprudence to attempt some arrests. But the people, quickly getting angry, intervened, and becoming infuriated, did not cease until they had obtained, or forcibly effected, the release of the prisoners. This want of respect for the uniform, these abrupt, though still mitigated refusals of obedience, were an omen of bad augury for the authorities.

When night fell, the agitation was of a different kind, but it did not become less. As on the previous evening, it was concentrated, in numerous gatherings; various public meetings, assemblies of propagandist groups, assemblies of Trade Unions; the halls overflowed with a feverishly excited audience, and the new comers, finding no vacant places, massed themselves round the doors. The speeches were sober. This was no time for lengthy chattering, but to consult as to the measures to be taken, and then to act with decision and vigour, in order to accentuate the strike movement, to hasten and extend it, until it became unanimous.

The committees of all the Trade Union organisations were in permanent session. The Confederal Committee, in their first manifesto, had explained the reasons for the strike, and stated their ultimatum to the Government, who were required to prosecute the assassins, to render justice to the working class.

A parenthesis is necessary here. On the threshold of this strike, the consequences of which were going to be so incalculable, the initiators narrowed it down to an ultimatum to the Government. But there is nothing surprising in this. It is the same with social upheavals as with living organisms, they are born from a cell, from a germ, which develops gradually; at the beginning the new being is feeble, the Revolution is shapeless.

The latter, indeed, is so unformed, that even its most ardent supporters, those who in their inmost minds call for its coming, and would carry it through to all its ultimate developments, desire it rather than feel a presentiment of its coming.

It has been so in all previous Revolutions: they have surprised their adversaries, and sometimes their most faithful supporters. But in the course of all of them, that which characterized the men who were profoundly revolutionary, was, that they knew how to profit by events, they have always risen to their height, they have never been outstripped by them.

It was so at this time.

This observation made, let us return to the Confederal Committee. At the hour at which we have now arrived, the thought which animated it, and which summed up the common aspiration, was to bring about a suspension of work so complete that the Government would be shaken by it. As to the rest, circumstances would decide.

Therefore, the Committee issued its manifesto, after which it came to an understanding with the Federal Councils of the Unions for the purpose of sending delegates into the provinces. These received the mandate to visit in the first place the strategic points from an industrial and commercial point of view, the great arteries of traffic, the centres whose productions were of primordial utility for the working of society. They had to explain there the reasons for the strike, to fan enthusiasm, to revive the courage of those who, weakened by false news, hesitated to take action. This was their work as they went from centre to centre.

The Trade Union groups were not the only ones in motion. All the Revolutionary societies, Antimilitarist groups, and secret organisations held meetings and occupied themselves with considering how they could help the movement, and what steps it would be advisable for them to take.

More than all others, the groups of Antimilitarists threw themselves into this work. Their activity increased tenfold with the strike in the building trades. A fertile field for propaganda offered itself; to remonstrate with the soldiers scattered about in the entrenched camp that it seemed Paris had become, reminding them that before being soldiers they were men, and that they owed it to themselves not to stain themselves with the blood of their working brothers.

To this work these societies gave themselves up with an untiring energy and fiery zeal.

If on the side of the people the strike was becoming more organized, the Government, on its side, did not remain inactive. Judging it to be superfluous to increase the already considerable defensive measures, which they had taken, they concerned themselves with guarding against the stoppage of work. They were besides very confident. The previous attempts at a general strike never having been more than partial, they thought it would be the same this time.

Nevertheless, they did not wish to be taken unawares, they wanted to show their ability to curb the social peril, as much to maintain their own prestige as to save the bourgeoisie from painful emotions. They could only do this by obviating the inconvenience of the strike by means of the manual work of the military. They therefore issued orders in this sense.

Rapid inquiries made amongst the employers' Unions and the great companies had made known approximately the number of soldiers that would be necessary to remedy the inconvenience of the strike, by more or less assuring the continuance of work. In consequence a mobilisation scheme was prepared for employing the army in various industries.

Some proposed that, without delay, soldiers should be installed by the side of the workers. They contended that none of the latter, seeing at his side a substitute prepared to take his place, would dare to go on strike.

The employers, better psychologists, objected that such a proceeding would have disastrous effects, and would make the most timid revolt.   They confined them-selves to drawing out a list of the trades, and divisions of industry in which, should the case arise, soldiers could be employed.

Then, whilst in both camps the last preparations for the struggle were being made, the night advanced.

The vast city became numbed in an anxious torpor; and, in contrast with the noise of the day, a gloomy silence spread over it It was only disturbed by the clang of the military patrols zigzagging from street to street.

CHAPTER III.

THE DECLARATION OF THE STRIKE.

The awakening of Paris, on the Tuesday, was like that of one paralyzed. The torpor of the night not only continued, but it seemed to grow with the day. The silence did not vanish with the darkness. There did not arise from the streets the usual murmur of the enormous beast, the symphony of various noises that from early morning was wont to announce the return of activity.

The stoppage of work, which on the previous day had been spontaneous, and was due to the accident of personal initiative and impulse, now became regularised and generalised in a methodical way, that showed the influence of the Trade Union decisions.

Popular indignation was at its height, and contributed to the hastening of this movement. The people felt such a profound pity for the victims of the Government, and their anger was so intense against the Government and its tools, that they threw themselves into the strike with a feeling of relief and satisfaction.

Nevertheless, it would be their own families, more than anyone else, who would be severely hit by these events. In addition to the inevitable disappearance of their wages, which for the workers would be the immediate consequence of the stoppage of work, the strike brought to them a whole series of inconveniences and calamities. In spite of all this they went gaily into the adventure, resolved stoically to endure the ups and downs that would follow in the train of the events in which they were going to be the chief actors.

The privileged classes saw the outbreak of the conflict
with a less tranquil eye. No combative mood stirred
them, no ideal cheered them. Their only dream was of
enjoyment without trouble. Now what they saw most
clearly in this strike with which they were menaced was
the disturbance it was going to make in their existence,—
their habits, and their pleasures.

Besides, except in cases where their own personal
interests were directly at stake, they tended to judge
social conflicts, not in accordance with their real importance, but according to the inconvenience and trouble
they caused them. For them, the strike of a quartet of
musicians, which prevented their seeing a theatrical performance, or that of a few dozen stable boys on a race
course which upset their bets, took on more serious proportions than a dockers' strike, which stopped the traffic
of a great port.

Therefore, it can readily be imagined that they were
moved and scared by the prospect of a universal strike!

Nevertheless, on awaking, they had one joy: the
daily papers appeared! They announced, indeed, that
they did not know if they would be able to appear to-
morrow; so far as a strike amongst their workmen was
concerned, it was only a question of hours. No matter!
They had appeared. It was a good omen.

On the other hand, one sight stupefied them, and
clouded their first joy, all the gas jets in the street flamed
away as they had done before midnight. The previous
evening, with special care, the lamplighters had gone
their usual rounds. After which, with a tranquil con-
science, they thought it superfluous to proceed to the
operation of extinguishing the lights, and had slept
through a full night.

Besides that, how many were the things in disorder,
and how many grounds there were for astonishment!
Each one took things according to his mood: some were
affected by the gravity and seriousness of events; others
jeered.

The Underground Railway no longer worked. This

was, however, served by a staff considered to be specially docile. The Revolutionists, with bitter irony, maintained that the risks of disease, which were very considerable there (consumption causing fearful ravages in the tunnel) together with the lowness of the wages, contributed to render this staff pliable and docile. Almost the only Trade Union which existed was a yellow one, formed with the approval of the Company. The red Trade Union was only a skeleton. Nevertheless, the metropolitan railway did not work!

In the morning, when the faithful staff wanted to set the trains in motion, they were not able to do so for want of electric current. The hours of the night had been taken advantage of to carry out effectively a work of unfastening bolts; and the electric force no longer ran through the cables. Besides, the generating stations were asleep. When their yellow staffs wanted to start the powerful dynamos, it was seen that a considerable amount of damage had been done: there was emery powder in certain places; some pieces of apparatus were disconnected, others had been short circuited.

The work had been done so effectively that starting the dynamos was, if not impossible, at least dangerous enough for whoever should attempt it. It was not tried, and the workmen were occupied solely in repairing the damage.

Neither tramways nor motorbusses were running. During the night, the Trade Union had held many meetings in different districts, in the course of which an immediate stoppage of work was decided on. Therefore, at the depôts from which the first departures should have started, there were very few employees. On the other hand, an animated crowd were stationed at the gates, determined to hinder the exit of any vehicles, in case some false brothers should wish to work.

The disordered and jolting run of the milk cart, which made rhythm with the clanging of the milk cans, in the grey hours of the dawn, had not disturbed the stones of the street.

The previous night the Trade Union had arranged so that neither the employees of the Trust Companies nor those of private masters mounted their seats on these carts.

Elsewhere, the aristocratic and commercial quarters had the benefit of a boycott that was disagreeable and evil smelling: the dust pails spread out the overflow of their rubbish on the pavement.   On the contrary, in the populous and workmen's quarters the street cleaners had as usual proceeded to the removal of the household rubbish.

The drivers of the municipal dust carts were not the only ones to adopt this choice of quarters where the strike should weigh more heavily.

In the same districts, the municipal street sweepers had abstained from cleaning the streets and boulevards, as well as from the daily watering.

Many Trade Unions carried out the same kind of boycott.

The workers thus proved that they knew how to ally to a clear understanding of the necessities of the class struggle, actions suited to the circumstances.

The General Strike had as its aim to employ the disintegrating power of the working class, and besides this moral demonstration, to attack their adversaries on the material side, to attack them in their needs, and in their pleasures.

Taking account of the social entanglement, it was difficult for the workers to deal blows at their enemies without hitting themselves by the rebound, but they decided, with a light heart, to face this necessity.

Nevertheless, they had no scruples about avoiding this rebound, whenever they could do so without endangering the principle of the General Strike.

Those workers acted from this motive, who, through cordial comradeship, (like the dustmen and street sweepers), endeavoured to lessen, in working class districts, the inconveniences of the arrest of work.

This clear vision of the accord necessary between

class brothers who were entering on a severe struggle, was a sign of the direction that the General Strike was going to take; to its first phase, purely dissolving and onesided, was going to follow a phase of effective solidarity, of social reconstruction.

For the moment, the significance of the conflict, which was still in its beginning, lay in its demonstration of the all powerfulness of the working class, as shown by a negative act: inaction, following on untiring activity.

And this inaction gained ground more and more!

At the bakers' shops bread ran short. A large number of the workers left work. The masters, striving to replace them, had to do the work themselves. However, in many bakehouses, the journeymen bakers, who were practised in strikes, took the precaution, before leaving, to make the ovens temporarily useless. And this without seriously damaging them, or throwing injurious substances into them. Owing to this fact a number of bakers found themselves at a loss.

Amongst the butchers, the meat famine was not yet noticeable. The strike only showed itself there by the smallness of the staff, a number of butchers' assistants having thrown down their aprons.

Amongst the grocers, and at the great provision stores, the same epidemic: a very limited staff carried on the business.

At the Markets, the morning obstruction had not the usual density. There was a calm instead of the daily jostling and uproar. Hardly any of the market gardeners in the neighbourhood had ventured out for fear of incidents. The majority preferred to abstain from taking the journey.

Thus, if it had not been for the consignments from the provinces, which still flowed in, the market would have made a very poor show.

This insufficiency had its echo in all quarters: the

greengrocers, fruiterers, and provision merchants were
scantily supplied.

Thus, from the first day of the strike, a symptomatic contraction affected the essential traffic, the provision trades. And, as the question of the stomach out-
weighs all others, this sign, the forerunner of a possible
famine, could only further excite uneasiness and increase
anxieties.

This disturbance, which revealed itself almost as
soon as the act of inertia by the working class had shown
itself, was a convincing proof of their power. It was
the workers, then, who made everything work in society:
they were the beast of burden, who, with his head under
the yoke, always bent towards the ground, had, without
end or respite, ploughed the hard furrow, fertilising it
with his sweat.

And here is the beast, tired of drudging under the
goad, stretching himself on the fresh earth; and raising
his head, is gazing into the future. What was going to
come of it? After having proved that he is the strong
and good worker, that without him only weeds and thorns
would spring up in the fields, that without him there is
nothing at all, is he going to have the audacity to want
to be everything?

For the present, he kept to a passive resistance.

In the industrial quarters, in the faubourgs, and
also in the surrounding districts, the workshops were deserted, and the high chimneys no longer spit forth their
black clouds above the factories.

In the Marais, the Faubourg du Temple, and the neighbouring districts where,—recalling the old time crafts,—
the artistic industries abounded and the hundred trades
connected with the making of "articles de Paris," the
workshops of the sculptors and carvers, jewellers, leather
workers, bronze workers, etc., were empty. Empty also,
in the swarming streets and districts which bordered the
Faubourg Antoine, were the cabinet makers' workshops. In

the St. Marcel quarter, on the banks of the Bièvre, the workers in leather left their work. The same thing happened at the Glacière, amongst the shoe factories, foundries, etc.

At Pantin, at Aubervilliers, the chemical works, soap works, match factory, were idle. It was the same at St. Denis, in the builders' yards, and the fifty other industrial prisons, where a population of immigrants from Bretagne and elsewhere withered away. At Ivry, at Batignolles, the blacksmiths took a holiday, the laundry workers at Boulogne, at Arcuel, the automobile makers at Levallois and Puteaux did the same.

Everywhere! Everywhere! In all yards, in all factories, in all workshops, the stoppage of work succeeded to the fever of production.

The workers simply folded their arms,—that was all!

Nevertheless, this unanimous suspension of work was not carried out at all points with the readiness desirable. On several occasions it was necessary to adopt the reverse of the "compelle intrare" of the New Testament; instead of compelling those to enter who refused, it was necessary to push the stubborn ones towards the door,—to compel them to go out.

The operation was carried out gently. The Trade Unions had mobilized a body of delegates, with the duty of seeing that the decision to strike should be generally carried out. These comrades acted as centres of union for bodies of strikers, who zigzagging from quarter to quarter, passed in review the factories and workshops, and made sure that the stoppage was complete.

Where work was not suspended, the demonstrators entered by assault. They at once cut the bands, turned off the commutators, let off the steam, extinguished the fires. These preliminary precautions taken, they explained to these thoughtless ones, who were continuing to drudge, how antisocial their act was, reproached them with this lack of the solidarity which workers owed one to another; endeavoured to make them understand that

they were injuring themselves, that they would suffer for
this treason, then, in conclusion to this short course of
Trade Union morality, "Off you go! Get out—all of
you!"

    Sometimes the delegates met with an attempt at
resistance; zealous foremen, masters infatuated with
their privileges, even workmen, thoughtless followers of
routine, interposed, and tried to drive back the strikers,
to prevent their entry. This resulted in some scuffles,
altercations, tumult. Then, if one of the champions of
order produced a revolver, or menaced the invaders, he
was at once deprived of the opportunity to do any injury,
the weapon was torn from his hands, and he was advised
not to repeat his offence.

    Nevertheless, if some of these incidents took a tragic
turn, they were very few, even when the masters decided
to call on the authorities for protection. The latter were
harassed by applications for assistance, not being able
to send either police or troops to the hundred different
points equally menaced, they did not know whom to listen
to, to whom to promise support.

    The measures already taken by the Government were
found to be quite insufficient and ineffective. Horse
patrols, indeed, rode up and down many of the streets,
bodies of troops were stationed at many strategic points,
but the delegates, who, like an element let loose, swept
down in a whirlwind, did not blindly drive on straight
before them, they knew how to avoid ambushes and to
march around patrols.

    At a favourable moment, they would double back,
and cross over to the right or left,—when necessary,
they would separate, in order to form up again somewhere behind; they did not resist the armed force,
they retired before them, refused battle, and went to work
farther on.

    At this game, the Government troops became ener-
vated and exhausted. They were the more harassed by
the useless and vain marches and counter marches that
were imposed upon them, because, in the majority of

cases, they arrived at the point they were ordered to
defend after the blow had been struck, having only the
disappointment of seeing the traces left by the strikers.

These last had on their side the superiority of initiative and spontaneity, they knew how to give their action
the dash that is favourable to success.

No monotonous repetitions, and acts that were always the same.

Thus, in order to vary their operations, they had
no scruple, on leaving a factory, against making for a
bazaar or draper's shop.

They made an irruption through all the doors at
once, they danced across the galleries, driving before
them the employees who were still at work. Their dis-
respect for the merchandise spread out was so complete,
that for fear of more serious losses, the directors hastened to liberate the staff, and immediately gave orders
to close the shutters.

And these crowds of workers, of shop assistants,
thus thrown on the streets of Paris, increased the excitement.

Whilst some of a domestic, timid disposition kept
out of the tumult and returned to their homes, others
found themselves in tune with it, they mixed with the
strikers, with the demonstrators, at first from simple
curiosity, then, led away by the excitement in the streets,
they were not amongst the least ardent, and they joined
heartily with their comrades.

Amongst the various scenes that the great city offered that day,—scenes where comedy was joined with
tragedy,—there was one which did not lack colour.

The stage for this, was the streets lying between the
Madeleine and the Opéra, between twelve and one o'clock
at noon.

Whilst the banks, and the shops for the sale of
luxuries, which swarm in this district, had judged it
prudent not to open their doors, the millinery and dress-

making firms, which also abound there, had required of
their staffs that they should attend to their work.

At the dinner hour the work girls, rather fearful,
but very curious to see the life and movement of the
streets, came down from their workrooms mutually em-
boldening each other.

The restaurants, generally extremely animated, where
gaiety dominated, and laughter was usually heard, were
almost deserted, and half silent; there was a murmur of
talk in an undertone, and the very limited service was
quite inadequate.

The strikers in the clothing trade, chiefly tailors,
judged this to be a favourable moment to lead the
whole body of workpeople to make common cause with
them.

In the morning, their efforts in this district had
failed: the display of police and military which, from
the Rue de la Paix to the Boulevard Malesherbes, was
very compact, placed an obstacle in their way. But now
these same strikers, being well acquainted with the habits
of the district, utilised the minutes of sauntering which
preceded the return to the workrooms. They mixed
amongst the groups of work-girls, explained the position to them, and led them to cry "Hurrah for the
strike!"

The authorities were alarmed by these half-serious,
half-joking shouts. They wanted to check them. It was
unlucky for them. What was at first chiefly amusement took a serious turn. In a short time, the Rue de
la Paix swarmed with a crowd, largely of women, who,
mocking and irritated, would not return to work.

Against this crowd, more exuberant than warlike,
who for arms could only brandish light umbrellas, the
police officers had the clumsy imprudence to use violence.
They ordered the police to charge them with their fists.
The men faced the attack, protecting the women as well
as they could. They only partly succeeded.

It was a savage scrimmage. Women and girls rolled
on the ground, struck and trampled on; others, frigh-

tened and maddened by the charge, suffered a mental and nervous reaction which made them ill with terror. Nothing was heard but cries of anguish, distress, and pain.

From the Rue de la Paix, the panic spread to the neighbouring streets. A rumour that women were being knocked down by the police spread everywhere, arousing the indignation of all.

It only needed this to empty tumultuously the work-rooms where work was still going on, in spite of the masters, who wanted to keep their staffs, and endeavoured to close the doors to prevent their going out.

The work girls, nervous and angered, dispersed like a flock of sparrows, and scattered to their various districts.

The recital of the events in which they had been the heroines and victims added a new grievance to the motives for excitement.

Thus the fermentation spread, not only from the fact of the strike,—intensified by the whirlwind of demonstrators,—but also because of the Governmental measures taken to stem the crisis.

Everything combined therefore, to give Paris the aspect of a city in revolt, and the pulsations of its vast organism of work and traffic became slower, approaching nearer and nearer to a total stoppage.

CHAPTER IV.

LET THERE BE DARKNESS.

What were the gas workers going to do? And what about the men at the electrical works? So far as the latter were concerned, there was no question. They had already given proof of the stuff they were made of. It was as good as certain that they would take part in the movement.

The Government were sure of it. But this hardly moved them, so sure were they of being able to remedy it. The sudden strikes of 1907 and 1908 had put them on their guard. They knew how the instantaneous stoppage of light, which occurred then, had impressed the whole population; they knew how this extinction of the electric light, coming without any warning, had disturbed and unfavourably affected public opinion, and had given the masses of the people the feeling that the Government had lost their power.

Therefore, the authorities had taken serious precautions against this happening again. After the stoppage of light in 1908, they decided to duplicate the staffs of electrical workmen by military staffs, who should always be ready to go anywhere, and take the place of strikers. Some detachments of engineers had therefore been mobilised, and there had been imposed on them a period of apprenticeship in the different works,—especially at the markets section.

The Government thus had, ready to hand, a military staff which was not altogether inexperienced. They already knew how to manage the apparatus, and would be ready,—it was at least hoped,—surrounded by engineers, managers, and foremen, to take the place, passably well, of the usual staff, in case the latter should fail them.

Further, the part these soldier-electricians were
to play was not to be limited to taking the place of
strikers; they were also required, at the first sign of a
cessation of work, to expel,—even by force of arms,—
the workers from the works.

These preventive measures were taken without delay. From the Tuesday morning, the various works for
producing electrical energy were occupied by parties of
engineers. Therefore, on this side, confident in the
measures taken, the authorities were absolutely tranquil.

For the rest, no sign of a strike, no effervescence
showed itself. The orders of the chiefs were promptly
executed,—and with the usual good will. It might have
been supposed that the electrical workers knew nothing
of the grave events that had just shaken so strongly the
torpor of the working classes.

The Government was still more confident with regard
to the gasworkers. Considering their Trade Union history, they were not to be feared; they were thought incapable of any energetic act. For years and years, all
their Trade Union action had consisted in respectful applications and requests to the authorities; respect for
legality seemed to have mummified them; they seemed
fixed in an attitude of submission. Therefore, the confidence of the Government was so profound, that, without
neglecting to take some precautionary measures with regard to them, at least those that were taken were not
overdone.

The day went by without incidents.

At nightfall Paris was lighted the same as on other
nights. The lighting up of the public electric lights took
place without any trouble. The same with the gas.

The light spread, dazzlingly. Not the least fluttering
or jumping. There was no hitch!

On the chief boulevards, the electric moons lighted
up with their whitish rays the already mocking smiles

of the bourgeois, quick to joke about these terrible men at the electric works, who were not going to make fools of themselves. Already, in the editorial rooms of the orthodox daily papers, envenomed pens were patching together the articles which should announce to the people to-morrow, that, thanks to such clever and intelligent ministerial measures, the electrical workers had not budged.

Suddenly, towards ten o'clock, when confidence was at its height, all over Paris, at the same moment, the electricity failed. Complete and instantaneous extinction!

The disillusion was severe. It was so much the worse because people had lulled themselves with hopes which the reality had upset. Smiles froze into grimaces, and faces grew longer.

The shopkeepers and manufacturers, accustomed to this inconvenience by previous strikes, had had the prudence to provide themselves with a mixed system of lighting, having recourse either to gas, acetyline, or simple oil lamps. They therefore turned to their alternative system of lighting.

Nevertheless, as far as gas was concerned, this method did not yield the hoped for results. The incandescent mantles blackened, the great circular chandeliers had no longer their illuminating splendour. The pressure fell with an alarming rapidity.

For a few minutes, this reduction of pressure was attributed to the great number of jets suddenly brought into use. There was nothing astonishing, they thought, that a diminution in the lighting power of the gas should correspond to an unexpected rise in the consumption. It was so much the easier to understand, as there was never any reserve in the gasometers, and a few hours consumption would suffice to empty them, unless more gas was made.

But when the light continued steadily to get lower, —soon to give no more light than a night-light,—then, no more at all!—Darkness!...Blackness!...It was surely necessary to seek some other explanation.

Nevertheless, the Government had carefully taken all sorts of precautions.

What had happened then? At the electrical works, as well as at the gas works?

In the electrical sections, the day-shift workers, when their working time was up, had retired without wanting to await the arrival of the night-shift men, who would replace them. But the latter, generally so punctual, did not arrive at all.

The menaces, promises, angry reproaches of the managers were without effect on the day-shift men who were leaving. All was in vain. Nothing made them go back on their resolution.

The workers having left, the managers thought of making use of the corps of engineers. There was bungling, contradictory orders, a nice dance. Before the soldiers went to their posts, which had first to be assigned to them, the fires under the boilers were almost extinguished, and several machines stopped for lack of steam.

The disorder increased,—became general. Contradictory orders, false moves, added to the trouble, and in a short time a good many dynamos were accidentally put out of action.

The confusion was still greater when it was found out that ill-will had been at work: emery powder had been thrown amongst the blocks, and in the bearings; certain layers had been watered with sulphuric acid, which after a short time set them on fire; some of the apparatus, and some of the distributing boards, had been short-circuited.

Many other acts of sabotage were reported from all over the place! It was desired that the machines should cease to work, and that was what had happened!

Who were responsible? Of course, there was no doubt that this damage, so carefully thought out, the effect of which was the suspension of the life of the works, was done by the electrical workers. Nevertheless, those who were used to reading faces thought they discovered in the attitude and on the faces of some of the soldiers the reflection of an interior satisfaction.

Were there saboteurs amongst this pampered corps of engineers, in whom the Government had placed its hopes? Were there amongst them any who had allowed themselves to be contaminated by the antimilitarist propaganda? Even this was possible!

Anyhow, the running of the works had become impossible. No one could go on under these conditions, and it was decided to stop the machines.

In spite of this, all did not seem lost. Some time ago, in order to guard against a stoppage of work in any of the Parisian works, all the latter had been connected up with a main station, situated in the suburbs. In this, the staff, carefully recruited, offered every guarantee for security, and it was carried on in a military way. There were no Trade Unionists there,—or so few that they were a negligeable quantity.

This electric station alone was capable of supplying nearly all the current required for Parisian consumption. For this, it was sufficient to make certain disconnections, and the electric energy would flow anew in the cables.

It was this course that the authorities at the disabled works on the outside and the centre decided to take, after having found out that they could not go on by themselves. Again all in vain. The current did not flow.

The explanation of this strange state of things was soon forthcoming.

An accident,—comparable to the rupture of an aneurism in the human body,—had suddenly brought the vast works to a standstill. A dull roll of thunder shook the ground, and they found the whole of the cables in an underground gallery were destroyed. The cables, although large and solid, were twisted, broken, cut up, and the heat of the deflagration had reached such a high degree that some of them bore traces of fusion. There was no possibility of doubt, this destruction had been caused by a powerful explosive. That was the

reason why the torrents of electricity they could have produced were not able to pass.

At the gas works,—contrary to all expectations,—
the staff of workers joined the strike. There, the movement was aided by the slight supervision exercised over
this staff, which was considered quite submissive.

It was the firemen who started the strike. They
formed a separate group, as in the electric sections.
There were amongst them men of a temperament that
became indignant at the weakness of their comrades;
who in a few hours well used, succeeded, first of all in
convincing the undecided, and then in preparing a strike
of the equipment.

At the hour agreed on, the firemen put out the fires,
and, going through the works, gave the signal to stop
work. Their inspiring audacity was contagious.

Not content with ceasing to produce, the gas workers took precautions, in order that, even if blacklegs or
soldiers were substituted for the strikers, it should not
be possible to make gas. Knowing the vulnerable points
of the piping, they opened or injured them, and from
the works arose a pestilence of hydrogen escaping from
gaping wounds.

The staff of directors and foremen strove in vain
to lessen this disaster. The gasworkers, who had for so
long gone astray, recovered themselves, and in their
anger at having hitherto been too sleepy, their hand was
heavy.

Nothing further could be done without important
repairs, which would take a long time.

Darkness spread over Paris,—a darkness that could
be felt!

During previous strikes only the electric light had
failed. Nevertheless, the disturbance had been very
great in spite of the fact that there had only been a
diminution of light—and not total extinction. As a matter
of fact the streets and boulevards continued to be lighted
by gas, which many shopkeepers also had. It was in

reality the system of lighting that was usual a quarter of
a century before, but Paris was not plunged into im-
penetrable darkness.

Now, both gas and electricity failed at the same
time.   This was no half darkness! The sudden extinction of light made the darkness appear still thicker
to unaccustomed eyes. The confusion was indescribable,
and the nervousness of the population, who were already
rudely shaken, reached a climax. Scared, perplexed folks
ran right and left, like a whirlpool, half mad.

The intense blackness that enwrapped the city was
pierced here and there by bright gleams.   It was the
glimmer of those establishments, which making their
own light,—electricity or acetylene,—were not affected by
the strike.

Now the pulsations of the great city began to get
slower; it seemed as though the darkness which invaded it was an omen of death. The theatres and all
other places were emptied in a roar of conversation, and
amidst exclamations which told of anxiety and panic.

The strike which had just broken out was going to
have other effects; to the privation of light was added
the privation of power. A number of motors moved by
electricity or gas fell asleep, compelling many workshops
to cease work.   .

Besides which, the darkness was going to aid the
further action of the general strikers. They would be
freer to carry out their plans, less at the mercy of the
Government's forces. Their power would grow from the
discredit with which the failure of light had covered the
authorities.

This phase of the struggle, through the reaction it
had on other trades, constituted a grave check for the
Government.   It was, with the strike of the railway
workers and postal employees, the pivot of the General
Strike, the triumph of which could be foreseen from this
moment.

CHAPTER V.

THE FUNERAL OF THE VICTIMS.

The funeral of the unfortunate men killed in the course of the Sunday's demonstration had been fixed for the Wednesday. With the consent of their families, their bodies remained at the offices of the Federations. The Government had not interfered. But they took great precautions, they brought together considerable forces, taking care to station them in the side streets, along the whole route that the procession would travel. They were, however, optimistic: it was their forecast that on the day of the funeral the stoppage of work would reach its height, and would then decrease.

The day began with an atmosphere of funereal gloom. The newspapers had not appeared, and besides, some of the Trade Unions, which yesterday had not moved, now joined the movement. Amongst others, the postmen and telegraphists stopped work, the telephones only partly worked, and on the railways only a very limited staff remained at work.

The entire city thus harmonised with the funeral ceremony for which preparations were being made.

As the meeting place, Rue Grange-aux-Belles, made concentration difficult, the funeral procession was formed in the Place du Combat. But, long before the announced time, an enormous crowd had come together.

The Trade Unions had fixed points for the assembling of their members, on the quays of the canal, the neighbouring streets, and the exterior boulevards.

Thus, there swarmed everywhere an innumerable multitude, from whom, in angry outbursts, arose imprecations and curses against the authorities.

Behind the funeral cars, which were hidden under mountains of wreaths, after the relatives, and after the representatives of societies, this huge crowd took its place. And then the procession moved. It was a human flood which flowed, swollen at every street corner by new torrents.

Over this ocean of heads, above which could only be seen dashes of red and black,—the banners and flags,—there reverberated, like the rolling of thunder, roars of hatred, shouts of vengeance.

This hardly fitted in with the Government's optimism. The fighting spirit, the heat of revolt, which for the moment, three hundred thousand throats expressed in angry cries, would it not burst forth in some dangerous form, if a pretext were given it by a collision, or some other incident?

This was the more to be feared, as in the districts traversed to reach the cemetery of Pantin, one felt that the heart of the faubourgs beat in unison with that of the crowd who followed the funeral procession. At every street corner, were crowds of human beings, who bowed their heads as the funeral cars passed by, replying to the shouts of the multitude by cries for vengeance.

And when, after a sudden calm, there burst forth, in one immense rhythm, which swept along the vast procession, the roaring strophes of "The International," one felt that, there and then, the song was transforming itself into action; that the "last fight" of which it spoke, was not for "to-morrow," but for to-day, now,—now!

Then along this human sea passed the thrill of fateful feeling; everyone was moved to the depths of his being.

But no obstacle hindered its march,—army and police became more and more invisible,—the funeral procession continued its journey, rolling its tumultuous flood up to the cemetery.

There, at the side of the graves, the speeches were short and vigorous. No one thought of fine phrases. And besides, beyond the few thousands who could hear what was said, there stretched away immense crowds to whom not even in the faintest whisper did any words reach. In exclamations that ended in sobs, in sentences cut short in the middle, and punctuated by clenched, uplifted hands, one after the other the speakers ended by an oath, which, under the low, grey sky, was re-echoed in decisive approval. The strike should have neither end nor truce until the Government had capitulated, until it had avowed its crime, until it had punished the murderers of these victims mourned by the people.

Now the stream flowed back to Paris,—like the flood tide which hurls itself against the coasts in a day of tempest. In colossal waves, the crowds of people advanced, thoroughly aroused, in a tension of revolt.

The authorities took a false step, they passed from an extreme reserve, to a provocative confidence, they departed from the caution they had observed up to then, and they took it into their heads to adopt measures that exasperated the demonstrators.

Instead of remaining hidden, and invisible, the troops, flanked by police, received the order to form barriers, to prohibit the access to certain roads, to dam up the crowd, and only to permit their re-entry into Paris along certain channels, and to do this in such a way as to divide and separate them.

At any other time, this method of dispersing the crowd and sending them on another track, would have been submitted to without too much protest. But now, this was impossible; the nervous tension and extreme excitement of the demonstrators had become too acute. This mass of people was so large, so compact; it was animated by such a force impelling it forward, that it was madness to try to disperse it, or even to hinder it. The barriers that were opposed to its progress were broken through, and it passed on.

The crowd advanced in ranks so closely packed

together that it was impossible for them to retreat, even had they wished to. They went forward with an irresistible rush : like an enormous wedge, they forced their way into the midst of the armed mass,—and the troops had to give way before their pressure. The infantry broke their ranks the more readily because they began to feel repugnance for the fatigue duties that had been imposed upon them, and they only obeyed in a sullen and lazy way. As to the cavalry, they were paralyzed by the human flood, surrounded—submerged !

But when the demonstrators, who had kept calm before the troops, found themselves confronted by police, they threw themselves on them furiously.

Their whole rage was concentrated on the police. They wanted to revenge on them the murder of those they had just escorted to their last resting place.

It was the police they always found barring the way. Therefore there commenced a furious struggle against them, and revolvers, which their hands had gripped all the morning, sprang out of their pockets.

The police officers grasped the fact, a little late, that they would have to let the storm pass by.

These skirmishes, however lively and violent they might be, were nevertheless only an incident underlining the gravity of this much more important fact : the intensification of the strike.

The hopes cherished by the Government gave way, the end of the day was marked, not by the slackening which they had hoped for, but by a still greater stoppage of work.

In the evening a great many meetings were held. Each Trade Union had summoned its members to special meetings, for the purpose of considering the situation, of examining the extent of the movement, and of discussing what attitude they ought to adopt.

The most important of these meetings were the district meetings held by the railway workers, by the postmen and telegraphists, and those held by the various descriptions of municipal employees.

The meetings held by the workmen of the various railway Companies, at which those connected with the transport department had the determining influence, decided that the strike, which on the railways had not yet become general, owing to waverings and regrettable hesitations, should continue, and to be carried out to its logical results. They took steps to ensure that the movement should not be limited to the Paris district; that it should extend from one end of the railway systems to the other, and that the departure and working of trains should be hindered as much as possible.

At the meetings of the P.T.T. (Postal Telegraph and Telephone Union) a rumour circulated, which stimulated all those who might have been undecided: they learned that the Government, as soon as the first stoppage of the service had taken place, had decided to have recourse to coercive measures. To this threat, they replied by very definite decisions. The stoppage of work which had, up to then, only been temporary, was transformed into a strike movement. This being agreed to, they at once considered the necessary precautions to take, to render ineffective any attempt to re-establish the service, whether by the aid of false brothers, or by the employment of soldiers in the place of the strikers.

The resolutions taken by the municipal employees were not less energetic, although of a more special character: all voted for an indefinite strike, without fixing its length. Only, according to the work done by the different departments, the use of the boycott which had already begun to be applied was confirmed.

By insertion on this black list, the middle class and wealthy districts would be hit without exception, whilst the workmen's districts would be a little relieved, and would not endure all the inconveniencies of the strike.

These discussions upset the optimism of the governing class. They had calculated that work would be resumed in the great public services after a twenty-four hours' stop. But nothing of the kind happened. On the contrary, the workers in these departments joined their comrades in this movement most heartily.

When these decisions became known at the many meetings held by various Trade Unions, the news was received with frantic applause. Resolutions of a similar character were adopted everywhere. Everywhere it was decided to carry on the strike to the bitter end, to continue the struggle until the claims of the mourners,—the whole people,—had been satisfied.

The satisfaction demanded was no longer limited to a simple capitulation of the Government, which, on consideration, it was seen, would be no more than a moral success. To the sympathetic strike, was now added the strike with new demands, in plain words,—the Revolutionary Strike.

In these meetings, where the actions of the morrow were being planned, weighty speeches were made. Whilst some called to mind, and explained again, the numberless claims which up to then had been made without success; —and added that the times were favourable for pressing them forward anew;—others saw much further: they proclaimed the administrative capacity of the working class; they urged that the psychological moment was near, and that it was necessary, from now onward, to consider the possibility of the fall of Capitalism.

In the furnace of these meetings, where brains were highly charged; and where, at the flame of reality, ideas surged up and became clear; by the side of those timid ones, who were always hesitating, there were those who were more impatient, who were exasperated by the slowness of events. The latter found the strides too short, and dreamed of doubling the pace. In their keen determination, they reproached those who showed signs of indecision, or hanging back; proving to them that, in the present circumstances, the greatest prudence lay in acting at once.

From this conflict of ideas, this mixture of proposals: arguments for the organisation of struggle
and resistance, arguments for the struggle to obtain
limited and special demands, arguments for the revolutionary extension of the strike, and the need for it to
end in general expropriation,—from all this discussion,
there separated out a compound, which constituted a new
phase in the struggle.

The people took a step forward in the path of the
Revolution: the period of the sympathetic strike that
was purely defensive ended, and the gleam of the first
rays of the attacking strike were seen, whose lightnings
illuminated the horizon with flashes of fire.

What made this outburst of revolt the more to be
dreaded was that the ferment was not restricted to
Paris: in the provinces it was at its height; they no
longer needed to take lessons in revolution from the
Capital, they did not wait for its signal before taking
action: the agitation was not less than in Paris.

CHAPTER VI.

THE POSITION OF THE GOVERNMENT.

The Government did not remain inactive. They were very anxious to weaken the strike, to minimize the inconveniences of the stoppage of work, and above all to reassure the wealthier classes, who quite lost their heads in the panic of the first days. One desire dominated them, to give the impression that the economic life of the community was not checked, that the economic circulation was only slackened, and not altogether held up.

They thought this was the best way of curing the wealthier classes of the fear which had them in its grip. Therefore, although their alarm was awakened by the great outcry in the capital, they endeavoured to disguise the strike by replacing strikers by soldiers, in the more necessary industries and services.

As soon as notice was received from any point, that work had stopped, a party of soldiers was sent there.

For instance, squadrons of soldiers were sent to the bakehouses, to make bread in the place of the bakers. Only in many cases, they were prevented from starting work by a variety of causes, the result of precautions taken by the strikers before leaving work : either the raw material was not at hand, or else the ovens would not work, or worked badly. These difficulties were got over more or less, rather less than more, by using the military ovens.

At the electric works, the military engineers, although long familiar with the work expected from them, were not able to start the dynamos. The strikers had taken their preventive measures so skilfully that nothing would work.

To combat the strike of the postal and telegraph staffs, as well as that of the railway men, the Government thought of mobilising the reserves. They drew up an elaborate order, by which all those who were inscribed on the army lists were called up, and their refusal to obey the summons would render them liable to be court martialed.

But, after consideration, they had to yield to the logic of facts, and to recognize that, at the stage events had now reached, this summons would have no effect. Giving up this plan, which would have been merely ridiculous, they endeavoured to re-establish communications by utilising military means.

Some soldiers were mobilised to carry on the railway traffic. But there, as elsewhere, special arrangements had been made; the essential parts of the locomotives had been taken to pieces and hidden: then again, in order to make it difficult to take them out of the sheds where they were kept, plaster or cement had been poured between the points, which prevented their working. The same methods kept the railway waggons and carriages idle on their sidings.

Besides this, before leaving work, the engine drivers had brought their trains to the stations, and had left them on the main lines, after taking care to make them incapable of being moved.

This accumulation, at the usually busiest points, of a multitude of trucks and carriages that are generally travelling backwards and forwards, formed an inextricable mass. Passenger carriages, and especially goods waggons, accumulated in such numbers that the stations were blocked by them. The obstruction was so great and so complete that movement, to say nothing of the carrying on of traffic, was made impossible.

Besides, along the lines, all signals had been placed at danger; this systematic blocking, whilst paralyzing the traffic, had the advantage of rendering any accident impossible. As a matter of fact, the trains that they succeeded in starting could only proceed with extreme slowness, the most elementary caution compelling the engine drivers to travel at a very low speed, as they did not know if the line was clear or not. What was more, in a great many places fog signals had been ingeniously put, so that, in case of traffic being carried on, their bursting would increase the confusion.

This stoppage of the railway service had been greatly helped by the support of the pointsmen to the strike. It was a very valuable assistance, as of themselves, the pointsmen are masters of the traffic.

By these measures, and others which tended in the same direction, the starting of the trains had become almost impossible, and also useless,—at least for the passengers. In fact, if it had been possible to start trains, they would have travelled empty, the fear of accidents damping the courage of the most venturesome.

The stoppage of the railways involved the stoppage of the postal service, even supposing that the postmen had continued at work: it stands to reason that the strike of the latter hindered it still more. To take the place of these, recourse was had to soldiers: the strike of postmen was met by organising an automobile service.

The Government tried everywhere, under these circumstances, to save its face, to mask its weakness. For this service did not give, and it could not give, the results that were expected from it.

This organisation was too imperfect, as well as too slow; for, in their journeys, one of the least of the troubles these automobile postmen had to endure was the meeting, along the road, of notices to automobilists to drive slowly, even when no feature of the road justified their being put up. The chauffeurs, who were soldiers knowing very little about the roads, only advanced therefore with hesitation, and at a very moderate speed.

On the other hand, when passing through strike districts, they were often asked to stop, and their machines were confiscated.

The disorder was still more complete in the telegraphic service. In the Paris offices the suspension of work was absolute. In order to render any work impossible the wires had been confused, or cut so much more completely because previous strikes had given the staff of the P.T.T. (Postal Telegraph and Telephone) some experience in the matter.

At first the upper classes were not much affected by their telegraphic and telephonic isolation. They thought this could be remedied by the military service of wireless telegraphs and telephones.

Here again they were greatly deceived. Amongst the strikers were men of considerable scientific attainments, to whom it was child's play to render wireless communication impossible. They established themselves in a workshop situated on a height and hidden from observation, having at their disposal about forty horse power, and an excellent dynamo, they erected antennae, taking care not to excite attention; and they threw into the atmosphere adverse waves that disturbed and confused the signals given out by the Government post offices.

Thus to the strike of arms and brains was added the strike of machines and material.

And this state of things was not restricted to the Trade Unions named above: in most of the Unions the tools and machinery had been intentionally put out of working order, and this was done in such a way that they remained unusable until the strikers returned to work.

In taking these preventive measures, the workmen had not acted from a senseless, mean, or wicked motive: they did not wish to destroy—for mere pleasure. Far from this. Their aim had been to take precautions which they considered essential; it is even very probable the most refined had felt a certain sadness in having recourse to such extremes. But they resolved on this course of action, because they were convinced that by putting industrial machinery and material, for the moment, out of action, they would save human lives.

Desiring keenly the end,—the triumph of the strike,—they had the courage not to ban any means that could bring them nearer to their aim.

They knew they were a minority,—numerous enough to checkmate the possessing and governmental minority,—on condition that no section of the people should lend its support to the latter minority. In order to make them the strongest, one condition was necessary : that the mass of people, whom the force of inertia has always inclined to the winning side, should be placed in such a position that it would be utterly impossible for them to give the enemy the support of their unconscious force.

This result was obtained by extending the strike of arms and brains to that of machines and materials. By taking the tools out of the hands of that part of the people who were still too ready to submit to the power of the capitalists ; by paralyzing the machine that their labour made fruitful ; by preventing this sheep-like mass from coming to terms with the common enemy, and betraying their friends by a return to work at an inopportune time, the Revolutionists proved their clearness of vision.

It was this which gave them the boldness that the circumstances of the moment required.

Against these tactics,—which were only the logical carrying out of the idea of a General Strike,—the army was powerless. Even had the army been capable of doing everything, qualified to remedy the strike of machines and equipment, qualified to do all the work that was indispensable, it was not possible to set the soldiers to everything, and send them everywhere. There was an insurmountable reason for their powerlessness,—they were too few.

In spite of the best will in the world on the part

of the Government to intervene, there was an obstacle to setting the whole of their army to industrial work and public services. They were not inexhaustible in number. It was necessary to keep some in reserve for the defence of Capitalism.

They had transformed the soldiers into bakers, electricians, gasworkers, railway workers, motormen, telegraphists, postmen, street sweepers, etc., but still this was not enough. There were other trades by the dozen still idle, where the troops could offer no help.

Very considerable numbers of troops were scattered about, guarding work-yards, factories, warehouses, shops, canals, railways, public monuments, and so forth. These constituted thousands of men taken away from real production, and taken away from their warlike function.

In normal times, the army was made up of about 600,000 soldiers, scattered about in barracks throughout France. Now, at that time in Paris alone, there were more than 600,000 strikers.

The numerical powerlessness of the army to combat the General Strike, was so much the more evident as the revolutionary upheaval was not confined to Paris. As a consequence, the Government had at its disposal, for purposes of repression, hardly any more than the troops in the barracks of the capital, or in its immediate vicinity. There were two causes which brought about this condition of things; they could not empty the provinces of troops, as "order" was gravely imperilled there too, and, on the other hand, they could not move regiments about as they wished, outside of their garrison districts.

They had tried to bring troops from the East to Paris,—and the attempt had been a miserable failure.

They organised some military trains, which they endeavoured to work in spite of the strike. They did not get very far. These convoys were blocked in the open country, stopped by the unfastening of rails, or by the destruction of bridges and tunnels.

The really reliable troops, whom the ministers regrette'd they had not ready to hand,—who would have punished the people with pitiless fury,—were the Algerian regiments, recruited from the Arabs, who still submitted, like the children of the mother city, to the blood tax. These would have been fine brutes to let loose on Paris! These soldiers were not embarassed by scruples, and would joyfully have revenged their race on the pariahs of France. But it was not possible to count on them. They were in Algerian barracks. If they had been successfully embarked, it would have been difficult to disembark them at Marseilles, or any other port, and still more difficult to get them as far as Paris.

Thus, scarcely had the economic war begun, than the army, the sole rampart of Capitalism, found itself outflanked. The rulers were compelled to face the facts; the soldiers were too few effectively to carry on the vast number of employments for which they were required.

This numerical insufficiency of the army was increased by a moral insufficiency still more dangerous for the authorities; the soldiers doubted the justice of their work, and they slid on an incline, at the end of which nothing was visible but disintegration.

The Antimilitarist propaganda was the initial cause of this depression. With savage, tireless energy Antimilitarists worked to break down the coercive power of the army, by showing them the hateful nature of the work they were required to do.

These symptoms, which were of bad omen for capitalist society, were superficially perceived by the Government. Hypnotised by the prestige of a centralisation which brought everything under their control, they believed themselves as strong and unbreakable as a rock. For this reason they only thought of checking the strike. It did not occur to them at any time to examine the claims formulated by the Trade Union organisations,—that they should investigate into the responsibility which they had incurred through the tragic events of Sunday.

To pay attention to the ultimatum of the strikers, to consider it, would be, they thought, to abandon their

dignity, to make terms with insurrection. They therefore supported all their subordinates; and, far from
inquiring into their acts, they drew up a plan of police
and judicial measures which they thought would be effective to disable and kill the movement.

They did nothing new. They acted energetically
in the traditional way in which Governments act. The
courts were set in motion, and for reasons of State, they
were ordered to proceed to a grand capture of militant
pickets, secretaries of organisations, and members of
committees.

The carrying out of this great plot was arranged
to take place on the Thursday. This day was chosen
because they considered that at this moment there would
be a slackening, and also because they did not dare to
make these arrests before the funeral, for fear of increasing the intense excitement.

This measure did not have the expected success.
The secret was not kept, and, in unknown ways, it came
to the knowledge of those concerned. A number of
those who were menaced by arrest took precautions;
they took themselves out of harm's way, and when the
police presented themselves the majority of them were
not to be found.

This was a check for the Government. The blow
missed, and it had not the demoralising effect upon the
people that was expected. But repressive measures were
redoubled. Besides, the slackening hoped for by the
ministerial strategists did not take place; on the contrary, there was an extension and intensification of the
strike.

It should be added that the authorities were deprived of one means of action, that, up to then, had been
a great support; the daily press.

Certainly it was annoying to get no news; but the
people gained by becoming themselves again, by thinking for themselves: deprived of newspapers, they followed their own impulses, they reflected and decided

according to their own reasoning, without being influenced
by the fiction mongers of the great capitalist dailies.
    And this was bad for the Government: as, not
having any longer at its command this formidable lever
of the press, it could no longer spread its menaces and
falsehoods.   From this fact, a balance was set up between them and the democratic societies, to the advantage of the latter.   Up to then, Trade Union organisations had only had rather rudimentary means of propaganda, consisting of leaflets, manifestos, placards, and
small journals.   But now it was in their power, in spite
of the strike, to have recourse to these other methods,
which enabled them, with the journal of the C.G.T.
(Confédération Générale du Travail) that punctually appeared, to counteract the effect of alarmist rumours on
public opinion.

    Thus, as a logical result of the strike, the Govern-
ment found themselves losing ground both morally and
materially.
    To recover their prestige, they threw themselves
more desperately into the work of repression, and redoubled their brutalities.   They only succeeded in making
themselves still more unpopular, more despised and disliked, and in involving in the detestation and hatred
with which they were surrounded the capitalist system
of which they were the combative expression.

CHAPTER VII.

THE BEGINNING OF THE SYNDICALIST ATTACK.

There remains no longer any hope that the crisis will become less acute, nor that it will be charmed away by palliatives or half measures. Conciliation has become impossible. The industrial war is declared, and it is seen to be fierce and implacable. The enemies are face to face, and no peace can be foreseen, until one of the two adversaries is defeated, and utterly destroyed.

It was not with cannon shots that the working class has opened fire on the wealthy classes. It is by an act at once formidable and simple,—by folding their arms. Now hardly has this attitude been adopted, when behold, Capitalism is shaken by spasms symptomatic of its death throes. This proves that it is the same with the body social as with the human body; all arrest of function, of circulation, is prejudicial and injurious for it.

A happy omen for the General Strikers! it gives encouragement to persevere, and the certainty of a near triumph.

Whilst the workers drew energy and strength from events as they unfolded themselves, the privileged classes only found in them emotions of a quite opposite kind: their panic reached amazing proportions.

From the first revolutionary upheavals, an unreasonable panic had seized the parasitic minority; whose artificial and superficial life was made up of snobbery, and puerile, foolish, and luxurious pre-occupations. These useless people were immediately rendered helpless, they were unhinged, overwhelmed. The fear of the people almost frightened them to death.

In the aristocratic quarters there was a mad helter skelter, a distracted flight. The last of the race thought the end of the world had come; they abandoned their princely houses; and many took themselves off to burrow in their country houses, where they naively believed themselves to be sheltered from the storm.

The great international caravanseries also became empty, the sumptuous hotels, select restaurants, and all the places,—bad and otherwise,—where foreigners of note flock, and where fashionable society and great money bags idle away their time.

The middle class who lived on the parasitism of these great parasites,—shopkeepers and suppliers of luxuries, were not less affected than the rich people. They uttered jeremiads on the difficulties of making a living, and above all mourned the bad state of business, and reckoned up the lack of profit-making that this strike had brought about.

On the Stock Exchange there was at first the uproar usual on days of crisis. Prices tumbled down with a promptitude the more disordered that the mob of financiers, gamblers, vultures and crocodiles was already less dense. The tenacious, obstinate, business men, who hugged the dream of raking in millions from the fall in Government stocks, were solid at their posts; although their anxiety was expressed by their less strident shouts; their voices became husky, the bawling became less noisy.

However, in the world of the possessing classes, the financiers did not cut such a bad figure when compared with some of the others. More accustomed to sudden changes of fortune, hardened by fantastic gains and sudden losses they instinctively scented the profits that could be made from a catastrophe. In the present circumstances, they were less readily overcome by the fever of fear, they could put their armour on before a peril, and try to face it. That is why the great masters of financial establishments, dispensers of credit, and regulators of the circulation of gold,—this life blood of capitalist society,—placed themselves at the disposal of the Government, ready to make sacrifices and to help them in all possible ways.

There were also some amongst the middle classes who preserved their clearness of mind, who had no weak and fearful soul, and they were inclined to defend themselves. They owed this elasticity to the modern education, which, by exalting physical culture, and turning them in the direction of outdoor sports, had endowed them with muscles. By motoring, by their infatuation for aviation, they had acquired a capacity for quick decision, a contempt for danger, and an energy that was not scared by the first shock. They compared themselves with the workers, and held they were muscularly as strong as the broadest-backed amongst them, and they decided to face them. Their attitude is explainable, even if it was a little boastful, as by defending their class, their privileges, they tried to maintain their position ; they fought for the continuance of their life of pleasure and idleness.

The clubs and societies, of which these people bourgeois by disposition, were members, deliberated, and decided to discuss matters with the Government offering to form themselves into corps of bourgeois free lances, who would fight against the people.

The Government were scared at this proposal ; they feared that this offer concealed some manoeuvre of the Royalist parties whose competitions and hopes were aroused. In order not to assist their adherents in any way, they did not accept this proposal. They had a second reason for declining this offer : they feared that to accept it would show that they thought the present situation was more grave than they wished people to think. They thanked them, prolix in words of gratitude, but affirming that the army would suffice to overcome this crisis.

This confidence which they pretended to have, and

wanted others to share, events gave the lie to. The army had indeed camped in Paris, had patrolled it in every direction, and had striven to take the place of the strikers, but the result achieved did not correspond to the efforts made. Faster and faster the strike spread. And the nervous tension in the atmosphere, which continued to grow, was increased by the lack of news. Disquieting rumours circulated; and these tales, which it was not possible to verify, increased the anxiety and worry.

Newspapers appeared more rarely than ever. The most powerful ones, by financial means, succeeded with difficulty in bringing out some rudimentary and intermittent sheets.

The city lost its background of luxury and pleasure. It was no longer the busy, commercial, manufacturing city. It took on the rust of a necropolis,—and also its mouldiness. The tremors that shook it suggested decay. The military occupation, which gave it in some respects the appearance of a camp, did not efface this impression of something dying. Its streets were gloomy and empty. There was no movement except in the great arteries of traffic, where there strolled about a motley crowd of unemployed workers and employees, and scared bourgeois.

The coming and going of vehicles was very much lessened: a few cabs, mostly driven by cabmen who in normal times spent the night in hanging about railway stations, and near places of amusement; a few motors, having at the wheel not professionals, but amateurs,—young and robust men of the middle class, who swaggered about proud of their biceps.

The majority of shops had put up their shutters; the exceptions, which remained half open, were cafés and wineshops, where the owners and their families did the work.

Life, reduced to its material necessities, became more and more difficult. The difficulty of obtaining food increased. In spite of every effort, the Government did not succeed in assuring the supply of food.

During the first days, all those who were able to rushed to the provision shops, to lay in stores of provisions. But if the bourgeois part of the population had succeeded in laying in stocks of provisions, there were very few amongst the people who had been able to obtain any,—either little or much.

Many workers, having no other resources than their wages, were taken unawares. By hard work they barely succeeded in making both ends meet. When the strike broke out, how could they have bought provisions? And now, when their wages vanished, now that provisions, become more scarce, were selling at excessively high prices, how were they to get out of their difficulties? If they remained with their arms folded, no other prospect was visible than distress and famine in a very short time.

At least as badly off as these were those comrades who had for a long time carried on a conflict with their employers; and who, even now, could only keep alive by the help of the Trade Unions, and the Communist kitchens.

It was impossible for the Trade Unions, with the funds at their command, to assure, even for a short time, a pittance to strikers, who from now on would number many thousands.

And also was it not to be feared that both of them,—the strikers of yesterday and the strikers of to-day,—gripped by hunger, would be driven to the cruel necessity of again taking the road to the factory or workshop?

Besides, was it not necessary to reckon with others who were in a yet more piteous plight, more frightfully unfortunate, the perpetual strikers, the unemployed? Multitudes at the end of all their resources, lamentable waifs and strays! The pawn shop having swallowed up their last rags, these poor wretches vegetated, lived no one knows how, or rather they died by slow torture. Now the hope of a meal, would it not bring up these reserves of flesh and blood to work against the strikers?

And then, was there not a risk that the class war would develope into a fratricidal war,—poor devils against poor devils: unemployed against strikers?

This is to say that the food question dominated
everything. It was the riddle of the new sphinx. If
the workers found its solution the road was open before
them,—wide and beautiful,—if not, they would be de-
voured. They would fall again under the yoke, a heavier
one than ever !

Since the declaration of the strike, the large Co-
operative Stores had made arrangements to supply bread,
not only to their members, but also to non-co-operators.

It was quite evident that, so long as the mechanism
of Commercialism hemmed in these Co-operative Societies, they could only proceed to free distributions of the
bread and other provisions they had in stock, in too
small quantities. It must also be added, that if they
had been able to do more, it would still have been insufficient to satisfy such a vast multitude.

At this psychological moment, which would decide
the future of the movement, the people had an intuition
of what it was necessary to do. Was it simply an instinct of self preservation, or was it a reminiscence of
social theories that might have been sown in their brains,
to sleep there, and suddenly to burst forth at the fateful
moment?

In any case, there occurred in the working class the
same phenomena of spontaneous inspiration and fruitful boldness that marked the dawn of the Revolution of
1789-93. This Revolution, whose political aspirations
have been specially extolled, was accompanied by acts
that showed the existence of profound economic tendencies. Before concerning themselves about the form of
Government, the people thought about how they should
live ; and they attacked the rich, and the monopolists.
Both in the towns and in the country the industrial up-
risings were innumerable ; here bands took by assault
magazines of wheat, and divided the stores they found
there ; there other bands took possesion of flour, took
it to the baker's, and, after it was baked, proceeded to

distribute the bread; elsewhere, the crowd demanded that provisions should be sold in the markets at cheap rates, in order that all could provide themselves with food. Everywhere, the main motive of the movement was bread; then, as they were carried away by events, the rebels sacked the houses of tax collectors, pillaged country mansions, and burnt the records of feudal rights and taxes.

The same state of mind showed itself in the working class on the proclamation of the General Strike; a breath of revolt passed over the miserable unemployed, until then so weak, and so incapable of any energetic action. They gave no thought to taking the place of the strikers, they only thought of how they should live. They, and all the unthinking ones who until the night before, bent their backs and trudged about without hope, caught a gilmpse of salvation, of an escape from misery. Amongst them there sprang up the same thoughts as those that aroused the people in 1789: to assure themselves bread and a means of living.

Bands formed here, there, and everywhere, who assailed the shops of bakers, grocers, butchers. To the injured shopkeepers, who naturally recriminated, the rebels, with superb coolness, gave signed orders of requisition, which they assured them would be paid at the Labour Exchange. After which they proceeded to a free distribution.

Against these bands, who sprang up spontaneously, without any warning, and worked at distant points, police and troops were sent. A futile intervention! The armed force often arrived too late. But, in the rare cases where they arrived in time to disperse the looters, they met with no resistance. The band, amongst whom were women and children, side by side with the men, allowed themselves to be dispersed without trouble. Those whom it was decided to arrest followed without resistance, the more readily that, knowing the prisons to be overcrowded, they foresaw that they would only make a short stay at the neighbouring police station. Such a passive revolt made it difficult to employ violent means against these bands. And thus it came about that, numerous and reiterated as these scenes of commandeering were, they rarely became tragic.

This non-resistance was, besides, a policy to which the crowd had recourse on many occasions: they had the prudence to decline to take part in useless and dangerous battles, which would have been for them wholesale massacres. But when they judged it was opportune to disappear their retreat was not a disbandment. After having fallen back this same crowd re-formed in another quarter,—and everything had to begin over again for the troops of "law and order."

Besides, the authorities could but observe how quickly the respect and fear they formerly inspired had vanished from amongst the workmen.

It soon became impossible for a policeman to go about alone. The police were chased, even to the houses in which they lived. As the greater part of them lived in workmen's quarters, where they found themselves next door to strikers, they were tracked, worried, and had to put up with reprisals.

Amongst the mass of policemen, there were some who had joined because they could find nothing better to do, pushed to it by necessity. These lacked the sacred fire, and when they realised that the occupation had become dangerous, that they got some hard knocks, they failed to report themselves, and hid so well that no one saw them again. As to the others,—the zealous ones,— in order to save themselves from popular anger, they demanded that they should be lodged in the police stations or in barracks.

Thus the hunt for policemen of all kinds was vigorously, pitilessly organised. Rapid investigations were set on foot about suspects, and speedily brought to a conclusion by those around them, their neighbours; and the districts where workers formed the chief element in the population were purged.

On their side, the Antimilitarist societies acted with redoubled boldness. They no longer limited their activity to lecturing squadrons of soldiers, they attracted them to meetings, told them of the example set by the French Guards in 1789, and by the infantry on the 18th March, 1871, and incited them to adopt a like attitude.

It even happened more than once, that the Antimilitarists passed from lectures on morality to action: to the disarmament of some sentries and then to that of all the soldiers at a post. Often the latter did not resent this violence, and took their disarmament with a friendly grin.

The restlessness of the army, and their moral depression became accentuated, aggravated by the deplorable material conditions to which their encampment in Paris subjected them. They also felt the effect of the strike; they were badly provisioned, badly fed. Besides that, overcharged with duties, and restricted to a war which they disliked more and more, disgust and fatigue broke down all their energy.

As to the troops mobilised to carry on the work of the strikers, they did this with slackness and indifference.

The results were pitiful. This work was hardly anything else than an unconscious sabotage.

The army, therefore, only obeyed unwillingly, and looked sulkily at the work expected from them. The officers were not deceived, they felt the illwill and discontent of the troops was increasing, but they were careful not to use severity, for fear of accentuating the failure of discipline which they observed. They tried to cheer their soldiers by haranguing and encouraging them; saying they would lead them to a glorious enterprise.

Thus this army, the only real force that the authorities had at their disposal, threatened to escape them. Within it, the effect of Antimilitarist preaching was still latent, but an attentive observer would have seen the

deep impression it had made, and would have foreseen
that on the least incident, more severe discipline, an
order considered to be rigorous or excessive, there would
be revolt.

It was felt that the soldiers were wavering, ready
to kick over the traces, more inclined to make common
cause with the people than to march against them.

CHAPTER VIII.

THE REVOLUTIONARY REQUISITIONS.

The unorganised requisitions, which bands of unemployed had made since the beginning of the strike, had been useful in giving a direction to the movement but they were inadequate and uncertain. Owing to the initiative of Trade Union organisations there was substituted for this a reasonable method of division, which although somewhat rudimentary, was passably satisfactory.

This initiative was essential. If the Trade Unions,—who claimed that they were capable of organising society from top to bottom,—had left it to the Government alone to look after the provisioning of the community, they would rapidly have been discredited. Their incapacity, when compared with the action of the Government, would have given renewed prestige to the latter, and would have proved that they were not so useless and harmful as their detractors asserted.

The Trade Unions, whilst checking the efforts of the authorities to feed the community, organised a competing system, which, however incomplete it might have been, was superior to that on the other side. This obvious superiority arose from its Communist tendencies: whilst the Government necessarily held to the Commercial system, according to which, at most, they gave charity to those who were without money; the Trade Unions established a system of equal distribution, which was inspired by principles of solidarity.

Their first care was to attach to themselves the mass who were not yet members of any Trade Unions for the societies were rare that included, not the whole, but even a majority, of the members of a trade.

Up to now, the Trade Unions had, with some rare exceptions, simply grouped together the élite amongst the workmen, who strove to gain general improvements, and benefited by the result of their efforts, the passive beings, the non-unionists.

Whilst sustaining, once more, the weight of the struggle, and whilst still undertaking the responsibility of the battle that was being waged, the active minority appealed to the non-unionists; they did not call on them to face any danger, but to join in the distribution.

Manifestos therefore gave notice to all workers, that those not yet organised must hand in their names to the Union in their trade, in order to be able to participate, on a footing of equality, in the distributions of food that were going to be made through the medium of labour organisations.

This distribution of provisions was not made with any narrow severity. Others besides Trade Unionists benefited by it ; intellectuals, shopkeepers, artizans. The latter still found themselves on the margin of Trade Union organisation, because that had been, in the past, an organisation for fighting ; but they would find their place there, now that it was to be transformed into a social organism.

The Unions in the provision trade constituted themselves into commissions for provisioning the town. The reserve stocks of the great commercial houses, depôts and wholesale warehouses, were placed under contribution, and it was in this way that the Co-operative Societies and the Communist kitchens,—installed in restaurants and wine shops,—were able to make distributions and partly to satisfy consumption.

With the spirit of solidarity that animated the Trade Unions, the first thought was for the sick, and they took care to reserve for them the best of everything, and the choice meat at the butchers'.

In the hospitals also, the sick did not suffer from the strike, the staff who cared for them having remained at work. But it is very probable that if they had had nothing better than the "Assistance publique"* to feed them and the staff, both of them would have had poor faie.

The working bakers had been the first to strike; they were also, bread being the basis of Parisian alimentation, the first to re-commence work, but on very definite conditions. They agreed to re-commence, provisionally, making bread as before, at the bakeries of those masters who consented to distribute bread free to all who could not pay for it; against those who would not subscribe to this condition, the strike continued; those who accepted it had the cleverness to recoup themselves from the rich, by charging them more for their bread.

In addition, the working bakers worked in Co-operative Stores and workmen's bakeries by successive gangs without stopping; further, they took possession of the bakeries of the great employers, which had mechanical ovens, and of the bread factories, like the great bread factory of La Villette, where they could bake, in twenty-four hours, some hundred thousand four pound loaves.

In order to obtain the flour and wheat necessary for this intensive bread making, expeditions were organised for the purpose of requisitioning it from the docks, as well as from the granaries of La Villette and Grenelle.

Sights were again seen of the same kind as those which unfolded themselves in Paris on the 13th of July 1789, after what was at that time the convent of Saint Lazaire, had been taken by assault, which convent afterwards became one of the prisons of the bourgeoisie.

The assailants, in 1789, had found in this convent a large quantity of corn and flour: they decided to

* This corresponds to some extent to the English Poor Law.

transport their booty to the Markets, and, in order to do this, they requisitioned by main force about fifty carts. The loading done, the procession started on its way, in a joyous cortège, whilst some insurgents danced round the cars, decked out in tinsel borrowed from the convent chapel.

Lacking the decorations, and with motor vans instead of primitive carts, one took part again in like processions.

The revolutionary tradition renewed itself to such an extent that there was with regard to these incidents the same attitude on the part of the armed force. In 1789, the French guards, in barracks in the Faubourg St. Denis, refused to bestir themselves when they were told that the convent of St. Lazaire was being assaulted; making the objection that they had no orders, and that they did not interfere with the work of the police: it was also the lack of orders that the military posts now used as an objection in order to prevent intervention, when they were told that the General Strikers were emptying the depôts of wheat and flour.

In most of the circumstances under which they were compelled to intervene, the troops only executed the orders given them under compulsion, and often grumbling, expressing in this way how much they disliked the work which was put on them. These feelings, which the soldiers took no trouble to hide, increased with the contact and relations that were established between them and the working population in the midst of which they camped: they gave them bread, and also wine, for there was always plenty of wine, and as the poor devils of troopers were badly fed, and irregularly, they were delighted with the present.

The Trade Unions did not only occupy themselves with assuring a minimum of food for all. Their more active militants were haunted by the saying, so much insisted on by Blanqui: "Twenty-four hours after the Revolution, the people must realize that they are less miserable,"—and this saying they tried to put in practice.

They concerned themselves with lodging and clothing. They smartened up those unfortunate men who were in the greatest destitution; they sought out the homeless and lodged them in the empty rooms of the hotels in the neighbourhood.

The hotel keepers and shopkeepers, a bit offended, protested. They succeeded in convincing them, by means of these "orders" of requisition, which, although they thought them but a vague kind of guarantee, still gave them the right to participate in the Trade Union distributions. To these "orders" were added some brief sermons on human solidarity, whose reign was at hand.

Not all the shopkeepers and not all the landlords were in an equally accommodating humour. There were some who were refractory, not willing either to accept visitors, or to submit to requisitions, and refusing the hypothetical "orders." These recalcitrants ran off to demand aid and protection from the police and the troops; and there resulted from this some more or less grave riots.

Thus the Strike grew. To the negative immobility of the first days, which was limited to social disintegration, began to succeed the period of affirmation and re-organisation.

Activity increased at the offices of the Confédération, at the Labour Exchange, at the Trade Federations, and amongst the Strike Committees. There, henceforth, was life,—a life still embryonic,—that was only at the stage of incubation; but which, to-morrow, was going to burst forth into vigorous organisms, taking the place of dead organisms.

And that which encouraged them, put joy in their hearts, was, that, thanks to the measures taken, the saying of Blanqui was being realized, the pariahs of Capitalist society saw the dawn of a new life breaking. Already some had more to eat than they had yesterday, and the atmosphere of misery that enveloped them seemed less heavy, less thick, less black!

CHAPTER IX.

THE REVOLT OF THE ARMY.

The period of social dissolution could not continue for ever. The Government was anxious to bring this state of things to an end; for the persistence of the strike, which strengthened the Unions, produced for the Government only increased disintegration and exhaustion. The State found itself dismantled; everything creaked; the vital organs of society, which had given it its prestige, cut off, it found itself reduced to little more than the machinery of repression; magistrates, prisons, police. They had, of course, the army,—but its fidelity became more and more problematical.

Wishing to end the insurrection, the authorities resolved to proclaim a state of siege. They had the approbation of Parliament. This was only a matter of form. The Chambers were only a remnant which survived; panic stricken, seeing red everywhere, they could, in the course of their interminable sittings, discuss, decide, vote resolutions and orders of the day,—but the real interest was elsewhere. They no longer represented anything. Parliamentarism was dying.

Although resolved on carrying out the sanguinary work of an implacable and ferocious repression, the Government were perplexed. The revolutionary movement that they wanted to crush out had this typical feature, that it was not centralized, but scattered about, which rendered the undertaking more difficult. Which were the suitable points for the decisive effort? To occupy with soldiers the office of the Confédération Générale du Travail, or even of the Labour Exchange,

hardly helped towards a solution. To imprison the principal militants, the members of committees and commissions? This had already been tried without appreciable
results. The arrests they had succeeded in making, and
they were numerous, had disorganised nothing. The im-
prisoned members had been automatically replaced,—
many times in succession in some organisations,—without
these organisations having been broken up, or even caused
to waver.

As a result of these attacks, and to guard against
their renewal, the Strike Committee took precautions:
they sat in permanent session in the public halls; where
day and night, many strikers were on guard.

And then it was not alone the committees that had
to be neutralised, annihilated,—there were also the people.
Where to attack them? How to strike at them?
They had the prudence not to lend themselves to repression; they knew how to steal away, to make themselves invisible, make it impossible to get hold of them.
Besides, how can they be coerced? To overcome their
inertia, to lead them back to work, to put them again
under their masters' yoke, it would be necessary to over-
whelm them with numbers; and the Government had
no longer the numbers on their side. They no longer
had the army in hand. Worse still, they could only
half trust the municipal guards; in their barracks they
hummed "The International." In fact, as far as soldiers
were concerned, they had only a few corps of élite,
chiefly cavalry, on whom they could certainly depend.
In addition, they had the police; but there too the severe
character of the police hunt had thinned their ranks.

But what did it matter? The present situation was
untenable. They would bring cannons and machine guns
into the streets if necessary; but they would anyhow end
this General Strike! To commence with they would
occupy with soldiers the Confédération, the Labour Exchange, the public halls, the Co-operative Stores, all the
centres of Labour activity. If they met with the least
resistance,—they would at once attack. And, in virtue

of the state of siege, it was not necessary to be embarrassed with scruples. No more half measures! Against the audacious people who should dare to resist they would be implacable.

Arrangements were made for the rapid realisation of this decisive plan. The troops were set in motion, and sent towards the strategical points of this great combined movement.

The military stir that the preparations for this blow rendered necessary, in which all the available troops should participate, was not carried out without arousing the attention of the strikers, and they also laid their plans.

Already the youthful elements in the Unions,—the most enterprising, the most resolute,—had formed some kind of bands who had undertaken, as their special work, to watch over the security of the committees and officials; establishing sentinels and guard posts, in order that the watch might never be at fault, and that they should not run the risk of being caught napping.

These groups had also sought to arm themselves; they looked after the military stores, commandeering useful arms amongst the gunsmiths and wherever else they found them. They did not however delude themselves about the value of their armament. The majority of the young people who were members of these bands were at the same time affiliated to the Anti-militarist societies, they knew well that it would have been foolish on their part to expect that they could hold their own against the army.

They knew that a Revolution had never been successful with the army against it, but only with the support of the army or at least its neutrality. They knew that in times of insurrection the people had only triumphed when the troops had refused to fire, and had rallied to their side. And they therefore came to the conclusion that, once again, the attitude of the army would decide the success or failure of the General Strike. On that account they concentrated all their efforts on building up friendly relations with the soldiers. They succeeded in this the more easily as the army were also fermenting with social aspirations,—disgusted, harrased by the repressive part which they had to play.

In the majority of the barracks and camps, valuable acquaintanceships had become established between soldiers and workmen. Things were worse even than that; in many companies the topic of conversation in the mess rooms frequently turned upon what soldiers owed to themselves and to humanity...and as a result various propagandist groups were formed within the regiments. In order to become members a preliminary promise was required,—that they would never fire upon the people. More than this, as it was impossible to keep the troops constantly under arms, some of the soldiers were not afraid to use their rare hours of liberty to mix with the people and attend meetings.

Such was the state of mind of the troops when the authorities decided to deliver the blow which they hoped would prove decisive.

During the night, marches and counter marches were carried out in such a way that, by the morning, military operations could commence at all points at the same time.

A little before the dawn, an incident, as unforeseen as it was disastrous, disturbed their plans. Just as the preparations for the battle were completed at the barracks of Chateau-d'Eau which, on account of their proximity to the Labour Exchange, and also to the offices of the Confédération Générale du Travail, was one of the centres of the repression,—cries of "Fire!" "Fire!" arose.

The barracks were in flames!

The alarm was soon given. In a disorderly pell-mell the soldiers descended into the court, and after the first moments of panic and disorder, they set to work to extinguish the fire. It had several centres,—a certain proof of malevolence,—and at various points it was already blazing furiously.

They exerted themselves to get all the pumps at work. But,—a terrible disappointment! No water came through! One after the other, all the water taps were tried. But all in vain. From no one of them did any water run. They had to face the fact: the water had been intentionally cut off.

Before they arrived at this disconcerting conclusion, precious time had been lost. By the time they gave up all hope of stemming the disaster, the fire was gaining on them more and more, crackling from story to story. One after the other the casements noisily crashed in, so that across torrents of smoke could be seen the red glare of the furnace.

When they tried to save the horses, that had brought cannons and machine guns, these animals, maddened, kicked, reared, and were quite unmanageable. After enormous difficulties, they succeeded in getting them away. On the other hand it was absolutely impossible, in spite of incredible efforts, to attach them to the pieces of artillery, so that these had to be abandoned in the court, together with their ammunition. And the terrible anxiety was increased by the formidable explosions that were possible.

This catastrophe upset all the arrangements that had been made for the attack. The soldiers, completely out of hand, half dressed, and without arms, went off at random. Although none of them had perished in the flames, it was with great difficulty that the officers succeeded in collecting together half their effectives. The other half had melted away, had disappeared.

Whilst the barracks of Chateau-d' Eau were burning, other events occurred which struck a still worse blow at the cause of Capitalism.

The Trade Union groups and the bands of Anti-militarists, who worked together heartily, decided that, whilst the Government was clearing its decks for action, they would attempt some counter operation on points that were necessarily uncovered. Possessed by the de-

sire to arm themselves effectively, these groups had maintained a keen watch on the State depôts of arms, resolved to take possession of them on the first favourable
opportunity.   This night, they found things just as they
would have wished them to be.

The store of arms and ammunition accumulated at
Vincennes,—as well as at other points,—had been almost
abandoned.   As soon as the Anti-militarist bands were
informed of this, the order was rapidly passed along
among all workmens' organisations ;   and, in small bands
that would not attract attention, the strikers marched
on the points indicated.

The few soldiers left on guard at the depôts were
very soon made harmless ;   and that done, they set to
work to empty the warehouses.   Before the military
authorities had information of this, some thousands of
men were armed with rifles similar to those used by
the army.

Of course, the strikers were not invincible simply
because they had now repeating rifles.   But this advantage gave them such boldness, such self-reliance, that
they feared nothing.   This was because, in addition to
the guns in their hands, they had profound convictions
in their hearts ;   they had the will and energy which
triumph over obstacles that seem to be entirely insurmountable.   ,Whilst the troops opposed to them, although superior on account of their military training,
were in reality much inferior, because they marched
under compulsion, without enthusiasm and without confidence.

From the early morning, the fever of great dramatic days sent all Paris into the streets.

The army, its last dispositions taken, dejected, and
spiritless,—with none of that energy that one attributes
to French soldiers even at the most critical moments,—
occupied the points that had been assigned to them.

Suddenly, along the ranks, the news of the night's
incidents spread like a train of gunpowder :   the soldiers

told one another the story of the fire at the barracks of Chateau-d' Eau, the sacking of the depôts of arms,—and that now the strikers were as well supplied with tools for fighting as the regiments on the side of "order."

On hearing these accounts, which were punctuated by ill-humoured comments, all that remained of the spirit of discipline, the instinct of obedience, amongst the troops, melted away. And whilst they stood there, fixed at attention, but perplexed,—a crowd, more curious than frightened, in which women and children were in the majority, inundated the pavement and the roadway. This crowd, continually growing larger, pressed around the soldiers, mixed among them,—in spite of the injunctions of the officers, who, impatient and nervous, nevertheless hesitated to order brutalities against them, they looked so inoffensive.

In the meantime, the strikers returned to Paris from Vincennes, in long columns; they were enthusiastic, they had a light in their eyes of force and confidence. They were armed! They went along, full of energy, marching to the sound of revolutionary choruses and fearing no collision.

As they had not been able to distribute all the arms and ammunition on the spot, they had loaded it on trucks, which they escorted to Paris.

On their departure from Vincennes, the Revolutionists were careful to take various precautionary measures; in order to guard against any trap or unforeseen attack, cyclists went in front and on the flanks as scouts. Other strikers to whom the handling of arms was familiar, formed an advanced guard, and some of the more intrepid were improvised as front rank men.

Now, with an extended front, the column descended along the wide avenue, and constantly growing, approached the Place de la Nation. Tragic, decisive moments!

A regiment of the line, sent to meet the insurgents, awaited them near Dalou's group of statuary. This monument then, baptised "Triumph of the Re-

public," was to be the witness of the downfall of the
bourgeois Republic. The irony of things! What joy
the great artist would have felt, how radiant he would
have been, if, when he baked the clay of his lions, he
had been able to conjure up the scene that was going
to unfold itself at their feet:—the revenge for 1871!

The officers wished to prevent any contact between
the people and their soldiers, and wanted to fire on them
from a distance. They were prevented from doing this
by the size of the crowd, which, continually getting more
dense and compact, surrounded their men, hampered
their movements, and, instead of dispersing when ordered, still more engulfed them.

But now this crowd, where women and children were
in the majority, instead of remaining passive, became
bold: remonstrances arose, haughty and tender, made
up of cries of pity, of sobs, of appeals to their humanity,
of ardent and panting prayers, of exhortations from the
women to the soldiers not to fire on their brothers, their
children, their husbands....

A few steps more, and the strikers,—who had begun
to sing "The International," and who were roaring out
the verses about soldiers and generals,—would join the
crowd, and find themselves coming to blows with the
troops. The officers, who felt that the latter were weakening and softening, gave the order "Fix bayonets!"

In order to facilitate the execution of this order,
and to isolate the troops from the crowd, they ordered
a sudden falling back of some steps. After these orders
had been given, which soldiers usually execute mechanically,—like automata,—hardly any movement was to be
seen.

Exasperated and furious shouts muffled the voices
of the military chiefs, destroying their influence; imprecations and curses spread around, and from the crowd,
who began to snatch the rifles from the hands of the
soldiers, there broke forth, roared, re-echoed the appeal,
"Crosse en l'air!"*

.* Hold up the butt-end of your rifles.

The superior officers tried to stem the imminent defection. Furious, foaming, they hurled their horses in front of the troops; at one moment they would reprimand their mutinous soldiers, promising them courts martial, the gallows,—at another, turning towards the crowd, they would threaten to have them shot by the soldiers.

This fit of rage, which recalled the anger of General Lecomte, on the 18th of March 1871, at Montmartre, only hastened the military revolt; the soldiers replied by the fatal movement, and stretched out their hands to the people. And, instead of a scene of horrible carnage, there were embraces,—shouts of joy.

The regiment broke up. Soldiers and strikers embraced each other; whilst the officers, (remembering the scene of the Rue des Rosiers), took themselves off, to the crackling of rifles that saluted their flight.

Soldiers and strikers divided themselves into several columns, and after a short halt, left the Place de la Nation; going, some by the Faubourg Antoine, some by the Boulevard Voltaire, some by the Avenue Phillipe Auguste, arm in arm, with an irresistible impulse and enthusiasm. Everywhere, as they passed, there were cries of enthusiasm, frantic cheering; the troops that they met on the road were disbanded, and carried away in their train.

The rumour of this first defection spread with astonishing rapidity. At all the points where the rulers had intended to carry out their repressive action, the soldiers, already demoralised, were definitely disabled by the pessimistic reports which they got; they refused to fight, and passed over to the side of the people.

At some points, there was a show of resistance by, picked troops, chiefly by the cavalry. But when these,— whose horses advanced with difficulty,—for the roads were strewn with obstacles, especially broken glasses and bottles,—had received some charges from quick firing rifles, with which the General Strikers were now supplied, their ardour cooled down. It was the same with some other troops that remained faithful, who, attacked in front, behind,—taken for targets from street windows,—could not stand it.

The insurgents were not intoxicated by their victory. They showed practical common sense. They showed useful initiative, and took the decisive steps which were necessary to secure that their success should have a morrow.

Bands were formed, in various districts, who were to make an assault on the barracks, and to occupy all the centres of repressive action, and all the Governmental centres, in order to render impossible any attempt at a reactionary rally.

But however urgent this work might be, there was another of still greater importance. It was necessary, at once, to strike at the heart of authority, to attack it in its living works. For this purpose, there were employed great columns, composed partly of soldiers in revolt and partly of strikers, who, starting from the Place de la Nation, marched towards the centre of Paris.

One, which went down the Faubourg Antoine and the Rue de Rivoli, occupied successively the Town Hall, the Police Offices, the Law Courts; then, crossing over to the left side of the river, they attacked the various Government Offices.

The other column, which marched along the Boulevard Voltaire and the great boulevards, fell like a thunderbolt, first of all on the Ministry of the Interior, then on the Elysée and the Place Vendôme.

The meeting place of these columns was the Palais Bourbon.

The march of these masses, who rolled on like torrents, was so unexpected, so sudden, so abrupt, that it had not been possible to take any serious step to oppose their passage. Along the route, they were joined by crowds, they grew,—became an avalanche,—carrying along with them both the people and the soldiers that they encountered; breaking, like bits of straw, the few bands of police or troops faithful to the authorities, that tried to oppose them.

Nothing could resist this human flood! It passed on, an element let loose,—it was a raging ocean....

Government and the Parliamentary régime were going to be engulfed beneath these waves.

CHAPTER X.

THE FALL OF PARLIAMENTARISM.

The events of the morning burst like a thunder clap on the Palais Bourbon. They were reported there in an imperfect, distorted, exaggerated way: anxiety was followed by stupor and perplexity. The Parliamentarians, who, until then, felt vaguely re-assured by the confident speeches of the ministers, by the military occupation of Paris, and the state of siege, now caught a glimpse of the abyss down which they were about to be hurled by the storm.

What was going to happen? Certainly they did not anticipate any immediate peril for themselves. The palace was well protected. At the entrance from the bridge, the Pont de la Concorde, battalions of Municipal Guards, in serried ranks, forbade any access from the right side of the river; on the side of the Rue de Bourgogne, in the square, around the palace, inside,—everywhere,—the place was overrun with troops.

How would this end?

In the corridors, at the refreshment bar, discussions were carried on in an animated tone, which soon attained a diapason of rage, modified by fear. The ministerialists overwhelmed their Socialist colleagues with maledictions, holding them responsible for all that was happening.

The sitting began in a feverish atmosphere. Amongst the few ministers present, the President of the Council tried to put on a good face, not allowing the anxiety

which oppressed him to show itself. He mounted the
tribune and explained the gravity of the situation, but
endeavouring to colour it with optimism, and refusing to
entertain any other attitude than that of resistance to the
uttermost. Several members spoke after him, making
absurd propositions, and engaging in recriminations
that were as tedious as they were beside the mark. No
one listened to them. The deputies, with anxious faces,
went in and out. They could not stay in their places,
they were eager for any news; occupying themselves
and with reason, less about the useless and empty speeches
made by their colleagues, than about what was happening outside. It was there that all the interest was cen-
tred!

The columns of strikers, interspersed with soldiers,
approached. They flowed in from all directions. The
bands coming from the Quay Voltaire, and those coming
from the Boulevard Saint Germain, arrived on the square
of the Palais Bourbon, whilst those who issued from
the Rue Royale, or the Rue de Rivoli, inundated the
Place de la Concorde.

And now, the roaring of the multitude, which advanced with the force of an avalanche, dominated all
other noises. The municipal guards, who barred the way
across the Pont de la Concorde, tried to oppose the
passage of this crowd. They drew their swords. All
in vain! They were tossed about, submerged, by the
flood of people who, when this dam burst, reached to
the peristyle of the Chamber. The defence on the side
of the Rue de Bourgogne was not more obstinate. There
were some machine guns in the court. They remained
there unused;—those in charge of them being reluctant
to level them against the invaders, in the midst of whom
they saw many of their comrades.

The presence of soldiers in the ranks of the strikers
counted for much in the slight resistance on the part
of the troops still faithful to the Government.

The Chamber of Deputies was thus invaded from
all sides with a pressure that was irresistible. The crowd,

clamorous, angry, had but one goal; the hall in which
the sittings were held. They entered it like a flood,
filling the tribunes, blocking up the hemicycle,—whilst a
number of the deputies thought it prudent to retire.

There were cries, shouts, roars. A shot came from
the public galleries,—obviously aimed at the Government
bench. An arm turned the weapon aside, and the ball
buried itself in the woodwork; whilst deafening cries
resounded,—"Down with Parliament!"—"Three cheers for
the Social Revolution!"

Some well-meaning citizens, desiring that the Revolution should not be stained uselessly with blood, and
who dreamed of it as being carried out without acts of
hatred and vengeance, sheltered the ministers from the
popular anger; whilst on the steps leading to the
speaker's tribune, groups of human beings clustered and
jostled each other. A demonstrator, climbing into the
presidential chair, pushed out the bewildered President,
took his place, and, frantically ringing his bell, quieted
the crowd, and obtained a relative silence. He profited
by this to proclaim in abrupt, vigorous phrases, that fell
like stunning blows, the downfall of Parliament, the
dissolution of the bourgeois State; and he threatened
with death any deputies who should dare to sit again.

His peroration, punctuated by the frantic applause
of the crowd, aroused protests from the deputies of the
extreme left, who, amidst the Parliamentary disorder,
had maintained their composure. The Social Democrats
had wished to give events a different turn; they wanted
to manufacture laws; their dream was to lead the
Revolution by State ways, to continue and complete it
by force of laws and decrees. They dreamed of living
the past over again, and shouted, "Let us proclaim the
Commune."—"To the Hotel de Ville!"

This proposal was received with hooting and cries. A
new tempest of exclamations arose, amidst which one
could hear a roar of protests and threats to crush any
Governmental renaissance. It was seen then how powerful
Syndicalist ideas had become. The shouts redoubled,

"No! No!—No Commune!"—"No more Parliamentarism!"—"Three cheers for the Revolution!"—"Three cheers for the Confédération du Travail!"

The leader of the extreme left, the powerful orator who had struck many rude blows at the fallen régime, pushed through the crowd, and reached the tribune. He was at first received with a redoubled volley of shouts. The cry, "Down with the Quinze Mille!" fused into one great shout, crackled forth, dominated. It proved that, in their hatred of Parliamentarism, the people made no distinction. The orator, in the midst of the uproar he had let loose, began to speak,—raised his voice. At first, one saw he was speaking rather than heard anything, whilst he moved his hands in calming gestures, asking for silence.

And now, like oil spread on angry waves, his words calmed the fury and exasperation let loose around him. The crowd wanted to hear; and, after some minutes, a relative calm was established.

With his wonderful gift for assimilation, the great orator defined the situation, lifted the veil from the future, and sketched out the part which would henceforth fall to his friends. He reproached the deputies of the extreme left, who had just talked of apeing the revolutions of the past. He begged them not to carry out their intentions, not to divide the workers, who, under present circumstances, needed, more than ever, to be united in aims and methods.

"The times have changed," he cried. "Let us have the courage to recognise it, without false shame, without bitterness, let us Parliamentary Socialists recognise the fact; we have played our part! We have dug the deep furrow, and sowed the good seed which has germinated well. Now, the time of the harvest has come, let us leave the harvesters to their work. Let us stand on one side! Let us leave the Trade Union organisations to act. The social axis has changed its position. It is no longer here, nor at the Elysée, nor at the Place Beauveau, it is not even at the Hôtel de Ville,—it is at the

Labour Exchange,—it is at the Rue Grange-aux-Belles.
Make room then for the working class. Let them come
on the scene and take first place. Let us return to the
ranks, without wounded vanity, without vexation. We
shall easily find means to make a fresh start."

Whilst the Socialist tribune held the invaders by the
charm of his eloquence, the majority of the deputies,—
especially those who knew they were heartily execrated
by the people,—as well as the members of the Government, slipped out of the hall, and stole away. So that,
when the orator had finished speaking, there was hardly
anyone within the walls, except the crowd, which was as
dense as ever, and the deputies of the opposition.

Amongst the latter, disagreement had arisen. There
were amongst them those who, seeing nothing beyond
Democracy, formally, and in good faith, disapproved
the thesis of the Socialist tribune; and who stubbornly
wanted to carry out their project of a "Provisional Committee," a "Revolutionary Government," or whatever
it might be called. They were more concerned about
the reality than about the label.

But the General Strikers were on the watch. Their
triumph was complete, and they were not in the humour
to leave the field free to the Parliamentarians, however
well-meaning these might be. After a short delibera-
tion, they agreed, that in order to guard against any
aggressive action by the fallen power, or any effort to re-
establish Parliamentarism, a certain number of their comrades should remain permanently at the Palais Bourbon;
and, if necessary, should oppose by force any counter-
revolutionary manoeuvre.

This definite intention of disorganising the State,
of dismantling and thoroughly disabling it,—in order to
render it impossible for the Government to recover itself, or rally round any point whatever,—was strongly
felt by all. This corresponded so exactly to the needs
of the case, that the various bands of Revolutionists, after
having taken by assault the Police Offices, the Government
Offices, the Elysée, etc., had taken the same precaution,

to leave behind them parties of General Strikers as guards.

The Hôtel de Ville was not neglected. It was occupied with the greater care, because, by tradition, there was the tendency to consider it as the centre of revolutionary activity. How many times, when the people had overthrown their Governments, did the men who had taken over the succession to power, come there, to receive from its balcony their revolutionary investiture! That belonged to the past. To-day, the Labour Exchange, the Confédération, the Trade Union centres, were the heart and soul of the movement, and it was towards them that the flow of the crowds set in.

The day,—whose dawn had been so dismal and threatening,—ended in enchantment. After the sudden changes of fortune that had made it famous, after the torpor of the preceding days, the night came serene;— disturbed only by the overflowing and wild delight of the people's joy.

The success of the Revolution was irresistible; the breakdown of authority seemed complete, beyond remedy. The men who had borne the responsibility for the resistance,—President, ministers, superior officers, great State dignitaries,—had disappeared, vanished! And in consequence of this overthrow, of this confusion, what remained of the army fell to pieces. The larger number of the officers had prudently disappeared; those who remained were the exceptional chiefs imbued with socialistic ideas, who, admired by their soldiers, were quite ready to share with them in the popular gladness.

As to the soldiers, returned to the people, mixing with them, they were everywhere fêted, everywhere they were fraternally received. Had they not in great part contributed to the success of the day?

After the terrible anxieties of the Strike, everyone, —bourgeois and workman,—enjoyed this lessening of the strain. For the former, however, this lessening of the strain was embittered by anxiety. What would the social reconstruction be like? For the latter, the unknown to-morrow only foretold joys, it was the realization of hopes so long cherished, the end of nightmares of misery!

CHAPTER XI.

THE ATTACK ON THE BANKS.

All the committees of Trade Union organisations met at once. They sat almost permanently, seized by a fever of activity that grew with the circumstances.

It was not everything to have overthrown the centralized, militarized State, an expression of Roman and Caesarian law. The real work began from the moment of this overthrow: it was necessary to start the social machine afresh; it was necessary, above all, and with all speed, to assure subsistence to everyone, to avoid famine.

On these difficulties of the first importance there were grafted the annoyances, happily quite relative, which the obstinate adherents of State Socialism raised up, infatuated with the idea of turning aside the Revolution into Governmental ways. Their disappointment at not having been able to install at the Hôtel de Ville some kind of authority had not cured them of their desire to carry out their project. They were defeated, but not converted. The frequenting of Parliamentary places, and the practice of law making, prevented them from comprehending the movement; its extent surpassed them,— and they thought the Revolution was lost.

However, their intervention was not dangerous, thanks to the habits of slowness, of wearisome discussions, continued endlessly, which Parliamentarism had taught them. The Trade Unionists gained on them by activity and speed;—amongst them, discussions were short, decisions prompt, and rapidly translated into action.

This superiority annihilated the Parliamentarians of
the Revolution, who, deprived of points of support, agitated in vacuum, exhausting themselves in efforts that
would meet with no approval, since all the social forces
henceforth turned in the direction of corporate organisation.

The return of a Government was thus avoided;
and, when once the ground was cleared of all useless
political arrangements, it was for those interested in the
matter, united in their Trade Unions, Labour Exchanges,
the Confédération, to bring about in a direct way the
conditions for the new life.

The first care was not to fall again into the mistakes
of 1871. The remembrance of the Commune, mounting
guard over the cellars of the Bank of France, whose
millions served to sustain the Versaillaise repression, was
too vivid, and too besetting, for the same fault to be
committed again. The Revolutionists had the sense of
social reality, and they did not think their victory was
altogether won, because they had beaten down the facade
of the old society,—Parliamentarism. Thus, during the
same night that followed the victory of the people, the
Confederal Committee, after an understanding with the
Trade Union of Bank employees, decided to take possession of the Bank of France, of the "Caisse des depôts
et consignations," of the great financial establishments,—
without making any distinction between the banks and
credit houses depending on the State, and those depending
on private capital.

It was decided that a provisional credit should be
given to those interested; and that this wealth, considered as social property, should serve until the normal
re-organisation, to provide for social needs, and to assure ordinary consumption. It was stipulated, in addition, that an account should be kept with individuals
of their respective deposits, which they could continue
to use, for the needs of exchange, in the form of cheques.

These arrangements gave rise to demonstrations of

a special character. The remnants of the reactionary parties,—which might be called Prehistoric!—thought it a propitious occasion to call attention to themselves. These slow-moving creatures, who imagined they could secure the acceptance of their cries of "Long live the king!" by mixing with them cries of "Death to the Jews!" caused some riotous assemblages. They hoped to mislead the people by stirring them up against Jewish capital only, and against Jewish banks. The reception they met with showed them how backward they were: they were spit at and hustled in a vigorous fashion by the workers, who did not allow themselves to be taken in by these subtilties of an earlier age. The lesson was severe enough, and this reactionary prank was without a morrow.

A scene of a quite different kind,—sad, because it brought to light the old miseries,—and cheering, because it announced their end,—without return,—was the operation of redeeming the objects of all kinds, of greater or less value, deposited at the Mont-de-Piété. The procedure was simple and expeditious: all the goods were handed over without any payment.

In the crowds who made a queue before the wickets were not merely the workers; there were also many shopkeepers, many employers, whom the dread of bankruptcy, and business difficulties had driven to pawning something. Now, as to these latter, although the order of things that was being installed did not inspire them with any great sympathy, in the depths of their eyes shone a flame of satisfaction; they could not help thinking that, if the Revolution had many vexations in store for them, at least it was inaugurated in a pleasant way.

Immediately after the victory, another step was taken spontaneously: staffs of revolutionary writers, as well as printers, considered how to assure the re-appearance of the newspapers. It was natural that, social conditions being overturned, the conditions of publishing were also overturned.

Previously, the daily papers had been hardly anything else than engines valuable for Capitalism; and they enslaved both printers and journalists. Both of them had to throw to the winds their ways of looking at things, their opinions, their class interests, and had to help in spreading ideas that they often considered were false, injurious, and pernicious; the necessity of receiving a wage from Capital, without which they could not live, compelled them to this.

Henceforth, the worker, being no longer a serf of the capitalist, wages being abolished, the conditions for the manufacture of the daily papers had to be different: they could only be the product of agreement and effort, both as to material, and intellect, of workers of all kinds, working together to put them into circulation. Therefore, they could but express the aspirations and reflect the hopes of the people.

Immediately also, all the Unions made their arrangements for the resumption of work in all branches. It was the end of a nightmare when the districts neglected by the sanitary workers were cleaned, and the pestilent heaps that encumbered them disappeared. And it was a feast for the eyes when the light burst forth from the electric lamps and arcs, and when gas flamed in the candelabras.

Above all, the urgent problem to be solved was that of assuring the food supply!

They hurried on as quickly as possible. Necessity often obliged them to set to work under defective conditions. It was a provisional state of things, which it was necessary to put up with, but they hastened to remedy it.

The taking of possession was organised with method.

The State abolished, no obstacle could any longer oppose the expansion of popular instincts: the spirit of agreement and fellowship was going to thrive, as well as the Communist tendencies, so long kept down by authority.

And the tradition was going to be renewed, between the new city and the communes of the Middle Ages, in the bosom of which had sprung up a rudimentary Communism, the development of which had been arrested by Governmental centralization.

CHAPTER XII.

THE GENERAL STRIKE IN THE PROVINCES.

Hitherto, in outlining the sudden changes of fortune in the struggle between Syndicalism and Parliamentarism, in which the latter was finally overthrown, it is especially the action of revolutionary Paris which has held our attention. It is necessary for us to go back a little and show the great part taken by the provinces in the movement, as it lights up and explains the wonderful success of the Revolution.

If the movement had been limited to the capital,— even supposing that it had gained some large towns,— the Government would not have been so rapidly disabled. But it had to fight a strike on such a vast field of action with such an extended front, with such numerous and strong centres, that the means of coercion which they had at their disposal were blunted from the very begining.

As we have shown, the army found itself numerically too weak to crush out the revolt; and what was more, the authorities could not, for lack of the means of rapid communication, send it towards threatened points.

When the slaughter on the great Boulevards resulted in enraging Paris, the economic crisis was as severe in the provinces as in the capital, and there were strikes everywhere. Therefore, as soon as the news of the massacre was heard there, the wrath which it aroused carried the ferment to its height.

In places where workmen were carrying on a struggle against their masters, the character of these conflicts was instantly modified, and without loss of time the General Strike was proclaimed.

The uprising was not restricted merely to the districts on strike. It spread rapidly, and in the majority of centres where Trade Union organisations had established flourishing branches, the stoppage of work was generalized with an unheard of vigour.

The appeals of the Confédération, and the measures arranged by the Trade Federations, fell on prepared ground, and had the result of increasing and strengthening the movement, more than of commanding and directing it. The value and superiority of the Confederal organism did not consist in its directing functions, but rather in a power of suggestion and of co-ordination. It was endowed, in fact, with a force of vibration drawn from its federal aggregate, which in radiating became amplified.

It was obvious then how superficial and exaggerated were the discords and divisions which were said to exist in the Confederation, about which a great ado had been made, which had helped to reassure the bourgeoisie.

All the Unions, whatever might be their tendencies, —those apparently the most moderate as well as those that seemed extreme,—made one " bloc " against the enemy. All found themselves in agreement. All dissensions were effaced and forgotten; and, from one end of France to the other, the working class arose everywhere at once. And everywhere also it was moved by the same ideas; everywhere the same ardent combativeness set it against Capitalist society.

It was noticed at the same time that men, who, in the Trade Union organisation, had a reputation for moderation and might have served as a brake to the agitation, were either carried away by the revolutionary current and rose to the height of the movement, or else if they remained as they were yesterday, without taking account of what was happening, they lost all their influence.

Everywhere, therefore, the strike spread with equal
vigour and with a like feverish impulse to that in Paris.
Even some Unions noted for their practical sense, and
having the reputation of never leaving work without
having first decided the question by a referendum, neglected all formalities, and were the most determined to
go on strike.

In the mining country, in the metal working districts,
the cessation of work was carried out with an amazing in-
stantaneousness and abruptness. At once, the Capitalists
claimed the protection of the troops. They claimed this
with the more insistence because they were very much
alarmed. They feared an outburst of the hatred which
they had drawn upon themselves. It should be understood that in these industries, long ago trustified by committees and sale offices, the conditions imposed on the
workmen were hard,—savage. And the foremen of the
works, and the managers of large factories and mining
companies feared their vengeance.

At first the Government did their best to satisfy
the demands they received for troops. They scattered
the troops about in the most menaced districts, according
to the persistent demand of the employers. But the appeals for help became so numerous that soon they did
not know whom to listen to. They were required to protect the mining basin of the East, that of the North, of
the Centre, of Saône-et-Loire, of Aveyron, du Gard, etc.;
also the textile regions, the slate country, the centres of
pottery, engineering, of fifty other industries, without
reckoning the forest and agricultural districts. From
everywhere, from all parts of the country at the same
time, came pressing applications for troops.

The Government had also to guard the railways,
being afraid the rails might be unbolted, the bridges,
tunnels, etc., injured; also they had to guard the telegraph and telephone lines in order to prevent their
being cut.

In the strike centres they needed soldiers to look
after the monuments,—they needed them equally, to take
the place of strikers in various essential occupations.

Where could they find the soldiers necessary for
this heavy work of protection? It would have needed
as many soldiers as there were telegraph poles, railway
signals, bridges, milestones. It would have required ten
times more than the authorities had at their disposal!

Things had arrived at such a point that everywhere, except in Paris, where the troops were concentrated in sufficiently imposing numbers, the army was so
scattered about that it was incapable of opposing any
band of strikers who had at their disposal a few arms
and the will to fight.

Certainly there were districts that were free from
the strike, but the disorganisation there was not less.
It was of little use that, in a third or fourth rate town,
the postal service was continued, considering that the
telegraph was stopped, and the postal service out of
order in the surrounding districts. Communications were
almost as much trammelled as if the stoppage of work
had extended everywhere.

The same thing could be seen on the railways.
There were stations at which there was no strike. But
traffic was not the less stopped, because for this it was
sufficient that, in some other stations, the employees had
blocked the line, set the signals at danger, clogged the
points, and then left work. Now, as these obstructions
recurred at frequent intervals, the very few trains that
succeeded in starting, with a scratch staff, could only
advance with deplorable slowness.

When the General Strike broke out, the spirit of
revolt was, in a latent state, more developed in the provinces than in Paris. This had been remarked more than
once. As a result of this, in a great number of centres the spread of the movement was very rapid; it

developed very quickly, and the strike, at first one of protest and solidarity, very soon changed into an insurrectional strike.

In the great cities, in the chief towns where there were Government Offices, the strike passed through the same phases on a small scale,—and with variations of intensity,—as those passed through by the revolutionary movement in Paris. To a period that was purely one of expectation, limited to the stoppage of work, and the suspension of industrial and commercial life, succeeded the period of attack: the General Strikers occupied the centres of Governmental action, and expelled the representative of the State.

Revolutionary action was taken with the more spirit that they attacked authorities plunged into inertia, for want of orders.

Government officials were too much accustomed to obey, to risk moving without instructions. Now, as they hardly received any instructions at all, they remained in a state of expectation,—they waited! Thus Centralization, a mechanism so exact and marvellous,—in normal times,—that all the prefects, from one end of France to the other, could be made to do the same thing, at the same moment, had only inconveniences during a revolutionary period.

The principal aim of the rebels was to place the army beyond the possibility of doing any injury. In garrison towns,—which were indeed, for the most part, almost empty of troops, as these had been chiefly sent to the large industrial centres,—their first care was to seize the superior officers; a simply provisional measure, carried out to make sure of their inactivity. A handful of determined men sufficed to carry out the operation successfully. This done, the soldiers readily allowed themselves to be convinced, disarmed, and sent home. After which, very prudently, the revolutionists armed themselves.

There were variations in the way in which the troops
were enticed away from their work. Thus, it happened,
that when a detachment was sent to some menaced point,
a crowd of working people would collect on the way,
reproaching the soldiers for their passive obedience, begging them to remember that they were brothers of those
they were going to fight against and repress. The women,
especially, showed praiseworthy boldness. They threw
themselves on the bridles of the officers' horses; heroi-
cally, they barred the road to the soldiers, crying out,
shouting, "You must kill us first before you can pass!"...
These scenes, of noble and epic frenzy, ended by demoralising the troops, who were already marching unwillingly; they made very little resistance,—they allowed them to snatch the rifles from their hands, they
became mutinous and disbanded.

In some special industrial regions,—mining centres,
centres of blast furnaces, of gigantic workshops,—the
workers had long since been prepared for the events now
happening; they had lived in a state of expectation,—
waiting impatiently for their coming. In order not to
be taken unawares they had obtained arms, chiefly improved army rifles; and, under the cover of gymnastic
societies, had familiarised themselves with their use.

As soon as the Strike was declared, without hesitation or delay, they passed over to the attack; and, as
they considered that everything belonged to them, they
pluckily took possession of the district. The employers,
the managers, their under officials, all those who had
drawn down on themselves the workers' hatred, fled
off in haste. Some were only roughly driven off; others
did not escape the anger and hatred repressed for so
long.

When the army arrived in these districts which were
in revolt, they were received by a population who had
decided to defend themselves, who were superior to
them in numbers, and who did not lack arms. The
strikers were ready for a fight,—they preferred however
to avoid it, and to influence the soldiers by persuasion

and good temper; they therefore received them in a friendly way, exhorting them to come to an agreement with them.

As the army was only retained in a state of passive obedience by the fear of punishment, its disintegration was only a psychological problem, the contagion of example would banish all its indecision. As soon as different bodies of soldiers, at various points, had passed over to the people, the news spread from place to place,—in spite of the lack of communication,—whole regiments, one after the other, gained by the epidemic of defection, laid down their arms.

In these purely industrial regions, where all the power of the Capitalist and the State had finally come to nought, the workers did not rest satisfied with their own victory. They did not forget the duty of solidarity, and they hastened to the assistance of their comrades fighting elsewhere. From these human hives, where hope arose, whole companies of rebels started out. They went to neighbouring towns, where their help would be of use.

These bands of people were an impressive sight, marching to songs of deliverance sung with wonderful sonorousness. They made one think of those who,—escaped from Dante's Hell, were marching to the assault on Paradise.

Along the roads, in the hamlets and villages which these bands passed through, the peasants gave them an enthusiastic and fraternal reception. They also had been carried away by the passion for freedom! And they cheered the rebels, grasped their hands, and offered them hospitality.

On their arrival at the town, the goal of the expedition, they were met by delegations from the Unions, and an excited crowd, with a redoubling of wild delight that elated the timid and confounded with fear the enemies of the Revolution.

FROM THE ABYSS INTO THE SUNLIGHT.

CHAPTER XIII.

THE MOVEMENT OF THE PEASANTS.

In their turn, the peasants began to move; their intervention made the Revolution irrevocable, put a decisive seal to its triumph.

It had been feared that the peasants might have held aloof from the movement. Besides the fact that the Capitalists would then have found a point of support in the country districts, they would also have drawn men from there to combat, and perhaps crush, the workers in the towns.

History proclaimed that there was no hope of a thorough and effective Revolution without the help of the peasants. The example of 1789-1793 was conclusive; it was the Jacquerie that implanted the Revolution in the heart of the nation; it was really won in the villages, it was there the old régime was uprooted. The bourgeoisie knew that; therefore they neglected nothing to set the peasant against the worker; a brother enemy. For long they had benefited by the mistrust and hatred felt by the peasants for the town workers;—for long they had had no better soldiers to march against these than the young recruits from the country. And it was in order always to keep alive and vivid the bitter ill-will of the peasants that they had spread in the villages the legend of the "Dividers"; of the proletarians always ready to revolt and fall upon the peasants, in order to take from them their piece of land.

However, many circumstances had contributed towards clearing up this cruel misunderstanding. In the first place the establishment of industrial works in agricultural regions, with the object of obtaining cheap labour, had begun to modify the mental outlook of the peasants. Then also, closer relations had been established between the town and the village; helped by the development of communications, by newspapers, and by the growth of education. On the other hand, the young fellows sent to the barracks often returned knocked into shape, transformed, filled with Socialist ideas, which they spread abroad on their return to the country.

If it is added that the country people suffered from the general distress, they complained of slow sales, and low prices, of the taxes, of mortgages, it will be understood that a day came when they uprooted from their minds the weeds of prejudice and hatred against the people of the towns which the privileged classes had maintained there.

The Agricultural Co-operative Societies had a considerable influence. They revived amongst the peasants the practice of association and common understandings which the bourgeoisie had done their best to stifle. As a large number of these Agricultural Co-operative Societies disposed of their produce by means of the Co-operative Stores in industrial centres, this contributed to bringing them together again.

Still more fruitful was the action of the Peasant Unions, that were affiliated to the Confédération, or which were constituted and developed under its influence. These Unions made the fighting tactics of the Confédération Générale du Travial their own; they heartily accepted its ideal, and spread it abroad. When peasants were seen taking part in Confederal Congresses no one could deceive himself about the social significance of this event. It was a demonstration that, henceforth, an agreement had been reached, the alliance between peasants and city workmen had been realised.

The wine-growers of the South and the wood-cutters of the Centre were the first peasants who federated. The others followed. The peasants of the North, the resin collectors of the Landes, the market gardeners of the Paris district. After that came others, and soon over the whole of peasant France there spread and grew a Trade Union network, alive and vigorous. The pariahs of the soil were no longer human dust; societies, solidarity, had given them vigour and force; they had ceased to be apathetic beings, dull of spirit, and they did not fear the future, for they familiarised themselves with the work of emancipation, and the taking possession of the land, of which they cherished the hope.

Thus, in many regions, the peasants responded to the appeal for a General Strike. They joined in the movement with a heartiness and impetuosity the greater that they did not interpret it in the restricted and narrow sense of a simple protest against the actions of the Government. To limit the strike merely to a stoppage of work seemed to them insufficient; and, instead of restricting themselves to folded arms, they dreamed of more positive action. In their opinion, the time had come for effecting the essential act which they had at heart,—the freeing of the land. They were therefore on the watch; they wished indeed to act, but not to be the only ones taking action. At the first symptoms of outbreaks that were clearly revolutionary, they became bold, their last hesitations vanished: they rose to seize the land. The land,—which, for the peasant, is life assured, freedom conquered!

The revolutionary shock therefore reverberated in the villages; and it was a new Jacquerie.

On the plains of the North, of la Brie, of la Beauce, and in all the districts where large farming had not left a square inch of soil to the peasants, revolt broke out and the great estates were seized. In the forests of the Centre, the wood cutters, veterans of Trade Union organization, and long familiarised with work in common, drove off the wood merchants, and took possession of the land and forests. In the South, the wine-growers marched; but no longer at the call of the owners, as in 1907; on the contrary, it was for the attack on them.

This Jacquerie was strengthened by one of those panics of which there are examples in history. From village to hamlet the rumour spread that "brigands" were invading the country; coming to divide up the land. It was a new edition of the great fear of 1789.

To what causes must facts of this order be attributed? Must the responsibility for them be thrown on the reactionists, who hoping to fish in troubled waters, thought, by means of these false rumours, to exasperate the peasants against the Revolutionists? Or indeed, did the Revolutionists, by a macchiavelian calculation, use this means to shake the apathy of the peasants?

Both these explanations are equally plausible, if the facts of past history are referred to: in 1789, both aristocrats and Revolutionists contributed to excite panic in the country districts...But the Revolution alone was benefited.

However this may have been, from wherever the impulse may have come, in the case with which we are concerned, the result was as in 1789; the peasants rose and armed themselves.

They came together, they united for action.

Once up, they did not see looming on the horizon the brigands announced; but, having shaken off their passiveness, they felt in their turn the effect of the revolutionary surroundings. They did what in many other villages had already been done: they discovered the true brigand,—the rich, the great landlord, the State and its bloodsuckers !

And then, like their ancestors in 1789, they were carried away by the land hunger. In a short time, the taking possession became general. Where Unions already existed, the initiative came from them; elsewhere, the rebels came together, and without delay, formed Unions destined to become the nucleus of the New Community.

What could the local authorities do against this

inundation? The mayor, the few State officials, and the few privileged persons that the commune contained were powerless. Besides, the majority of them were not endowed with a combative temperament; and, much as they would like to have been defended, they were little disposed to defend themselves. But no power of compulsion existed any longer. The few gendarmes of the canton, whose mercenary ardour had fallen to pieces, looked on the revolt without disfavour. As to the army, it visibly melted away and dispersed. Many soldiers returned to their village, happy at being free before their time was up; some who, when leaving the barracks, had carried away guns and ammunition, joined the ranks of the Revolutionists, and distinguished themselves by their spirit of initiative and their mettle.

Without doubt it often happened that the rebels in a village were no more than an audacious handful; but they were sure of the tacit approval of the majority, and, however few they were, the privileged classes were still fewer. The latter, isolated and scattered, found themselves swamped in a hostile environment. Nevertheless, some refusing to recognize events, and also refusing to emigrate, attempted resistance. They were proud of their sporting education, they knew they were strong and robust. But they lived too much in the memory of the past: they counted on the prestige of their declining splendour, they depended on the respect with which they were accustomed to be surrounded.

When they saw themselves abandoned, alone, having to depend on their own powers, when they realised that their own servants refused to fight for them; when they saw themselves boycotted, treated like lepers, they had to recognize how little their physical strength served them, now that their privileges had foundered.

However, the Revolutionists had no sanguinary soul. Their attack was less on individuals than on wealth, knowing that, deprived of this means of corruption, the most feared capitalists would be incapable of doing injury. Nevertheless, there were, in some cases, rough executions;

vengeance was taken.   But these dramas were only incidents, not a system.

Amongst all the possessors, the most scared, the
most crushed under the weight of events were those who
fled from Paris, or the industrial centres, in order to
take refuge in their country houses or châteaux. They
had come to their estates in search of calm;   hoping to
await there, without hindrance, the end of the storm.

And here it was let loose about their heads, at least
as tumultuous and relentless as in the town!   And here
are the peasants,—freed from all respect, speaking to
them like equals,—coming to summon them to abandon
those great estates from which they draw pride and
profit!

To give up the land in favour of those who cultivate it,—that was the end of all things,—that was more
frightful than the Terror of 1793!

If this land, which was haughtily claimed from
them, had opened up under their feet, their fright could
not have been worse.

CHAPTER XIV.

THE END OF COMMERCIALISM.

We must now return to Paris, which we left in the full crisis of re-organization. This was a chaotic and confused time,—but it was also one of magnificent energy. No one looked askance at trouble. Men overworked themselves with delight. They brought to their work an incomparable fervour and tenacity. It was for themselves they worked. They felt themselves masters of the future!

All kinds of problems presented themselves at once, and it was necessary to find a satisfactory solution to all of them. But amongst them all, none were more pressing than that of the food supply.

Paris could not do without the continual flow of food products. And it was the more urgent to re-establish regular arrivals as, during the time of the General Strike, stocks had been exhausted. On the other hand, it was to be presumed that, at first, there would not be enough confidence in the new régime for market gardeners, graziers, and various producers and dealers to send supplies to Paris, without having the certainty that they would receive payment for their consignments.

These difficulties were met by various expedients. The Unionists drew from the cash reserves in the banks; and, whilst waiting for the dealers to become accustomed to other methods of exchange, they paid them according to the old commercial methods.

The various Unions connected with the food supply, each in its own sphere, drew up an inventory of the provisions in the warehouses, and made out some approximate statistics of the quantity of goods that would be required daily. At the same time, delegates were appointed to travel amongst the centres from which supplies were obtained, giving to the senders the required guarantees, in order that regular consignments might again be forwarded. To fulfil this mandate, there was no lack of goodwill. In addition to the militants of the great Distributive Co-operative Societies, and amongst others the Co-operative Wholesale Societies, who, on account of their established relations were a valuable help, other assistance was eagerly offered. The Unions could make use of the experience and knowledge of deserters from the bourgeoisie, who, having occupied important places in Capitalist society, came over quite frankly to the Revolution, anxious to make themselves useful.

These delegates for the food supply had not only work to do of a purely material and commercial kind, they had also a propagandist mission. In the districts where Agricultural Societies, and Co-operative Productive Societies had long been at work, their mission was simplified; there the minds of the people were prepared for modes of exchange less rudimentary than that of the exchange of their products for gold. In the districts where social life had only commenced with the Revolution,—and still more in refractory corners,—they had to use all their powers of persuasion. In no circumstances could there be any question of resorting to force. This was legitimate for overcoming persons in authority, and destroying Capitalist exploitation, but not for convincing the people.

If there were any peasants, artisans, small owners, little bourgeoisie, whom the missionaries of the Revolution could not make share their convictions, time and example would remedy that.

With all speed, the Unions of bakers, butchers, milkmen, grocers, and others were placed in a position to assure the distribution of goods, and to perfect its mechanism. It was they who henceforth, each in their own special line, were charged with seeing to the supply of needs;—distribution becoming a social function. The system of competing shops, scattered about or facing each other, was too absurd to be maintained.

Whilst awaiting something better, a hasty census of the useful shops was drawn up, and those considered superfluous were closed. In most cases these measures were taken with the consent of the former owners of these small businesses. The small employers, bakers, butchers, grocers, were invited to join the Union of their trade, and instead of shopkeepers they became distributors;—in their own shop, when this was kept open. Those amongst them who refused these proposals were simply boycotted: they found no men to work for them. Besides, as it was necessary when dealing with them to buy according to the old system, they had a very small trade. Most of them profited by the lesson, and quickly came to an agreement, which they had no cause to regret.

The trustification of certain branches of the food trades facilitated revictualing and distribution; this was the case, amongst others, with the milk trade. The services of the trusts were started again, and it was only necessary to modify the system of these monopolies to make of them social organisms.

The Distributive Co-operative Societies, which, in bourgeois society, had been useful to compete with ordinary trade, to free consumption from the Capitalist imprint, were going to fade away, now that the functions of distribution, which they had performed until then, again returned to the Unions. However, during the whole period of groping and re-organisation, they rendered good service, and were valuable auxiliaries.

In the various branches of former trade, the organisation of the service of distribution was carried out on the same plan as it was in the case of the food supply; the Unions of employees in each trade aimed at serving as intermediaries between producers and consumers, whilst simplifying this work as much as possible. As it was no longer a question of doing trade, of gaining a profit from the service which these intermediaries rendered, the working of the shops recalled the system of the Co-operative Stores.

Instead of the multiplicity of shops, which formerly keenly competed with each other, there was substituted a network of general stores, with district depôts. This simplification had as its first result a considerable reduction in the mechanism of distribution, and a large number of employees, useless now in the shops, threw themselves into production. The methodical organization of these general shops and depôts was not carried out without resistance. Many small shopkeepers were timid, and persisted in living in their former way. With these no violence was used. They were left to vegetate in their corner. Others allowed themselves to be coaxed, and with them an arrangement was come to, the same as in the food trade: some of their shops were changed into district depôts, and the fears which had, from the first, haunted these ex-shopkeepers disappeared. They soon saw that they had lost nothing by the change; their existence,—often full of cares, anxieties, confusion,—had given place to an easier, larger, life; without fears for the morrow.

The distribution of absolute necessities was carried out in a Communist way. They simply required, at the shops, the presentation of a consumer's card, which was issued by the Trade Union to which each one belonged. Provisionally, except for bread and sugar, (there was an abundance of wheat and considerable stocks of sugar,) it was necessary to resolve on a moderate allowance,— which did not constitute a privation,—but which was justified for the moment by the fear of an insufficiency or irregularity in arrivals.

No regulation was made making an exception of those formerly wealthy. The Unions did not think they

had a right to starve them.   They had, with regard to
them, more generosity than they themslves had shown
with regard to the unfortunate, the workless, the victims
of Capitalist society.   They were allowed to provision
themselves, either by means of money, or on presentation of special consumers' cards issued to them at the
Labour Exchange.   This was only provisional, until their
situation should be decided on.   As a matter of fact,
the question of parasitism would certainly arise, for in
the social hive there could be no place for hornets.

At the same time that the food problem was solved,
the Unions thought also about the suitable clothing and
lodging of the disinherited of the old régime.   Gradually
everywhere, by districts, by streets, by blocks of houses,
societies were formed; groups for inquiry, and for initiative, which did for these unfortunate ones what they
would not have dared to do for themselves: they provided
them with clothing, linen, furniture;   they took a census
of the uninhabited houses, and moved them in.   They
did the same for the families who grovelled in wretched
dens.

This constant thought, how at once to improve the
lot of the masses, was the dominant characteristic of
the Revolution.   The most thoughtless felt that something had been changed;   that the air was more fit
to breathe, and life less bitter, less sad.

And   because   the   revolutionary   elements   were
dominated by this thought,—at once to increase the
general well-being,—the Revolution was made invincible,
it would triumph over all resistance, overcome all difficulties.

CHAPTER XV.

THE RAILWAYS AND POST OFFICE.

The re-organisation of the great services of communication and circulation was one of the most urgent things to be done. This was begun as soon as the Government had been annihilated.

The administrative incapacity of the State had been so notorious that autonomous management by the groups interested appeared, even to men who looked upon the Revolution with dislike, to be the logical and only practical solution. This transformation of former public services was simplified by their very form, and for each of them the staff proceeded to do this with relative ease. There was but one aim, to adapt them to the needs for which they had been created, in such a way as to obtain the maximum of result with the minimum of effort.

In the postal, telegraph, and telephone services it was naturally the Trade Union Federation of the "P.T.T." which had charge of the work of re-modelling.

Whilst communications were hastily re-established, a Congress of all the services was organised, and committees of administrative revision received from it a mandate to proceed to the weeding out of the staff. The unworthy, incapable, parasitic chiefs were swept away; after which these committees, basing their action on all the information which they received, thought out a system of re-organisation which should substitute ability for authority. The engineers, the specialists, the administrators, in a word, the men with real knowledge,—of whatever kind it might be,—were neither disdained, nor unrecognised; they were placed in a position to utilise their capacity.   This was a change from the past, when intrigue and official influence were of more importance than knowledge.

This preliminary work finished in a satisfactory way, they considered the simplification of the service.   Red tape paper-scribbling, which in the old parasitic system was madly developed, was reduced to its simplest expression.   There resulted from this such a lightening of work that the real work could be carried out better and quicker, and with a smaller staff.   Naturally, these committees of revision did not settle things by themselves, and did not decide arbitrarily on re-organisation.   The task was made easier by the division of the services. When once the general plan was elaborated, it was those interested, who in their sphere of action, in their group, or in their section of work, undertook the re-modelling and re-organisation of the service.   By this method, there was no stifling of initiative, and by means of this co-ordination of common efforts directed into one convergent course, it was possible to gain a unity of action never before realised.   ·

What the postmen did in this emergency, and what was done in the various public services, was only a repetition of what was easily carried out, during the Revolution of 1789-1793.   Only at this remote period, it was within the military sphere, and not the industrial sphere, that revolt was materialised in significant acts.

Thus, during the first days of April 1791, in the reign of Louis XVI., the regiment of Auvergne, in garrison at Phalsbourg, turned out all its officers, and replaced them by men of its own choice.   An eye witness has told us the story of what happened.

"Towards one o'clock in the afternoon, the regiment, led by its sub-officers, drew up in square on the Place d'Armes.   The officers who were nobles, were in the Café drinking and playing.   The drums beat, three old sol-

diers stepped out of the ranks, and one of them drew a
paper from his pocket, and read. He notified to Sergeant
Ravette that he should step out of the ranks. The latter
advanced, rifle in hand, and the old soldier said to him:
'Sergeant Ravette, the regiment recognizes you as its
colonel.' Then, continuing to read, he named successively
the lieutenant-colonel, the major, the captains, the lieu-
tenants, etc.

" The officers, attracted and enraged by this
scene, wished to interpose. The new colonel said to
them in a dry tone: 'Gentlemen, you have six hours
in which to evacuate the place.' After which the regiment returned to barracks; and, on the morrow, not
one of the former officers was in the town."

This military weeding out was of the same kind,—
although in a different sphere of action,—as that which
the postmen of the new Revolution had taken in hand.
This proves that there is a persistent identity in Revolutionary tactics at different periods, merely modified by
changed surroundings.

Whilst the Federation of the P.T.T. successfully
carried out the inner re-organisation of the services, they
examined and solved the difficult problem of their relations with the public. The system that was adopted;—
the free conveyance of correspondence, and telegraphic
or telephonic communications,—had existed in germ for
a long time: it had been anticipated even in bourgeois
society, which had progressively travelled in that direction. In reality, was it not almost free transport, the
stamping, with a penny stamp, a letter that was intended for the colonies? And was it not a relative Communism to require the same stamp for a letter sent a
few miles as for one carried across the sea?

With free transport, the mechanism of the services
was reduced to useful functions only; it was freed from
the work of book-keeping, and all the complication that

was involved in the monetary system. This transformation had the result which had been noticed before, each time that the cost of postage had been reduced: there had been an increase of correspondence.   But parallel to this increase, there was a considerable falling off, which was due to the suppression of commercialism, and of the affairs of the Stock Exchange.

Therefore, henceforth, it was only correspondence with foreign countries that was still subject to the methods of the monetary system, to the formalities of stamping, or the payment of fees;   inland, the sending of letters, of telegrams and even of telephonic communications, was effected by the presentation of the Trade Union consumer's card.

Of course the communization of the services of the P.T.T. implied a reciprocity which would place their staff in a position to satisfy their wants.   This was provided for at the Congress of the Confédération du Travail;   where questions of a general kind were decided, and in the course of which the proposals to communize completely, and at once, the great public services, the P.T.T., the railways, and others, were discussed and approved of.

As a corollary to this decision, it was agreed that the staff of the communized services should receive "cards, and "consumers books," enabling them to satisfy their wants.

The revolutionary action, which transformed so radically the service of communications,—which might be called the nervous network of society,—was repeated, in almost exactly the same way, for the working of the railways,—which might be compared to the arterial and veinous network.

The Railway Workers' Union took the place of the Private Companies and of the State;   taking possession of the stations, of the rolling stock, and of the engineering workshops for manufacture and repair.   This done, committees, just as in the Postal Service, drew up useful measures for establishing as perfect a working system as possible. They attended to the unification of the systems, to the suppression of budget-eaters, to the weeding out of the staff, to the cutting down of all bureaucratic superfluities, such as paper scribbling, and foolish book-keeping. These various measures enabled them to divert to active service a large number of employees, formerly immobilised on idle and superfluous work.

The transport of passengers, as well as that of goods, was free; and in order to provide for their wants, the employees received, like their comrades in the P.T.T., "cards" and "consumers' books.'

This free transport was, in fact, only the extension to all of a privilege until then reserved for the great personages of the State, for deputies, and other notabilities, as well as for certain officials and railway employees.

At first, of course, this possibility of travelling at one's pleasure, without having to unfasten one's purse, was abused. So many of the industrial disinherited,— especially amongst the women,—had never left the shadow of their factory, had never seen a mountain, or the sea shore, so many peasants had never spent a holiday in a town, that the passion for travel which seized both of them was excusable. But the inconveniences that resulted were less than the moral benefits. The mixing of town-dwellers with peasants destroyed many prejudices, and the joy of travelling proved to the dullest that the Society whose era was beginning was better than Capitalism.

CHAPTER XVI.

THE LIFE OF THE CITY.

Whilst in the post office, and railways, Trade Union management was substituted for State management, a like change was successfully carried out in such national services as those of highways and bridges, water transport, etc. In the same way the town services were reorganised, which formerly, had been either municipalised or carried on by companies or contractors. In both cases, the Trade Unions interested became the centre of the reconstruction.

The Municipal Authority was an administration over which the Municipal Council had only an illusory power of control; it depended on the State; like it, it was incompetent; like it, it was bad;—and it foundered with it.

As to the Municipal Council, really a miniature Parliament, it was a democratic excrescence as much out of date as the Chamber of Deputies. But as the Hôtel de Ville had behind it the prestige of a revolutionary tradition, the Trade Unionists had to watch, as we have seen, in order that this attraction might not be exploited, and to avoid any medley from the past,—any resurrection of the Commune.

Public life had henceforth other centres: it was wholly within the Trade Unions. From the communal and departmental point of view, the Union of local Trade Unions,—the Labour Exchange,—was about to gather to itself all the useful functions; in the same way, from the national point of view, the functions with which the

State had adorned itself were about to return to the Trade Federations, and to the Confederation, a union of district and national organisations,—Labour Exchanges and Trade Federations.

Thus, on the ruins of centralisation, whence had flowed the suppression and exploitation of the individual, there was installed a society decentralised, federal, where the human being could evolve in full autonomy. It was a complete reversal of the terms: up to now, man had been sacrificed to society;—henceforth, society would exist for him; it would be the soil from which he would draw the sap necessary to his growth.

To the reign of law, imposed on individuals by an outside authority, would succeed the system of contracts made by the contractors themselves, which it would always be possible to modify or revoke. For the abstract and unreal sovereignty which the citizen of a democracy enjoys, was substituted a real sovereignty, which he exercised directly, in all the spheres where his activity found expression.

At the same time that wages disappeared, all trace of subordination had to disappear too. No one must be, in any case, either the hireling, or the subordinate, of anyone whatever: between human beings there would be contacts, contracts, associations, an intermingling of groups,—but each would render service to his fellow on the footing of equality, to be paid by some service in return. And because the new society was going to be like this, any legislating assembly was out of date,— whether a national, departmental, cantonal, or communal one.

Consequently, the Unions of workers on whom the life of the city depended, and who from the first were eager to re-establish the services, showed equal eagerness to arrange the conditions of their autonomous working.

The Unions of the workers who supplied water, electric energy, gas, motorbuses, and who found themselves confronted by Companies,—groups of capitalists, of shareholders,—proceeded, according to the method inaugurated by the postmen and railway men, to the revision and indispensable weeding out of the staff, as well as to a simplification of the services. As to the Unions of sanitary workers, and the services that had been municipalized, the taking possession was carried out without any difficulty, municipalization having been a step on the road towards collective property; they had only to re-organize the work.

In the trades where the Unions were strong before the Revolution, the transformation was accomplished very easily; the Trade Unionists,—who formed the conscious framework of the new order of things,—carried their comrades along with them, set the fashion. On the contrary, in those trades where the Trade Union centres had remained weak and inconsistent, difficulties arose; they resulted from the apathy which up to then these classes of workers had shown: having been incapable of revolt, it was to be expected that they would be at least as incapable of taking the steps necessary to carry out the administrative and technical re-organisation of the services of which they had charge.

Amongst others, this was the case with the staff of the underground railway system. The Company who exploited it had intimidated their workmen and had put down all attempts at organization, so that they held together no better than a rope of sand. It was not possible, however, under cover of this apathy, to allow the Capitalist form of administration to continue; neither was it possible to run counter to the mentality of the workers interested, and to set about a re-organisation of which they would not have understood the urgent necessity. This would have been a bad solution, for it would have consisted in substituting a Proletarian authority for a Capitalist authority.

In order to solve this difficulty, the Trade Unionists in the service of this Company, all too few, with the help of the militants in other groups, undertook the conversion of their comrades. They called a meeting, and explained to them the working of the new social order; and their joy was great at finding they met with less obstinacy, incapacity and inertia, than they had expected. This showed that if these workers had remained hitherto scattered and divided it was not for the lack of social feelings, nor from dislike to organisation, but it was the consequence of Capitalist repression, which had opposed their desire for cohesion and hindered their Trade Union grouping. Freed from the yoke that had destroyed their initiative and their will power, they formed a society, took the advice given them, familiarised themselves with the work and responsibilities that fell to them, and gained the necessary skill.

These were not alone in bowing to events which they had in no way been prepared to accept, or to submit to. Many others did the same, and had recourse to the mutual education of this new life, which, given without pretention, was received without mental reservation.

Then was seen also the evolution of the yellow Trade Unions, on which formerly the Capitalists had founded so many hopes; these, without offering the least resistance, allowed themselves to be carried along in the wake of the Revolution. There was nothing paradoxical in this. These conglomerations of workers, created artificially for the defence of the masters, were unstable; and it was natural that, being set free, they should cease to act like tamed animals, and should occupy themselves with the real interests of their members.

Indeed, each time that the bourgeois, in order to secure their future, and prevent the spread of subversive ideas, had favoured the formation of workmen's societies, with the hope of keeping them in leading-strings, and using them as tools, they had met with disappointment.

The most typical of these cases was the formation, in Russia, under the influence of the police, and the direction of Father Gapon, of yellow Trade Unions, which quickly evolved from conservatism to the class struggle. It was these Unions who, in January 1905, organised the

demonstration before the Winter Palace at St. Peters-
bourg;—the starting point of the Revolution which, although it did not overthrow Czarism, succeeded in
weakening the Autocracy.

Economic re-organisation, therefore, met with no
insurmountable obstacles; the whole working class, even
those most opposed to new ideas, followed the current.

This ready acceptance of change was not simply
due to the material improvement caused by the overthrow
of Capitalism, it was also a result of the more rapid
evolution which marks all revolutionary periods: human
nerves vibrate then with great intensity, the brain works
quicker, and adaptation to the environment takes place
at once, and swiftly. It often happens that the most
cold, the most sceptical, are stirred and carried away,
they become impassioned and roused.

Whilst the Unions, whose working was essential to
the life of the city, went on with the weeding out of
their staffs, and the re-organisation of their services, they
did not remain isolated. The water-tight partitions, that
characterised former administrations, did not exist
amongst them; they did not ignore each other, and
they succeeded in establishing relations between the
Unions which gave the municipal services a co-ordination
that they had never before enjoyed. There followed from
this an arrangement of work that was without the bungling of the former system. For example, there was no
longer seen the successive breaking up and repaving of a
street for the carrying out of various works that, with a
little arrangement, could have been done at the same
time.

The rule was, to act quickly and well; but its application came from the social structure itself, and not
from orders and authority. No one had any longer an
interest in making work hold out, in running up the hours
spent on a job, nor in scamping work, in cheating, or
wasting materials. To do these things would be injuring

everyone else, as well as oneself, without gaining anything by it.

Besides these Unions, who undertook the municipal work, societies were formed, and meetings held, in which all took part who wished, whatever their occupation might be; as inhabitants, and not as producers.

The City was thus covered and bound together by a federal network, which had the advantage of familiarising the entire population with the new life.

These societies concerned themselves with measures of hygiene and health; and by their advice and criticism took part in the administration of the City. They undertook the work of the moral administration of house property, now proclaimed collective property, and, as a matter of course, placed at the free disposition of all: they looked after its upkeep and repair; they drew up statistics of empty houses, they regulated removals; they also drew up lists of unhealthy houses, and in order that the necessary alterations might be carried out, they entered into arrangements with the Builders 'Unions; they marked out for destruction all the jerry-built houses, and the slums which hid within their hovels all kinds of pestilences, and the germs of all manner of infectious diseases.

In this work, these societies were helped by committees of architects, contractors, and engineers, who had rallied to the Revolution, and who co-operated heartily in increasing the healthfulness and beauty of the town.

Amongst the many labours undertaken by these societies, none had so much of a compulsory character as those which consisted in a fair distribution of dwelling houses. So long as the question was limited to turning the miserably poor out of their hovels, and installing them in better houses, the matter was relatively simple. It was another matter when it became necessary to satisfy the claims of occupiers who found their houses inconvenient. In the majority of cases, their complaints were well founded; the houses of the old order having seldom been constructed with a view to comfort, but always with a view to rent and profit. Even the princely mansions of aristocratic quarters, although of an imposing aspect were not practically useful; comfort was only possible there, with the help of a large number of servants.

There were many schemes, which, when carried out, would enable everyone to be housed according to his liking. Now that land had only its usefulness, and all its financial value had vanished, one dreamed of the erection of comfortable, luxurious buildings, unsparing of space, which would be suited to needs born of the social transformation. People dreamed also, that, instead of being packed together in huge, narrow cages six or seven stories high, they should swarm towards the outskirts of the town, and there build cottages, where they would be better able to understand what home meant.

That belonged to the future,—a future which would soon be realized. But, whilst waiting to have Paris such as they would wish it to be, it was necessary to decide on inhabiting it as it was. They did the best they could.

Moreover, as the distribution of houses was not made by any authoritarian method, as it was the inhabitants themselves who decided it in their societies;—first of all by streets, then by districts, then for the whole,—the work was carried out with the minimum of trouble.

To begin with, it was decided that a certain number of princely houses, flanked by splendid gardens, should be reserved for the aged. Then, the arrangement was agreed to, that each should continue in his former house, on the basis of one room per head; and that those who were worst lodged should move first.

Those of the formerly wealthy who had not left the country, were invited, with the tact desirable, to choose, in their houses, the rooms that they wished to reserve for themselves; as the majority, deprived of servants, attended to their own housework, they did this without their pride suffering too much from it.

Then, after a census of the available houses,—in which number was counted the houses abandoned by those who had left the country,—they undertook, in the house societies, and in the street societies, a collective inquiry; and, by common agreement, a list was drawn up, with marks of urgency and necessity, of those occupiers who on grounds of health ought to change their dwellings.

These first inquiries, sent to the district societies, received there a new classification,—always based on their urgency and necessity,—and those who were living in the worst conditions were the first to be given the choice of new lodgings. Thanks to this system, those who in the bourgeois society had the hardest lot now found themselves the best housed.

CHAPTER XVII.

THE ORGANISATION OF PRODUCTION.

The taking possession was not restricted to the services whose remodelling we have just sketched; it was carried out, with equal vigour, in all branches of social activity.

Trade Unions, which, under Capitalism, had been societies for combat, changed into societies for production; and, each in its sphere, set itself to the re-organisation of its work. For the most part, they were not taken unawares; previous discussions and papers, at congresses and in Trade Union journals, as well as the popularization of Social Democratic and Anarchist ideas, had given their militants a view of what was wanted, and of the work to be undertaken under the circumstances.

Therefore the Unions in each industry, in each profession, took possession of the factories and workshops which were indivisible from them. This was not always easy. Some masters kicked, would listen to nothing, refused any discussion,—as surly as a mastiff defending his bone. Some with a feudal mentality, proud of their privileges, decided to fortify themselves within their factories, determined to renew the exploits of the Crettiez family, at Cluses; they shut themselves in; and, rifle in hand, awaited the Unionists.

But the times had changed! When the Crettiez shot at their workers from behind their walls, the latter were without arms, and the soldiers who mounted guard at the gates of their factory allowed them to fire without hindrance;—far from interfering, they prevented the workmen from breaking down the gates in order to attack those who were shooting.

Instead of that, the masters who imitated the Crettiez found themselves alone, face to face with workmen resolute and armed. The parts were reversed: these had the numbers and the force! The struggle was unequal; the masters were beaten in advance.

These incidents hindered but little the re-organisation of the methods of working. A census was taken of the factories, their possible output was estimated, as well as the number of workers in the trade. After which, the Unions drew up statistics of the goods that could be manufactured in a given time; they showed also the proportional quantities of various raw materials that would be required. This information they sent to their Trade Federation, and to their Labour Exchange, which henceforth were the centres where the statistics of production and consumption were drawn up. The offers and demands flowed there; from there radiated the information as to the utility of producing in larger quantities such and such things,—which were in more demand than others; from there came the information about sending to such and such points raw materials and manufactured products.

An immediate effect of this re-organisation was to modify the absurd system of incoherent and disordered production so much practised during the Capitalist régime. Formerly, the manufacturer often worked in the dark, without being sure that he would be able to sell the goods made by the men working for him; in the future, he would know what he was about, being certain that this production responded to some need.

Another great and extremely important change was that of bringing into production a loyalty until then unknown: things were made for use, and not for sale, for utility, and not for profit. This fact caused the disappearance of the abominable "sabotage" which had been usual at all degrees of the industrial scale, which had enriched many an unscrupulous employer and contractor: defective, bad, adulterated, falsified merchandise, ready-made slop goods and trash were eliminated.

Why should valuable time be lost, and raw material wasted, over such production? It was natural formerly, when the well-being of one was based on the misfortune of others. To-day it was the contrary; the interests of the producers were the same as those of the consumers, they were bound up with them; therefore it was of no advantage to anyone to deceive or cheat his fellow man.

This tendency to frankness and good faith in economic relationships, this contempt for falsehood, this disdain for the spirit of lucre, were shown from the first. These qualities became more and more pronounced; especially as they were not due to individual culture, but resulted from the social structure itself.

There was no rigid and sectarian formula in the methods of re-organising work; account was taken of different temperaments and sympathies. There were variations, according to what was being dealt with, whether with large or medium-sized establishments, or with survivals of craftsmanship. When once the taking possession was carried out, if certain comrades expressed the wish to work alone, as artizans, no opposition was made to their preference. In the same way, the formation of working gangs, in both large and small establishments, did not result from arbitrary orders, but from agreement between comrades, from mutual recruiting. The distribution of various functions was also carried out by means of deliberations and agreements between the working parties interested. The tasks of co-ordination, of direction, and of specialization did not obtain for those in charge of them any larger income; therefore the competition for these jobs was reduced to a minimum, and the choice was often a judicious one. Furthermore, in bourgeois society, the working classes were already used to this selection of competent men, by the practice of work "en commandite," and by the working of Co-operative Productive Societies with a Communist basis which had already been largely developed.

The resistance of the masters was broken down, without hesitation, when it came from large employers; on the contrary, negotiations were entered into, and persuasion was used, with those who did a small or medium trade. To the latter it was demonstrated that socialisation would relieve them from the worries of business, from the hunting for orders, from the fear of failure. Those who were obstinately resolved to vegetate in the old way were left to themselves; they were left to live on the borderland in their own way, with all the disadvantages of the old society. As there was no lack of machinery and tools, theirs were scorned, so that they could only use them in a very imperfect way, for want of workmen willing to work for them.

Side by side with these obstinate ones, many others, —masters, contractors, engineers,—tried to adapt themselves to the new conditions. Sacrificing what was artificial in their former mode of life, they submitted to existence in this new environment, an existence which was for them a painfully simple life. To soothe their regrets, they argued; "Supposing I had failed, that I had been ruined, I should have had to work in order to live. This is what has happened to me now, with this difference, that I am ruined in company."

Now, it being granted that the human being has considerable plasticity, that he quickly adapts himself to conditions, to environment, to the most diverse climates, these "ci-devant," with their breastplate of optimism, adapted themselves to the new life, living happy hours, discovering satisfactions and joys of whose existence they had been ignorant, during the artificial, and even excessively ostentatious life, that they had led under the old order.

At the same time that the Unions, within their sphere of action, had effected the taking possession, had presided over the co-ordination of work, and had taken in hand suitable measures for making work less irksome, by a better management of the factories, and by an improvement in the equipment, other work was being carried out.

The Trade Federations, which bound together the Unions connected with the same industry which were scattered over the whole territory, held congresses, in the course of which the general conditions of production were worked out.

There was one fear: that the output would not be enough, without overwork, for absolute necessities. The statistics and information collected reassured the pessimists. They were convinced that with a reasonable utilisation of the existing equipment, and the suppression of unemployment, formerly in many trades so cruel and so long, the production of manufactured goods would reach the necessary level. In the trades and for the work about which any doubt existed, it was decided to appeal to the good-will of all those who, in bourgeois society, had been occupied with useless or harmful work, and who now returned to normal production. In the first place were the few hundred thousand soldiers of the vanished army; then the workers in military equipment, those manufacturing arms, powder, and those in the arsenals; then the custom house officers, the employees of the octroi and the excise, tax collectors, magistrates, lawyers, bailiffs; then the whole series of middlemen, courtiers, merchants;—finally, servants of all kinds. They were so many that their help sufficed to increase production by more than a third.

This census of the available hand-labour reassured the timid, gave them the certainty of a life of ease for all, and increased their confidence in the future.

In each Federation they estimated the number of supplementary workers who would be necessary for the various branches. Those who were unoccupied, as well as the parasites of yesterday, had only to choose: they were allowed to decide what work they preferred to take up.

The estimates of the quantities of raw material, of the heaps of manufactured products that would be indispensable, as well as those connected with the distribution of work in the various centres, were facilitated, in the case of certain industries, by the mechanism of committees who had formerly controlled these industries, or had even secretly trustified them. This was the case with coal-mining, blast furnaces, and the great metallurgical workshops.

The offices of these committees, which, under a harmless exterior, had for certain branches of production, formed a kind of industrial dictatorship,—violently combative with regard to the workers in the trade,— were occupied, from the first days of the victory, by the General Strikers. They found there valuable documents, and important statistics, of which they took advantage in their social reconstruction.

Each of these congresses brought together the Unions of workers taking part in some one of the varied functions of social usefulness: there were congresses of miners, of railway men, of teachers, etc.

The workers in various industries of luxury, those working in rare metals, jewellers, goldsmiths, also held congresses. They considered what amount of utility could be attributed to their work. Whilst holding that their skill should not be despised, for the needs of art and of luxury must be satisfied,—widened, not crushed out,—they decided that, for the moment, they should turn their hands to making things which were more urgently needed.

The workers in useless industries, in occupations or employments now abolished,—the workers in military establishments, powder factories, marine arsenals, and custom house officers,—also met, in order to examine together to what work it was better that they should transfer their activity.

Thus, in the conferences of their own organisations, the workers in various industries drew up plans suited to their special conditions, and prepared themselves to take part in the work of general co-ordination which sprang from the Trade Union Congress.

CHAPTER XVIII.

THE TRADE UNION CONGRESS.

Delegates came from all parts of France. They came there from all trades, from all professions. In the enormous hall in which the Congress was held, peasants, teachers, fishermen, doctors, postmen, masons, sat beside market gardeners, miners, and metal workers. An epitome of the whole of society was there.

It was a stirring scene this assembly, where were gathered together the most energetic and the most enthusiastic of the combatants for the Revolution, who, inaugurating a new era, were about to disentangle and sum up the aspirations of the people; to point out the road along which they were resolved to march.

The old militants,—who had seen so many Congresses,—who had fought rough fights, who had known the bitterness of struggles against the employers and the State, who, in their hours of anxiety and doubt, had despaired of ever seeing their hopes materialize, were radiant with joy. Their bold thoughts of past years were taking shape. They lived their dream! A happy moment it was, when old comrades greeted each other. They met, their hands held out; and trembling, deeply moved, they embraced each other,—transfigured, radiant.

The new delegates, out of their element at first, in the midst of this fever of life, were soon caught by the atmosphere of enthusiasm. Many of them were the product of events. Before the Revolution, they were ignorant of their own capacities; and if it had not come to shake them out of their torpor, they would have continued to vegetate; passive, indifferent, hesitating. Thanks to it, their inner powers were revealed to themselves;   and now, overflowing with passion, energy, and enthusiasm, they vibrated with an immense force.

Still more marvellous and cheering than the picture of the general enthusiasm which illuminated the Congress was the spectacle of the oneness of thought and of action which animated it.

The opinions which had so much divided men, had brought to naught so many efforts, had raised up so many hatreds, which had caused such floods of ink to flow,—and how much blood!—were unknown in this assembly.   There were no political parties there.   They had disappeared in the storm, foundered with the State. They were destroyed, done with,—the Revolution had killed them.   All the sub-divisions, all the classifications which Parliamentarism had engendered, belonged to another age.   Thus, when the flood of delegates rose and broke into foam, it was aroused by high and noble plans for the future, not by the baseness and vulgarity of the ambitions and desires that were endemic amongst the legislating assemblies of the régime that was abolished.

There was not within these precincts any deputy, unknown to his electors, having nevertheless received from them an unlimited power, and substituting, without scruple, his personal way of looking at things for the aspirations of his constituents;   his views often varying according to the whims of ministerial winds.   But here were workers, sitting there for the moment, and having to decide on points previously discussed by the comrades who had sent them.   And then, this great difference, after some days, the work of Congress ended, all these delegates would return to their Unions, and again take their place at work in the factory, the builders' yards, or the fields.

The change was vast.   And men who, formerly, led astray by the morbid influences of the State environment, had taken themselves for adversaries, (on account of differences in their theories of Government,) found themselves to-day in full agreement,—the governmental question, altogether eliminated, not being even mentioned. The one thought which dominated and possessed the Congress was that of working for economic agreement, and to create, or try hard to create, an environment favourable to human development.

What was aimed at was, in a practical way to co-ordinate and unify the views of the different corporate and federal organisations, in such a way that there should result an equilibrium that, far from injuring individual liberty, would extend and intensify it, by the support that each would receive from agreement with his fellows.

In the first place, a resolution was taken which there was no need to discuss,—or even to explain,—it was so logical and inevitable: the charging the community with the care of the children, the sick, and the aged. This was a question of principle which had the advantage of demonstrating, to those who still retained prejudices with regard to the new régime, how little the future was going to be like the past.

It was agreed that no difference should be made between the aged of different classes, and that the formerly wealthy and the proletarians should have a right to equal treatment. Neither could there be any question of parsimoniously restraining the possibilities of their life by rationing them at a ridiculous minimum, and by giving them, as before, insufficient pensions. It was therefore decided that the greatest possible comfort should be provided for them.

Next, it was laid down that the age for work should begin, on the average, at eighteen years, and should finish, at the latest, at fifty years; this age limit was only provisional, and would be lowered to forty-five, as soon as the social working should make it clear that there were more hands than were necessary.

The examination of comparative statistics on the probabilities of production and consumption, which were furnished by the Labour Exchanges and the Trade

Federations, involved the fixing, for one year, of the average length of the day's work at eight hours. In the occupations where the length was already less than this the former hours were maintained, and for work specially hard and laborious the average of eight hours was reduced.

In this connection they discussed and decided the old problem of "major" trades and "minor" trades, as they were called in the Italian Republics of the Middle Ages. Would there still be such distinctions? Were they going to reconstitute a kind of aristocracy of work called "intellectual," and would the "minor" and laborious trades be placed in an inferior position?

Long before the Revolution, the question had been debated by Trade Union organisations. All of them had, on many occasions, pronounced in favour of equal wages; which, even then meant that they could not imagine the setting up of any distinction between this or that work. This point of view could but grow stronger; so that, at the Congress, there was hardly any defence of the theory of inequality.

On the contrary, the theory that was put forward, as a subject for argument, was, that the "minor" trades logically had more right to a specially favourable treatment, just because they were more laborious than the "major" trades.   -

The delegates who expressed this opinion explained that the doctor, the engineer, the professor, should consider themselves as being "paid" largely by the joy of cultivating their brains, the satisfaction of enriching their minds; they affirmed that if any had a right to extra payment it could only be those drudging at heavy work. They did not demand that their proposals should be discussed just then. But they insisted strongly on the urgency that existed for giving up the methods of production used in certain chemical works and elsewhere;— methods injurious in the highest degree to the health of the workers. It was necessary to abolish these barbaric survivals as quickly as possible; it was not compatible with the new state of things that these monstrosities should be continued. And they concluded; that, as it is necessary and indispensable that each person should give a definite amount of work, therefore it is inadmissible that this work should be carried on under hurtful conditions.

This question brought on another, of the first importance; it was laid down that no Trade Union, no Public Service,—although autonomous from the point of view of management and working,—could have an isolated life, could set up for itself special accounts, separate itself from the community. If it had been otherwise, if groups had been able, under the guise of Co-operative Societies, to make for themselves special interests, outside those of the whole community, it would have been the germ of collective privileges, of advantages for special Trade Unions, which would have developed on the ruins of the individual privileges of Capitalism.

Attention was called to this peril, with overwhelming argument, by many delegates,—and this dangerous rock was avoided.

With this decision was bound up the solution of the problem of the lightening of work; of the scientific management of factories.

If the system of organisation with a Co-operative basis had prevailed, Commercialism and Competition would have continued: the richer Unions would have been able to equip themselves better; and the interest of all would have been subordinated to that of a few.

With the method that was adopted, agreement between the general interest and special interests was inevitable, and was secured automatically: the Unions, the working groups who needed either equipment, or the repair of plant, informed the Federation interested, or, more simply, the producing group able to accomplish the desired work, and it would be provided without any further procedure. It would not be necessary, in this case, to establish a balance of "debit and credit" between the group demanding and that supplying; equipment, material, management, were not considered as capital, not even as representing capital, but simply as wealth, used to increase the wealth of all; therefore, to contribute to and to increase, the well-being of each.

In order that this decision should be put into practice, it was agreed that large inquiries, rapidly carried out, should point out what needed to be done for the repair of works, factories, and workshops. The stocks of machines and tools already in the warehouses, enabled them to provide, in part, for a great many needs. Besides, there was no lack of constructors: instead of military stores, for the army and the navy, the making of which material was already suspended, the making of useful tools and equipment was substituted. Beyond this, in order to get on better and quicker, it was agreed to appeal to the councils of scientists, of engineers, of practical people, of professionals,—to the good-will of energetic men, young or old.

The problem of remuneration and distribution was strictly connected with the preceding one. Besides, when the data of the social problem were carefully considered, it was seen that all questions fitted into one another; all were linked up, in such close, such dependent relationships, that it was necessary to bring to all a solution based on the same principle.

In what proportions should each take part in consumption? How would each one be admitted, and what fare would he have at the social banquet?

It was a formidable question!

On this subject the discussions were long, animated, and thorough. The solutions proposed and advocated were held very strongly by the delegates, and each one explained and defended his theory with an ardent and lively conviction. All felt it was not a matter of obtaining a majority, of gaining this by subtle rhetoric, by oratorical methods; but of evolving a system of connections and relations, (between producers and consumers,) which, in spite of inevitable defects, and although not corresponding fully to the ideal of anyone, would, however be accepted by all as a solution that was so much the more reasonable in that it did not bar the future.

Two tendencies were shown; one, that of the pure Communist, who advocated complete liberty in consumption, without any restriction; the other, which, whilst inspired by Communist ideas, found their strict application premature, and advocated a compromise.

This latter view predominated. It was therefore agreed as follows :—

That every human being, whatever his social function might be, (carried on by him within the limits of age and time indicated above), had a right to an equal remuneration which would be divided into two parts: the one for the satisfaction of ordinary needs; the other for the needs of luxury. This remuneration would be obtained with regard to the first, by the permanent Trade Union card; and with regard to the second, by a book of consumers' "notes."

The first class included all kinds of commodities, all food products, clothing, all that would be in such abundance that the consumption of it need not be restricted; each one would have the right to draw from the common stock, according to his needs, without any other formality than having to present his card, in the shops and depôts, to those in charge of distribution.

In the second class would be placed products of various kinds, which, being in too small a quantity to allow of their being put at the free disposition of all, retained a purchase value, liable to vary according to their greater or less rarity, and greater or less demand. The price of these products was calculated according to the former monetary method, and the quantity of work necessary to produce them would be one of the elements in fixing their value; they would be delivered on the payment of "consumers' notes," the mechanism of whose use recalled that of the cheque.

It was, however, agreed that in proportion as the products of this second class became abundant enough to attain to the level necessary for free consumption, they should enter into the first class; and, ceasing to be considered as objects of luxury, they should be, without rationing, placed at the disposal of all.

By this arrangement society approached, automatically, more and more towards pure Communism.

The Congress saw no inconvenience in keeping, for the products of luxury, the method of fixing their value transmitted by Capitalist society: they considered that to take for the standard of value the hour of work, instead of the gramme of gold, was only playing with words. Certainly, there had been great evils engendered by the sovereignty of gold, by its monopoly; but this metal, henceforth dethroned, reduced to being no more than a simple article of merchandise, was deprived of its poison; it had no more power of absorption, nor of exploitation;—consequently, its use was no longer fraught with danger.

For this reason they no longer feared to leave to the money, still in circulation, its power of purchase. Besides, circumstances rendered it necessary, at least during the time of transition. But it was laid down that, when once this money had returned to the public chest, it should not be again put in circulation, except in very special cases; either to get exotic products from abroad, or to buy from those refractory people who did not yet agree to the new social system.

It was necessary, in fact, whether one wished it or not, to take account of these refractory people; were it only in order to gain them by persuasion.

With regard to those who, in the districts in full work of transformation, obstinately persisted, through narrowness of mind, or from the fear of losing by the change, in living the former life, no measure other than the boycott was decided on. They wished to remain

apart;—they were left apart! They would find themselves in such an inferior place that their position would
be untenable; they could not, by their isolated work,
compete with collective productions; and, if they wished
to trade, they would only have a very small number of
customers. And on the day when they amended, which
would not be long delayed, they would be received without ill-will.

A less expectant, less indifferent, attitude was taken
up with regard to the slow-moving population of certain
regions,—chiefly peasants,—who remained outside the
movement. It was the rural masses especially, still
easily frightened, who had to be convinced. Therefore
the foundation was laid of a vast campaign of propaganda, methodically carried out, in which both delegates
from the towns and peasants took part: they went together into these districts, explained the mechanism of
the new society, and demonstrated its advantages and
how far it excelled Capitalism.

Another set of refractories was that of the former
privileged classes. They had not all left the country,—
which would have simplified the problem. Some, taking
their part in events, had set to work, had adapted themselves, and had become part of the new society. Therefore it only remained to treat them as comrades. There
remained the others;—those who were not reformed, and
who, provisionally, lived on the margin of society, continuing their former parasitism. What attitude should
be adopted towards these? Should society still maintain them in idleness? This was out of the question, and
no one thought of doing it. It was decided to ask them
to choose some occupation; and, if they refused to do
this, they should be asked to emigrate; if they did not
willingly consent to this, they should be considered to
be in the same class as the "Apaches," and treated like
them.

Of course, there was no question of re-constructing
prisons, and of re-establishing, on their account, a repressive system that had been abolished. No, indeed!

The syndicalists limited themselves to clearing the territory of their encumbering and harmful presence: they
would be transported, furnished with a little money, to
the country which they preferred.   Consequently, no violence was used against them.   Since they refused to join
in the social contract, since they had not the character
suitable for living otherwise than as parasites, divorce
was a necessity.

In order not to be exposed to the mutual quarrels
that might follow from a rupture, they took the precaution with regard to them that was the least harsh;—
banishment.

It would be wearisome to follow the Congress step
by step, to set forth and enumerate the list of its works
and its decisions.   We have wished, in calling attention
to some of these, to point out the main lines of its action,
to show that its resolutions were always inspired by an
intense feeling of human solidarity, and by a broad Communist spirit.

Let us add that not a single discordant note came
to trouble the atmosphere of good comradeship.   Certainly, there were vigorous discussions, the diapason of
voices mounted high;   but at no moment did the tone
become bitter;   and it was possible to realize how artificial were the disagreements which, under the reign of
the bourgeoisie, had agitated the Confederation, and put
at cross purposes Reformists and Revolutionists.   In the
fire of battle, quarrels were ended: reconciliation came
on the ruins of Capitalism.

As soon as the Congress was over, the Confederal
Committee, which consisted of delegates from the Trade
Federations, and the Labour Exchanges, began its work.
This work was not direction, but condensation and analy-
sis: it drew up statistics as to the indispensable minimum
of production and consumption, and it served as a bond

of union between all the groups. It was like the centre
of a vast telephonic network, to which there arrived, and
from which there came, the information which secured the
regulation of the social working, the maintaining everywhere an equilibrium, in order that there should not be
excess at one point, whilst there was scarcity at another.

CHAPTER XIX.

THE LAND TO THE PEASANTS.

In the country districts, the taking possession was continued and increased. It spread like an epidemic, from village to village, but it was not effected in any uniform way, nor according to any previously arranged plan.

Nevertheless, the direction taken by the movement was towards the Communist solution. The peasants rallied to this by instinct, more than by reason. They were carried away along this road by ideas of agreement and solidarity, survivals from the older Communist customs, which, in spite of its age long efforts, the State had not been able to extirpate; and also by the current of social aspirations with which the country districts had been more and more filled.

From the North to the South, were seen again the 'days of unanimous revolt that, in 1907, shook the vine-growing districts of the South. As then, the dominant note of the movement was hatred of the State. Now again, the rallying cry was, "No more politics!"

And in many a village, where all the peasants went forward with the same spirit, if they had been asked, "Who are you?" they would have replied, as the vine-growers of a village in revolt in 1907 replied, "We are men who love the Republic, men who hate it, and men who do not care a hang about it."

The truth is that hatred of the State had been for a long time,—always, indeed,—strong and lively in the country districts. It was hated there as much as the monopolist of the land. A legitimate hatred! Was it not the State which,—monarchic or democratic,—had

legalised the theft of the land from the peasant, in order
to give it to the lord, or to the bourgeois?   Without
going back beyond the reign of Louis XIV, was it not
the edict of this monarch, promulgated in 1669, which
allowed the lords basely to take for themselves the larger
part of the communal wealth? And since then, what have
all the Governments done which have followed?

Nothing but sanction this spoliation, and render it
more complete.

The peasants had not forgotten! Therefore, in their
revolt, they were animated by a double feeling; love
of the Land,—hatred of the State.

For this reason, since the time of open Revolution,
in spite of some hesitation, they had rallied to the form
of organisation which best suited their needs; the Trade
Union and the Agricultural Co-operative Society.

These societies were substituted for the former
municipality; and, for the solution of all questions, they
had recourse to village assemblies; which, making another
vigorous start, brought the peasant back again to social
life; which economic isolation, and the deviation into
politics that the Capitalist system had imposed on him,
had made him unaccustomed to.

We have said above, how a wave of panic and anger
had shaken the torpor of the peasantry, and had made
them arm themselves. A fact which had increased the
gravity of this rising, and had caused it to evolve so
rapidly, was, that, added to the action of the Unions of
the Confédération du Travail, was action by thousands
of Agricultural Unions, which, by their constitution and
membership, did not seem like subversive elements.

In these Syndicates, formed long since, there were,
unfortunately side by side, small and great owners. The
latter had at first pampered these groups, thinking to
themselves that they might use them as electoral tools.
But, little by little, a new spirit had penetrated these
organisations: the influence of the small owners had
became preponderant in them, and a peasant Syndicalism,

of a rather special type, had grown up there, and had vivified them.

The work of Co-operation and of Benefit Societies had been, originally, the only reason for the existence of these groups. Little by little their horizon had enlarged, and they had caught glimpses of an ideal of social re-organisation, on a Co-operative basis; which, besides meaning liberation from the yoke of the State, would allow them to cultivate the soil in a more rational way.

When the Revolutionary crisis arrived, these Syndicates, at first distrustful and hostile, had been carried away by the movement. And as, in times of revolution, successive stages are very quickly gone through, they took these at a rush; and soon joined the Federated Syndicates.

The grave problem, for the peasants, was that of their farms. How would they solve it? The rigid Communist solution contended for the putting in common of all the fields, and the collective working of the whole. But if, in the districts where large farming prevailed, this solution could be readily enough adopted, it was different in the districts of small holders, where this was, at first, generally disliked.

Therefore it was not spontaneously, and at first sight, that the peasants found themselves in agreement on the transformation of the system of agricultural production. They proceeded by measures which met with no opposition, that all, whoever they were, approved: they freed the land from charges that weighed on it and crushed it; they suppressed rent, and mortgages. After this preliminary arrangement, the peasants, following the form of land culture on which they vegetated,—and also following out their own stage of evolution,—decided to cultivate the land seized from the rich in an individualist way.

If it had been proposed point blank, to the small owners that they should break down their hedges and enclosures and reunite their lands, the majority would

have refused; in spite of the fact that, with their method
of cultivating small portions in different places, their
toil was hard and crushing. They had not, at first, to
come to a decision on this point.

All the land cultivated directly by the holders was
left outside the revision which was carried out by means
of the Syndicate. The scruple was pushed so far as to
leave in individual possession the medium sized properties, which the holders continued to cultivate themselves,
or with the help of their families, without employing paid
labour.

The revision only concerned those properties worked
by wage labour. All these were proclaimed common property, and the Syndicate took over their management.
Again, in many cases there were arrangements according
to the districts, and according to whether the holders were
small farmers, or "métayers," cultivating with the help
of their families. In these cases the lands were held as
communal land, which in certain districts had survived
the pillages of the former systems; these lands, distributed in usufruct, returned to the commune on the death
of the holder, or on his leaving the village.

As to the large farms, the great estates, the vast
enterprises,—that were almost agricultural factories,—the
taking possession of them was carried into effect without
the least hesitation. There was, indeed, some trouble
caused by some managers and farmers, who found it disagreeable to be reduced to the common level; nevertheless, those were few who obstinately espoused the cause
of their landlords; the majority accepted the situation,
and took their place in the young community, where they
were called on to do different kinds of work according
to their abilities.

The Syndicates did not limit their activity to modify-
ing the system of ownership; they employed themselves
at the same time in ameliorating the situation of the
pariahs of the land, the wage slaves of yesterday. It was
necessary that they should at once find their life a better

one; it was necessary to link their fortune with that of the Revolution, in order that they might be its furious defenders. This work fell to the conscious syndicalists, for too many amongst these modern serfs, baffled and uneducated, would not have dared to do it. It was no longer admissible that these should be reduced to the animal existence that had been theirs up to then;—an existence like that of beasts of burden; with this difference, that employers did not take the care of them that they took of the animals, the latter having a market value which farm servants lacked. The young men on the farm, the cowherds, and the shepherds, returning after their day's work, wet through, worried and depressed, had no other couch than a bundle of straw, in the stables, the cattle sheds, or the barns.

That was set right. It was seen to that each one had a home,—at least, a room and a bed. There were,—for this thing which seems so natural and so simple,—material difficulties which they did their best to get over. In order to do this, they placed under contribution the furniture of bourgeois dwellings and of large country houses: the superfluity that was found there served to provide what was needful for those who had been for so long deprived of it. The proletarians of the land were thus raised to the state of comfort demanded by the environment. This did no one any harm.

Those who were lately farmers, the managers for the large owners, even the masters of yesterday who depended on the work of servants,—when they consented to adopt the new life,—did not suffer any diminution of their comfort; they found no change, except that they no longer had the pride of commanding, that they were deprived of servants, and had to put their hands to work.

The work was, besides, less rough, less severe, better understood, and very much lightened. Instead of the interminable days of last year, which, in many districts, began with the daybreak, and only finished with the fall of night, the average length of work was reduced to eight hours.

This limit had not the rigidity possible in other forms of industry, but so difficult in the country, where work is subject to climatic conditions. In pressing cases, —when a storm was feared, or for any other urgent cause,—they toiled with a will, without counting the hours. No one refused to do his share. Each one went at it with energy, without grudging the trouble, forgetting weariness;—they were working for themselves and not for a master!

The exodus from the towns towards the country made it possible much to reduce the duration of work. The "back to the land," preached in vain by so many economists, came about of itself,—as soon as the Revolution was over. Many of those uprooted from the land, who had been drawn away by the attraction of the artificial life of towns, the bait of a rapid fortune, and above all by disgust of dull work without respite, for a wage ridiculously insufficient, returned to the village, when it offered the possibility of an assured and healthy existence. They received a joyful welcome there. The good nursing mother, the land, only asked to be fertilized. She offered herself everywhere. The time of monopoly and misery was ended. The more the workers, the heavier would be the harvests,—and the greater the well-being for each. Therefore, the new arrivals were received like prodigal sons, with the greatest heartiness, and in the most friendly way a place was found for them in the productive groups.

Henceforth, the number of workers was nowhere a charge on the community. Far from it; as much in the country as in the town, everywhere, they brought a common lightening of work, and an increase of wealth for all.

Besides this abundance of hand workers, other agents helped to intensify the productive power of the soil:

mechanical tools, more and more improved, as well as chemical manures, forwarded in abundance from the industrial centres, enabled a better return to be obtained, and also enabled them to effect great works of permanent improvement, which, for lack of capital, could not be dreamed of formerly.

The example of this working in common presented a convincing contrast, when compared with the culture of small plots of land in different places by the small owner, who, in spite of hard labour, only obtained a moderate return; this did more to demonstrate to him the superiority of association than a compact and solid argument.

The peasant loved his land with a deep, violent love. He loved it for itself,—and because it assured him freedom and independence. Now, he had feared that by associating with his neighbours, by joining his bits of land to theirs, his freedom and his independence would be lessened. Experience showed him how illusory were these fears: he saw that, by culture in common, with an economy of tools, and an economy of work, better harvests were obtained. The working in common, and the division of work, enabled them to do at one point, and at one time, work which, in the individualist village, was done in an isolated way, and was repeated as many times as there were small cultivators.

The draught animals, collected together in healthy stables, were looked after more easily; and the same with the flocks and herds. No longer each man went to his little piece of land, with his plough, and his more or less suitable cart; instead of dispersion, loss of time, and useless toil, there was agreement, symmetry; and the waste of energy was reduced to a minimum.

This transformation of the peasants' state of mind had been prepared by the Co-operative Societies for the sale of agricultural products, and by the associations for buying seeds, manures, and machinery; which, under the auspices of the Syndicates, were greatly developed during the last years of the Capitalist period. These societies, which had at first only an immediate and restricted aim,—to eliminate the middleman, the speculator,—had prepared the way for a better organization.

At first, the peasants had joined them in order to obtain manures, seeds, and tools at a lower price; then they found it an advantage to buy machines, which would be owned in common by the members, and used by them in turn; and later on, to establish Co-operative bakeries and flour mills. Others were grouped together to found Co-operative wine cellars, dairies, and cheese factories; they, too, only thought of freeing themselves from the yoke of the buyer, who oppressed them. The inspiration of the movement carried them on, and little by little, they began to appreciate the advantages of mutual aid, and to accustom themselves to the idea of the Co-operative cultivation of the land.

These Co-operative Societies had entered into relations with the working populations; they had found valuable outlets in the Co-operative Stores of industrial cities; from this contact, the workers in the country and those in the cities had learned to know each other better, and mutually to appreciate each other.

Thus there were various causes which helped to lead the peasants towards economic changes. But, in order that these germs of Communism should spring up, there was needed the warm and passionate breath of the Revolution. Without it, the high hopes that a keen insight would long ago have discovered in the villages gained for Co-operation,—the hopes which foretold a grand blossoming time,—would have remained indefinitely in a latent state.

In those villages where Communist methods were adopted, Co-operation was doubly useful; it was the foundation on which the peasants built the organisation of the rural community; and, on the other hand, it made much easier the work of agreement between the towns and the country for the purposes of exchange.

The Syndicate centralized all the operations of exchange, and took the place of the small shopkeepers, for whom commerce had often been only an additional source of income. It was the depôt for all industrial and manufactured goods, the shop for general supplies, and it was the better able to satisfy all demands, as, connected by telephone with the general warehouses, it could, without delay, provide for the most varied needs.

Communilization was not limited to commerce: both milling and baking became Communal services; and this was the resurrection, in a more perfect form, of the common mill and common oven of the Middle Ages. In the same way, the crafts of the village,—shoemaking, and locksmiths' and wheelwrights' work,—were raised to the rank of Communal services.

The village became, in its internal organisation, like a great family, where the family groups nevertheless kept liberty of action, and of consumption. As to the relations which it maintained with the outside world, they were carried on according to Federal principles: the village forwarded to the town societies its surplus production, sending it to the points designated. Keeping in constant communication with the Labour Exchange of the nearest centre, and also with its Agricultural Federation, it was aware of the demand; and, according to the nature of its soil, it increased such cultivation or such breeding, intensifying the one or the other, according to what was needed, and the information given by statistics.

In exchange for its harvests, the village received the quantity of tools, agricultural machinery, and chemical manures that were necessary for a good return from its land. It received also, in sufficient quantity to supply the needs of the community, the manufactured goods necessary, for life, which were placed freely at the disposal of all.

Besides that, each of the villagers was entitled to his share in the consumption of luxuries; in the same way as the members of town centres. The person entitled to this could obtain it at once, by sending, through the agency of the Syndicate,—or even directly,—to special warehouses, for the objects of luxury, (or those of which the consumption was regulated,) up to the maximum of his power of purchase. This method was, of course, not a formal necessity; he could go to whatever centres he wished, and there obtain for himself the rare products or luxuries that he desired, in exchange for his "consumer's notes," or even for the former money.

In the villages where the principles of the Federation were not yet accepted, and where, consequently, the Communist arrangement was not yet working, goods were exchanged according to the old commercial methods. The isolated peasants, or their Co-operative Sale Societies, bought and sold as they pleased. The produce which they disposed of was sent to town warehouses, and they were paid for it in the old money; on the other hand, as they could not claim as Trade Unionists, they had no right to any free consumption, and they had to provide themselves with goods for ordinary consumption, as well as with agricultural machines, tools, and manures, by means of money.

This survival of the old order was partly broken down by the delegates sent from the towns to establish and assure the supplies of agricultural produce and cattle, as well as by the Federal propagandists, who, for the most part, were themselves peasants. Both showed and proved the advantages that the cultivators would gain from their complete adhesion to Federal principles;— for the lightening of their work, as well as from the increase of comfort; they drew a parallel between the method of commercial exchange, which did not allow them to obtain anything except for money, and the Federal method, which placed freely at their disposal the most perfect tools, and assured them the satisfaction of their needs; they explained to them that when they wanted to undertake some great work, some great constructions in the commune, or to make their houses more hygienic, if hands were lacking, they had only to appeal for volunteers, who would come from the town, in sufficient numbers, to aid them in their work.

This propaganda which, if it had been merely theoretic, would not have been convincing, became so, owing to the power of example: the results already gained in the neighbouring villages spoke louder than any argument. Thus, in the districts where the Revolution was at first limited to the seizure of the estates of the rich, Communalization extended, creating there plenty and well-being.

CHAPTER XX.

THE ARMING OF THE PEOPLE.

The work of re-organisation had not caused the neglect of a contrary, but indispensable, labour: the destruction of the institutions of violence and coercion that had assured the power and duration of Capitalism. The Parisian Revolutionists had occupied themselves with this without a pause: to begin with, they scattered the staff who lived on these institutions, or gravitated around them.

They did more. Through an excess of prudence, in order to paralyze, by making concentration difficult, any attempt at attack by the bourgeoisie, in order the better to uproot the institutions of the past, they destroyed the buildings which had given them an asylum, which had been their symbol.

The Préfecture de Police (Police Offices) had been one of the first Governmental dens occupied, and it was one of the first to be pulled down. The Palais de Justice (Law Courts) had the same fate, with the two adjoining prisons,—the Depôt and the Conciergerie.

The police, and the sergents de ville, were nowhere to be found. The way in which they had been hunted, during the course of the General Strike, in the districts where they lived, had given them warning of the dangers they ran. Therefore, as soon as they saw that the triumph of the people was only a question of hours, they disappeared, they vanished.

At the Palais de Justice, there was a queer crowd. In this place there swarmed, trifling their time away, a population of barristers, lawyers, employees of the courts, a lot of dubious people, who, wretchedly under-rating the extent which the transformation now being accomplished would have, supposed they would be able to continue their operations, and to live still at the expense of the community. Their illusions were deceptive. All these persons were informed that their functions had no longer any meaning, that all parasitism was ended, and that they must select some useful trade or profession. They were advised to take time by the forelock and to join the Syndicate of the profession for which they had a fancy, or which best corresponded to their taste.

The prisons were attacked. They were emptied of all their political prisoners; as well as the common law prisoners. But with regard to the latter, a few preliminary formalities were gone through.

A Federal Commission was charged with the consultation of specialists who had the best repute for knowledge and integrity; they were given the task of examining those amongst the prisoners who, considering their physiological defects, were sick people to be cared for; whose sudden liberation would have constituted a danger, and who would be transferred to lunatic asylums.

Then the Federal Delegates called together the prisoners,—including with them the warders and prison officials. They explained to all of them the conditions of the new life; they explained to them that the Revolution had been made to suppress idlers, parasites, thieves and criminals of all kinds; and that consequently, henceforth, it was necessary that all should work, and that no able-bodied person should avoid work. Then, addressing without distinction both the warders and the prisoners, they added:—

"It is for you to decide whether you feel yourselves capable of adaptation to this environment, of reforming yourselves? If so, you will choose some profession or trade, and you will be admitted as a member of its Trade Union. There, you will only find comrades; they will treat you as friends, and will be ignorant of,—or will

forget,—what kind of man you have been. In case this
life of healthy labour, the foundation of well-being, does
not attract you, you are free to refuse the social contract
that we propose to you. In that case, you will be banished
from the territory, and sent to whatever country you may
name. But in order that, on your arrival, you may not
be entirely unprovided for, we will furnish you with a
small sum of money."

These words,—ringing between the thick walls, behind the bars, and in the dull light of prisons; in the
damp atmosphere of jails full of mouldiness and of the
offscourings of human society; there, where so many
sorrows had been born and died away;—addressed both
to the prisoners and the warders, who heard them on a
footing of equality;—these words proclaimed the full
extent of the social upheaval, and they moved and convinced their hearers.

The warders were glad to give up an occupation for
which they had nothing but dislike, and which they had
adopted through want. As to the prisoners, the frankness and sincerity of the language used to them,—a
change from the hypocrisy with which they were generally
surrounded,—impressed them, and the majority agreed
to accept the contract that had been offered to them.

The demolition of the prisons and court houses,
and the dispersion amongst producing groups of the
parasites who had lived on fraud, theft, and crime,—either
directly, by taking part in it, or indirectly, under the
pretext of repressing it, as policemen, judges, and gaolers,
—did not result in placing society at the mercy of brigan-
dage and idleness.

In future, anti-human acts were dealt with by the
working group or by the Trade Union of which their
authors were members.

Each one was therefore "judged by his peers,"—to
use the old expression. But either the "guilty" man was
recognised as being diseased, and received the care that
his state needed; or there was pronounced in his case a

verdict which, instead of bodily punishment, involved merely a moral punishment, in the form of boycott and contempt. This quarantine was stopped, as soon as it was judged that the person sentenced to it had reformed.

In some exceedingly rare cases, banishment was decreed, by decision of the general meeting of the Syndicate, from which appeal could be made to the Trade Federation, and even to the Confederal Committee. But it was only exceptionally that it was necessary to have recourse to this measure. For the most part, the boycott was sufficient to reform evil-doers.

To accept being thus placed under a general ban, one had to be strongly tempered, and sustained by a great and generous idea; this was the case, in former days, with the Revolutionists; who, strong in their subversive ideas, faced public opinion, and laughed at the sheeplike and unanimous censure which was accorded them; or else a man must know that he is approved of and encouraged in certain quarters; this was the case with common law criminals; who, for the prison world, were heros.

But as it now needed more energy to face general reprobation than to fall in with the conditions of work that were established, and as there was no longer a flash population to admire hooligans, no longer a press to write up their exploits, these sad specimens disappeared.

The régime of a plague-stricken person to which evil-doers were subjected was so heavy, so painful, that misdeeds became more and more rare. This moral curb was more efficacious than the penal codes of bourgeois society had been. By this method a result was obtained that a recourse to imprisonment and tortures had not been able to reach,—anti-human acts were, to a great extent, dammed up.

Besides that, to begin with, these acts diminished automatically, by fifty per cent, because there were no longer any crimes and misdemeanours caused by misery, inequality, or the evil deeds of Capitalism. In addition, the offences which were the consequence of physiological defects, of degeneration, of mental diseases, had a tendency to disappear, under the influence of the environment. There only remained then crimes of passion, and those due to accidental causes; for which already, in bourgeois society, there were always excuses, extenuating circumstances, if not acquittal.

It certainly happened sometimes that, impelled by indignation, the eye-witnesses of some odious outrage allowed themselves to be led into acts of summary justice. Thus, the seducers of children, the violators of women, taken in the act, were executed without pity.

These sudden violences, however merciless, rough and sanguinary they might appear, were healthy and fruitful. They gave security to all the weak. The wild beasts, who had the misfortune to carry about within them ancestral savagery, were, as far as possible, put on guard against their perverted instincts by the menace suspended over their heads. If these monsters could not contain themselves, so much the worse for them. They did not repeat their action twice.

However cruel and inexorable this system of immediate repression might be, it was less repugnant than the former procedure, with its judicial paraphernalia; and it had the excuse of a genuine anger, which the magistrate working in cold blood had not.

Whilst the prisons were being destroyed, the barracks and forts surrounding Paris were not forgotten.

The army was disbanded. The soldiers of all descriptions were sent back to their homes. Already a large number had forestalled this; and, on their own initiative, had dismissed themselves. Above all, the disarmament of the so-called select corps where an aristocratic spirit was maintained, was watched over carefully.

These prudent measures were completed by the closing of the military schools.

As to the barracks, they were pulled down without hesitation. They had menaced Paris for too long for any scruple to be felt about their demolition, under the specious pretext that they could be transformed into dwellings. The anger of the people was furiously aroused against these, and it was with enthusiasm that gangs of demolishers were formed, who worked with pickaxes and mattocks to pull them down.

The forts met with the same fate. They set to work to dismantle them with the more energy because they were a constant menace to Paris, in case of any reactionary attempt. In fact, they had been constructed and improved more with the ulterior thought of using them to overcome and bombard the great city than with the idea of defending it against an outside attack. And, if the Government had not had recourse to their cannons, it was because the Revolution had had an unforeseen and rapid development, that had made them incapable of using all their means of defence. There happened to them what had, in the course of previous revolutions, ruined Governments, which, on the eve of their fall, had seemed unshakeable;—they had been dazed by the extent of the insurrection, and its vigorous attack.

The demolition of the forts had more the character of country festivals than of Revolutionary expeditions. They went to the work of dismantling them in joyous bands; they feasted gaily on the glacis; singing, dancing, and drinking in high good humour. They preluded with merriment the levelling of the ditches, the overthrow of the casemates, the break up of the cannons, the destruction of the ammunition.

They only respected the rifles, and the arms that could be easily managed; these were removed in triumphal processions, and taken to the Labour Exchange.

These were good and sound tactics. They proved that having been capable of winning, the people would also be able to defend their victory; since, the more they held that it was indispensable to destroy all offensive armament and means of attack, the more they valued the advantage of preserving their defensive arms. They remembered how much they had suffered from the lack of rifles. They remembered the disappointments they had

experienced, when there had been opportunities for freeing themselves, and they could not profit by them, for lack
of arms. Therefore, they did not disdain to arm themselves, although their triumph made the need problematical.

The people had always detested military servitude;
they had always execrated wars between nations, and the
bloodshed of which their children were the victims, and
it was not with light-heartedness that, after having bent
their backs under oppression, they lent their arms for the
exploitation of others. This, however, had never meant
for them the resignation and non-resistance preached
by Tolstoi. They had always sought to arm themselves
to counterbalance the military and other forces, which,
under the old order, held them under the yoke. They had
provided themselves with revolvers. They had bought
rifles, when they could. They had made explosives and
used bombs. And therefore it was to be expected that,
being placed in a position to arm themselves effectively,
they hastened to do so.

Under these circumstances, the Syndicalists only
walked in the footsteps of the Revolutionists of 1789,
who showed as much eagerness in seizing arms, where-
ever they could be discovered, as they showed in attacking the Convent of Saint Lazare, or the Bastille.

At that remote time, the best arms were cannons;
and the Parisians, who prized them more than flint-lock
rifles, considered them as the best of arguments. Therefore they went to take them wherever they were to be
found.

Expeditions were organized against those large coun-
try houses known to possess cannons; the Chateau de
Choisy-le-Roi was despoiled of its cannons, and also the
Chateau of Chantilly, of l'Isle-Adam, of Limours, of
Broglie, and many other residences of the nobility.

When, on the return from one of these expeditions,
the Parisians brought back their booty to Paris, they
were not naive enough to listen to the treacherous advice

of Lafayette, who was distressed to see the people arming themselves; and who, in order to disarm them adroitly, wished the districts to hand over to him their cannons, under the pretext of forming with them a park of artillery. The Parisians did not fall into the net, they did not listen to this treacherous advice; they kept their cannons in their sections; and this was their strength on the great days of the revolt.

Therefore, imitating the Revolutionists of the eighteenth century, their grandnephews of the twentieth took arms wherever they found them. The engines of war being more perfected, they had not the same esteem as their ancestors for simple cannons; on the other hand, they did not disdain mitrailleuses and quick-firing guns. With great care they laid hands on all kinds of defensive arms; and they were distributed, in the Trade Unions, to all able bodied comrades who wished to arm themselves.

To the arms found in the forts were added those coming from the disarmament of the troops, those piled up in the magazines and war depôts, and those collected from gunsmiths.

The radical purification of which we have just narrated some of the details, was not limited to the capital. With equal energy, the provinces put themselves in unison; the law courts and prisons were pulled down, the barracks and fortresses dismantled.

Soon, in the whole country, there was not a single battalion in arms. Simultaneously with the dislocation and dispersion of the army, a census of defensive arms was taken; and, by means of the Labour Exchanges, they were distributed to those in the Syndicates who wished for them.

In each Syndicate a group for defence was formed, to which flowed voluntarily the young and active elements; they exercised themselves in the management of arms, and the methods of resistance; in order not to be taken unawares in the case of any reactionary conspiracy. These groups arose from the Labour Exchanges; and, whilst entering into relation with like groups in the same district, and with distant centres, their members did not cease to be active members of their Trade Unions. They did not consider themselves excused from their share of daily production, under the pretext that they were giving themselves up to the practice of military gymnastics.

These Syndicalist battalions were not a force external to the people. They were the people themselves; who, having freed work, had the common-sense to arm themselves in order to protect their conquered liberty.

This organisation for defence, with a Trade Union and Federal basis, made impossible any intrigue tending to divert this armed force from the end that it was intended to serve. Mixed elements, and suspects could not be included in it; there one was amongst comrades, and in order to be admitted to one of these groups, it was necessary not only to be a member of a Union, but to be known to, and proposed by, members who made themselves responsible for you. Rather distrustful precautions; but useful for preventing the infiltration of any doubtful characters from the formerly wealthy classes.

Now bristling with rifles and bayonets, with mitrailleuses and quick-firing guns, Trade Union France was on guard; these powerful arms were handled by men of temper and resolution; and they had,—over the France of 1789,—the advantage of being entirely cured of all Lafayettes.

CHAPTER XXI.

THE DEATH THROES OF REACTION.

From the beginning of the troubles, a number of privileged persons had taken the precaution of placing themselves in safety. When the crisis became acute, there was a rush of emigration.

Amongst those who fled from the Revolution, some were superficial frivolous people, loving their ease and fearing worry; others had more serious reasons for seeking a change of air: their name had such an evil notoriety that it seemed to condense the popular hatred. Besides, for both of them, leaving the country was a trifling incident. The habit of going long tours in automobiles, excursions to the banks of the Nile, or the fiords of Norway, had made them thoroughly cosmopolitan. Knowing that they could find their ease no matter where, expatriation was a light matter for them. And then they had the same illusions as the emigrants of 1790; they counted on soon returning; and only saw in these momentary troubles the occasion for a journey, unexpected, but not disagreeable.

After all, there was nothing easier than going out of the country. In a few hours, by motor, the frontier was gained. The only risk was in passing through villages where revolt growled. Still, it was less as emigrants than as motorists that the fugitives had anything to fear. As a matter of fact, motors were not held in esteem in the country districts,—they ran over chickens, and also people. And when wrath broke out there was a danger that it might be turned against them. Nevertheless, reprisals were rare. More rare still, were those that ended tragically.

Emigration was not hindered by the Revolutionists. Far from that. It was desired by some, who saw in it an opportunity for continuing, without hindrance, the expropriation of the Capitalist. As the Revolution was made more against institutions than against persons, the result of the exodus of privileged persons was to avoid difficulties and disputes with them. The emigrants could carry away their gold; but not that which constitutes real wealth; their land, their factories, their buildings. Their departure therefore facilitated the occupation of their estates by the peasants, the using of their factories, and the new management of the buildings that they had abandoned.

But the possessing class did not all leave the country. There were some, as we have already said, who refused to leave a free field to the Revolution, and who, now that Parliamentarism was overthrown, tried to defend themselves. At the same time, the Government was trying to reconstitute itself in the provinces; its members;— ministers, deputies, superior officers,—had rallied at the camp at Châlons; and there, surrounded by some remnants of the army, they tried to re-organise a military force, hoping that an occasion would present itself for taking the aggressive.

The bourgeoisie counted on its numerous rallying centres to give substance to their attempt at direct opposition to the Revolution: in the first place, on the Chambers of Commerce, and the masters' Syndicates; then on the central committees, which, in certain industries, had controlled production;—the central offices of ironmasters, committees of coal owners, and of textile factories;—they counted equally on the masters' Federations for assurance against strikes, and on many other different associations.

On account of this network of societies, those who were formerly wealthy who wished to defend themselves, could still imagine they were capable of resistance. They cherished illusions. Their social horizon had not enlarged, and they were always looking back to the former state of things, paying no heed to the transformation that was going on.

Their means of action were above all of a financial kind, and the organizations which they hoped to make the pivot of their opposition were adapted to Capitalist society. So long as the problem was limited to guaranteeing an employer, or even a whole industry, against a strike or a partial rising, these associations, well armed financially, would have been able to provide against the danger. This case was different. The Revolution had broken out, and it was necessary to withstand the disorganisation of the whole system. A tremendous work, for which these societies were the more powerless in that their industrial or commercial domination was destroyed.

Could the bourgeoisie hope for anything better from the varied organizations, mixed and hybrid, sandwiched with masters and resigned workmen, from which, some good souls had believed, would come forth the elements of a reconciliation of classes?

These foundations were not firm. The workers who joined them formerly, through timidity or the spirit of imitation, were not the men to set themselves in battle array for their masters. What was more, a transformation took place in them: it had been necessary for them, in order to live, to join Federal societies; and, in contact with comrades with whom they were there side by side, they became new men;—more disposed to defend the Revolution than to combat it.

The bourgeoisie therefore found themselves, with rare exceptions, reduced to their own strength, and deprived of that which, until then, had made their power, financial influence. Gold had lost its enslaving attraction. Life was possible without it. And because a living by work was assured to all, the recruiting of mercenaries became very difficult.

The formerly wealthy classes, until then used to being defended, were reduced to paying the piper in their own persons. And what pitiful persons they were! The former kings of finance, of iron, of coal, all the trust magnates, all the giants of Capitalist industry, after having kept armies of workmen under the yoke, having dominated the State, and enslaved ministers, now had their privileges cut off. They were now more feeble than abortions, and were disabled to such an extent that they did not know if they would have anything to eat the next day!

They could do nothing really effective against the Revolution. It was no longer a question of overthrowing a Government, but of destroying the creative power of Trade Unions, and of replunging a whole people into the wage system. Now, whence could they attack the New Society? There was no longer any State centralisation, and the means of communication and transport were in the hands of Federations of workers, who would paralyse the reactionaries, without much difficulty. The work of counter-revolution was therefore impossible, for it implied the abdication of the working class.

We have seen that, since their triumph, the Revolutionists had acted swiftly, not hesitating to take the measures that were necessary: at the same time that they seized the factories, the banks, the whole social equipment, they occupied the offices of the trusts, and' all the points where the reactionaries might have been able to concentrate, and to plan amongst themselves. The latter were thus deprived of the rallying centres on which they had counted. Everything tottered around them! Their disaster was without remedy. They could only busy themselves to no purpose.

They gathered together, with difficulty, in some stagnant towns, far from all economic activity, in corners to which the Revolution had not extended. They were little more than a general staff without soldiers. There came to join them there some adventurers with the mentality of gorillas, and some officers of the former army.

As for the officers and under officers of the industrial

army,—the staff of managers, of engineers, of foremen,—
they came in small numbers; the majority, who indeed
had suffered, as a real intellectual proletariat, refused
to espouse the reactionary adventure, and frankly passed
over to the people.

Against the collection of parasites and exploiters
who urged some counter-revolutionary action, the Confederates only used the boycott. The places where the
"ci-devants" gathered together were cut off from all
communication, ruthlessly isolated. They allowed neither
convoys nor provisions to reach them,—nothing! And
in order that the circle of the boycott should not be
broken, they redoubled their activity so as to arm especially well the Syndicalist battalions in these districts:
they were furnished with mitrailleuses and quick-firing
guns, which, mounted on automobiles, were formidable
engines. Not that they desired to act on the offensive
against the reactionaries; but in order to be in a position
to repel them, in case they should decide to attack.

They could not attack!

They lacked arms, ammunition, everything. The
positions were reversed. The proletariat were armed;
they, hardly at all;—and none was on their side.

Their situation was as insecure as that which the
people had endured for so long, with this difference,—
making things worse for them,—that they only strove to
reconquer privileges, whilst the people had been sustained in their martyrdom, by an ideal of freedom.

With regard to the phantom of Government which,
at Châlons, tried to keep up an illusion, which did its
best to seem alive, and tried to unite in one group the
scattered remnants of Capitalist resistance, they were
treated with much less respect.

Extremely severe was the boycott with which the
camp was fenced about. The Governmentalists only succeeded with difficulty in revictualling it; as to arms and
ammunition, it was impossible for them to renew them,
for want of the power to obtain supplies from the public

stores. This inconvenience was more felt by them than all the others; it reduced them to the old means of defence and attack, without any means of possible improvement or modification. The more easy it was, in fact, for a Trade Unionist to obtain, through the agency of his Union, the most varied kinds of metals,—steel, aluminium, or others,—the more difficult was it for a refractory person, as there was no longer any trade in metals.

On this account, the Governmentalists had to live upon the past; and this was the cause of their inferiority, as opposed to the Federalists, especially in what concerned the formidable engines that aeronefs and aeroplanes had become.

When the Governmentalists had been shut in by the boycott, as in a vice, methods of terrible destruction were used against them, which did not involve any military mobilisation. These methods were known long before this time. But Governments had never wished to have recourse to them. When they hurled the peoples one against the other, they preserved in these butcheries a certain diplomatic decorum, and they would not carry on a war of real extermination, which would have been as perilous for the general staffs as for the mere "food for powder."

At the dawn of a radiant day, a flotilla of aeronefs set out to fly above the camp of Châlons. The aviators who had taken the initiative in the expedition, and who went of their own free will, were of an unheard of coolness and boldness; they made evolutions at a low height, and with a precision which the fire of the enemy did not affect, they did their work of havoc.

They bombarded the camp. And the bombs they rained down like hail were of two kinds; some contained a violent explosive, others hid within their flanks asphyxiating gases.

The effect was terrible! The almost silent bursting of the asphyxiating bombs, which, in a large circle,

mowed down men, overthrew them and withered them
without noise, was more sinister and still more horrible
than the explosion of the detonating bombs. These let
loose on the plain a hurricane of fire, mixed with sharp
hisses, and heavy blows.

In less than an hour, there no longer remained a
building, or even a casemate standing. The cannons lay
scattered about, dismounted, with broken wheels and gun
carriages. The men had been seized with an unutterable
terror. Those who, during the first minutes, had tried
to carry on a useless struggle, quickly gave it up. And
there was a headlong, mad flight in all directions.

The survivors were allowed to escape, without arms.
The Federalists had no other object than that of defending themselves, of definitely crushing out the reaction;
and not of beating the vanquished. Some succeeded in
passing the frontiers....

That was the end!

Thus, in spite of all the bitterness which they felt
about the social overturn, and the ruin of their privileges, the bourgeoisie could do nothing effective against
the Revolution; they were no more than human atoms,
without cohesion, and without means of action. There
were certainly amongst them some personalities with
energy, capable of personal courage and heroic acts,
but who, lacking ground on which to place their feet,
struggled in empty space; it was as impossible for them
to combat triumphant Federalism, as to grasp the ocean
in their arms.

CHAPTER XXII.

EXPROPRIATION AND EXCHANGE.

The last convulsions of Capitalism did not hinder the work of social reconstruction. In all directions, the Syndicates completed their work of re-organisation. In the very few branches where, either through ignorance or inertia, or as the result of Capitalist intimidation, the workers were not previously organised, this was remedied, with the aid and counsel of the Federal delegates. So well was this done that, little by little, the enclaves which, at the first revolutionary outbreak, had remained outside the movement, were influenced and gained.

Mistrust had disappeared. The fear of losing by the change, of falling from bad to worse, which, at the beginning of the Revolution, had prevented the timid from rallying to it, had vanished. The facts were there, proving the absurdity of these fears. Thus in backward regions, where now the transformation was being carried out, difficulties which at first had caused serious perplexity were settled without trouble.

For instance, the question whether compensation should be granted to the small employers and small dealers, who were eliminated by the new order, was no longer discussed; whilst, during the first days, this question of expropriation, with or without compensation, had been a stumbling block. The Confederal Congress had debated it, and had decided in the negative.

Expropriation without compensation,—which was indeed an accomplished fact,—was agreed to by all, when it concerned great fortunes, great properties, the great industry. On the other hand, some sought to establish a

distinction between other kinds of capital: they classed on
one side, that due to the ordinary increase of capital, and
consequently having no right to compensation; and on the
other side that due to the direct work of its owners, the
fruit of their savings, and deserving compensation. This
compensation, they said, might consist of a power of
consumption, given to those among the expropriated, who
were recognised as having a right to it, according to
some definite percentage to be agreed upon.

To this argument it was objected, that the bettering
of life, and the certainty of the morrow, with continuous
well-being and its indefinite increase, which the Revolution
brought to that class of privileged persons who were considered to be deserving of an indemnity, more than compensated them,—and much more than compensated them,—
for the loss of their small capital. For instance, had not
the small owner, when he arrived at the age for retiring, a
really wider and better life than the life he could have
hoped for with his small income of last year? The former small shopkeeper, and the former small manufacturer,—who were besides left free to stagnate in their
corner,—had they not greater comfort than before? As
to the peasants and proletarians who had saved, penny
by penny, just enough to take a small mortgage on a
neighbour's property, or to buy a few shares, were not
they also very amply compensated for the loss of these
slight privileges?

And then, added the partisans of expropriation pure
and simple, so many inconveniences would arise from the
proposed arrangement that this should be sufficient reason
for giving it up.

First of all, how should we draw a line of demarca-
tion between the capital entitled to compensation and the
other? Then, supposing this first difficulty overcome,
others would arise, equally troublesome: it would need
a bureaucracy to make the inquiries and estimates for
the purpose of the compensation; besides, it would arouse
and excite greed, this mirage of still living as parasites.
This would be to perpetuate the old order in the new.

This would be to graft a cancer on the heart of the young society. No! No! No compensation!

To this argument, the opponents of compensation added the example of 1789. They said they must not repeat the dupery of the night of the 4th of August. In this famous sitting, with a great noise of words, the Constituent Assembly decreed the abolition of feudal privileges,—with redemption,—Why? Because the members of the Constituent feared the peasant insurrection, and because they counted on checking it with illusory promises.

After the 4th of August, the old feudal system continued, with its tithes and dues, and it would have lasted, if the peasants had not taken things into their own hands, and suppressed, by their own might, the privileges that they detested. They were tenacious. During four years they remained at the breach. It was only after this period of unwearied revolt, that, in 1793, the Convention was obliged to sanction the abolition, pure and simple, of feudal rights.

Who can say what force this Revolution would have had if, at its origin, in 1789, the members of the Constituent Assembly had had the good sense to reply to the popular revolt by the abolition, without redemption, of feudal privileges?

They concluded by saying, that to-day the situation is identical: the privileges of capital are equivalent to the feudal privileges of 1789; but whilst the members of the Constituent Assembly, who were of either bourgeois or noble origin, were interested in the conservation of these privileges, it is not the same with us; our interests are the same as those of our comrades, and we have no right to weaken the Revolution by half measures.

As a result of this discussion, it was decided that capital, whatever might be its origin, should give no right to compensation. It was considered that the assurance of a full and easy life, which, in return for a moderate amount of work, society guaranteed to everyone, formed that part of the repayment which each one could equitably claim.

This decision only concerned capital which was in the form of estates, buildings, warehouses, factories, titles to rent, and shares. As to the money held by private individuals, that was left in circulation. In the same way, the holders of deposit books in Savings Banks could obtain possession of their deposits, and persons having deposits at the banks could obtain repayment of them up to a maximum of some thousands of francs, about as much as was required to live upon for one year, estimated on former prices. The inconvenience of these various measures was very small, considering that this money could henceforth only serve for consumption, and must, necessarily and rapidly, return to the Syndical Bank.

It was by basing their action on these considerations that the Federation of Bank employees assured the working of the Syndical Bank and its branches : this Bank, as we have said, was founded with the funds of the Bank of France and of the Credit Houses, and with the treasures of the Jewish, Catholic, Protestant, and other Banks. It was the general reservoir whence the community drew. As it was only a question of keeping the balance of incomings and outgoings, as there was no longer any debit and credit, the book-keeping was not very complicated.

For the return of money, the mechanism was simple : those individuals who bought from the public shops, according to the former method of exchange, paid in gold or silver. This money (with which the warehouse could do nothing, for its supplies were obtained by a simple demand, through the agency of the Federations and the Labour Exchanges), was not kept in a safe, but sent to the Bank. This registered the sum it received, and whence it came, without however carrying it to the credit of the warehouse which paid it, for the obvious reason that there was no account with it.

For the paying out of money, the working was not more complicated. It concerned two cases ; that of home supplies, and that of foreign supplies.

The organisations which required supplies from the interior,—for example, to buy from peasants, or stock raisers, who had not yet accepted the social contract,—demanded from the Bank, or from the branch in their district, the advance in money or cheques which they thought necessary, and they made their purchases, according to the old system. Now, as the sellers, who were paid in money, also needed supplies of all kinds, they applied to the public warehouses; and the money which had been paid to them returned to the Syndical Bank whence it came. All did not return; there was a difference between the amounts paid out and the amounts paid in, caused by the hoarding craze of some weak-minded people. This was of no importance, for the Bank concerned itself, not with keeping its funds at the same level, but solely with fulfilling its function of a pump drawing in products which it poured out over the community.

The Trade with other countries was also carried on according to the commercial method: the goods to be exported were sent either to maritime or river ports of embarcation, or to the railway docks. In the same way imported goods arrived. The Dockers' Union and Federation took charge of the various operations of export and import.

The imported goods were according to the orders received,—or in proportion to the quantities in stock and the demand,—forwarded by the Dockers' Syndicate to such and such centres. Commercial operations naturally ceased as soon as imported goods entered into the home circulation.

Only the surplus was exported, for with Capitalism had foundered the absurd and evil system of producing for exportation, while at home people lived miserably, for want of the goods that were sent far away. The degree of a country's prosperity and wealth was no longer guaged by the extent of its exportations, but only by the amount of well-being spread through the whole population.

The shipping system was, as a result of its special situation, carried on in two different ways; it remained commercial in its relations with foreign countries; and became Communist in its relations with the interior.

From the first, the sailors of the mercantile marine joined the Revolution; and, without hesitation, their Syndicates took possession of the vessels of all kinds; those belongiug to ship-owners and those freighted by Companies.

The first measure that was necessary was to re-constitute the crews according to affinities and sympathies; for on the sea, more than anywhere else, homogeneity and agreement are necessary. In order to secure this, the crews recruited themselves, with the friendly help of the Seamens' Unions.

It was also by a common agreement amongst the crew that a choice was made of the captain, and other men charged with the management of the ship. This no longer involved any position of authority, but was a natural division of labour, which made no one inferior, and gave to no one any superiority as a right.

Whilst they were going on with the reconstruction of the crews, they drew up the new conditions for shipping. It was agreed that, so long as they were on French soil, or in French ports, seamen should have the same advantages of life as all the comrades. Whilst at sea, it was unavoidable that they should submit to restrictions made necessary by the rationing that had to be made at sea. As to facilities for living in foreign countries, in the course of their journeys, this would be assured to them by an advance of money, which they would get from the Syndical Bank at their port of embarcation.

The vessels, like their crews, worked in two different ways; they carried without charge travellers who were members of the Confederation, whilst they carried foreign travellers according to the money regulations of the old order. In the same way, whilst merchandise coming from French sources was embarked without payment,—but charged with a freight rate which the buyer paid,—the merchandise imported was unloaded without being charged with any dues.

The ships which carried on commerce with foreign countries received information, based on the orders for goods received by the Dockers 'Unions and the Seamens' Unions; a wide discretion was left to them for these buying operations, and the Syndical Bank gave them the necessary sums.

On their return, the ships paid to the Bank the sums which they had received, in payment for goods exported, or for the transport of travellers, but without their having to establish an equilibrium between their receipts and expenditure.

Such was, in its main lines, the mechanism adopted for exchanges with other countries.

It was feared that foreign countries, through hatred of the Revolution, would break off all commercial relations with France. The Governments would have wished this. But the desire for gain won the day. All attempts at an international boycott failed; there were foreign capitalists ready to take advantage of events, and to obtain larger profits, because, under the circumstances, the French did not hesitate to pay a higher price for the raw material that they needed.

This method of exchange, which would remain in use as long as neighbouring countries were not freed from Capitalism, was only an extension of the attitude adopted in the interior, towards the refractories to the Confederal pact.

The circulation of money, therefore, had only a commercial aspect with regard to those who were strangers to the social contract; with regard to members of the Unions, the Bank worked like a communal reservoir, from which they drew according to their needs. The kingdom of gold was therefore abolished in the new society: this metal was deprived of the means of increase which in other days was the source of its power, and it was reduced simply to assisting exchanges; a function which would steadily decrease.

CHAPTER XXIII.

THE LIBERAL PROFESSIONS.

The "intellectuals," as they were formerly called, did not look too gloomily on the Revolution. Many rejoiced to see it break out, and had aided in its triumph.

Nevertheless, amongst them, there were some that the transformation injured; for whom it put an end to advantages of fortune or position. These were not the less enthusiastic: the new life seemed to them a deliverance. They were stifled in Capitalist society. The material satisfactions that they found there did not compensate them for the annoyance, disgust, and hatred which they felt for the defects, the miseries, and the injustices which were everywhere in the bourgeois environment.

Men of great worth,—in science, art, and literature,—all of whom enjoyed advantages under the old order, felt for it such dislike that they were delighted with its downfall. This state of mind hastened the fall of Capitalism; its overthrow was so much desired, so much expected, that these impatient wishes formed an atmosphere favourable to the Revolution.

Among the students, many took part in the movement, some were deserters from the bourgeoisie; others, intellectual proletarians, for whom life promised to be hard; they joined their lot to that of the working class, they took their place among the combatants. They brought their energy and their good will, and they were received fraternally.

This collaboration of intellectuals with the Revolution was of much assistance in the re-organization of the schools, of the methods of education, and also the transformation of the liberal professions.

Henceforth, doctors and surgeons were not obliged to make a trade of their knowledge and experience. Their profession became a social function, accepted and fulfilled from professional zeal; from a desire to lighten human suffering, and not from a commercial interest. Already, in Capitalist society, some signs of this transformation were visible; after a doctor of great reputation had attended the rich, at exorbitant fees, it pleased him to attend poor devils for nothing;—and sometimes even to help them from his own purse. The majority thus obeyed a sentimental impulse, without attributing to their acts of human solidarity the meaning of a social criticism. But whatever was the motive of their acts, these were none the less a protest against terrible inequalities, against compulsory commercialism; and they tended to re-establish an equilibrium. For this reason these doctors, who thought themselves merely charitable, were more prepared than others for the Communist ways of the new life.

Equally, the architects, designers, engineers, chemists, and others, lost their former privileged positions; they became useful collaborators, and gave valuable aid towards the good working of society, but their abilities did not give them a right to more favourable treatment.

The associations which existed previously, in professional society, were transformed into Syndicates, and federated. These societies had an autonomous life, exactly like the other Unions; and, like them, participated in the life and acts of the Confédération du Travail.

Thus, as we have explained, the liberal professions had no different conditions of life from those of other Unions; their respective Syndicates distributed to their members the consumers' cards,—which were like those of all the other Confederates,—giving them the right of consumption for all products of which there was abundance; they distributed also, to each one, a book of "notes," which allowed them to consume or to obtain, in a proportion equal for all, rare products or articles of luxury.

Of all the goods, all the objects the smaller quantities of which made rationing necessary, the share of each was theoretically equal; but their mathematical division, besides being impracticable, would have been absurd, and would have given very poor results. The exact distribution that one would have vainly sought for by this method, was brought about naturally by the free play of special tastes, of individual preferences; some wanted one thing, others another, and this diversity of desires, this variety of tastes, caused an equilibrium between supply and demand. Each one was allowed to satisfy, in a proportion equivalent to the social wealth, his desire for luxury.

This equal power of consumption, given without distinction to all, only seemed excessive to those who shut themselves within the narrow circle of bourgeois life. Others, who knew what long preparatory work had been carried on since the middle of the 19th century to bring about the new social order, accepted it, if not with joy, at least without too great bitterness.

In truth, the ideas of equality and of the equal value of various kinds of work, with which the working class was imbued had not arisen suddenly. For a long time its more active members, after having condemned the privileges of wealth, taught that a human being does not acquire, because of his knowledge, rights superior to those of other men, and that he has no right to claim a remuneration on the basis of the more knowledge the more pay; they demonstrated that he who is furnished with knowledge owes it to his teachers, to the accumulated work of past generations, to the whole environment in which he is steeped, which has allowed the development of his faculties. And they added, that as the masons, the sewermen, the bakers, the gardeners, have need of the doctor, so he has need of them; between the former and the latter there is an exchange of services, therefore there should be an equality of rights; and it is an abuse for anyone to boast of his knowledge in order to cut off a larger share for himself, to the injury of his fellow workers.

All were not inclined to accept this levelling without complaining. To those who lamented it, a doctor with a great reputation, who under the Capitalist régime, had analysed the artificial pleasures of great wealth, poured the philosophic balm.

"Have you forgotten," he said to them, "that what the rich man could consume personally was but little compared with his growing fortune?

"He had but one stomach, and had to treat it carefully. When he had eaten two or three dishes, twice a day, he had reached the limit of his digestive power as to quantity. His food was of the finest but the best quality was soon attained.

"Potatoes, one of the best of vegetables, could be procured, of perfect quality, at a low price. As to very early fruits and vegetables, and products out of their season, their price might rise enormously, without their agreeableness growing in proportion. The majority of them were not worth as much, so far as taste went, as the fruits or vegetables in season.

"A man had only one bed; for the successive use of several would disturb his sleep without compensating advantages. Clothes are like beds. To change them rather causes discomfort. It is necessary to try them on when new, to fit them to your body, to suit yourself to them, this drove the multi-millionares themselves to having a wardrobe not very much larger than that of a shop assistant.

"This man had only one bedroom, for the same reason that he had only one bed; and the same applied to the one or two rooms that he really used, his office, dining room, and private room. The other rooms were for receptions, were for others.

"He could travel? But frequent journeys perturbed his existence, and exposed him to a thousand discomforts, that, for many persons, were greater than the distractions they sought.

"He could associate others with his pleasures? But outside the fact that it may be more or less agreeable to organize amusements for the benefit of strangers, the pleasure was not consumed personally. In this case, there was a beginning of the Socialization of wealth."

In conclusion, the optimist doctor preached to his colleagues adaptation to the new surroundings: he explained that their science and their talents would be appreciated there, and used; but would not give them any privileges; he set forth the joys and compensations they would feel in being social entities, equal to anyone else, joys and satisfactions much better than the relative and artificial pleasures which had flown away when their wealth vanished.

Besides, if a man, belonging to a liberal profession, spoiled by success, could consider himself as poorer with regard to his power of personal consumption, on the other hand, from the professional point of view, he found himself so rich that he could not wish for more.

There was placed at the full disposal of scientific organisations, and their members, an improved equipment, splendidly installed laboratories, and the means of making all the experiments and researches they could desire. From this it followed, that if men of science could argue that their personal superfluity was reduced, in compensation, provided they were passionately devoted to their art, they had to avow themselves more truly rich than before.

The medical and surgical organisations, in concert with those of the sanitary staff, each in its own sphere, had charge of the reorganisation of the services of public health and hygiene, taking the place of the wasteful and hateful administration of the "Assistance Publique," which had been suppressed without regret.

The asylums and hospitals were transformed, they were excellently managed, with all the hygiene desirable, and the maximum of comfort. Nothing was neglected that could make, of these palaces of pain, places where the sick man would find in pleasant surroundings, if not relief of his physical sufferings, at least pleasure for the eyes, and a mental consolation.

It should be added, that it was not compulsory to send patients to the asylum, or the hospital, except in the case of epidemic diseases. Each person could arrange to be nursed as he wished, either in his own home or in a communal house. For the rest, the hospital attendants,—previously engaged under bad conditions, because they were a badly paid class,—now took up the work from sympathy; as a vocation, and not under the goad of necessity. Therefore, nurses and attendants brought to the exercise of their duties a gentleness and courtesy formerly too rare.

In addition to the reorganization of all the services connected with health, the Syndicates of doctors, surgeons, and chemists worked actively at remodelling the special schools, which, henceforth, would work with the full autonomy claimed in vain under the old order: the schools would be autonomous, the students would choose their professors; the teaching, without losing anything on its theoretical side, would be more thoroughly practical, technical, and clinical.

CHAPTER XXIV.

EDUCATION.

The teachers, whose societies had, for a long time past, taken part in Trade Union activities; who, from the first, had declared the necessity of freeing teaching from State tutelage „ of reorganising it on a Syndicalist basis, with full autonomy, were amongst the warmest supporters of the Revolution. Only, whilst taking part individually and according to their temperament in the insurrection, they did not make the General Strike a pretext for suspending their classes. They said to themselves that a strike in the schools would more inconvenience the parents than the Government, and they remained at work, thinking they helped the cause of the people more by looking after their children. The pupils could therefore still attend school, up to the time when, following the example of those around them, they made in their turn a General Strike,—played truant.

When the phase of battle was ended , when the time of triumph came, the Federation of Teachers' Unions called a Congress; to discuss methods of education, and to lay the basis of a rational education, in accordance with the social transformation that had been made.

The older classification, into primary, secondary, and higher education which penned in the children of the people in the "lay" schools, and reserved the Lyceums and Colleges for the children of the bourgeoisie, could no longer be tolerated.

The system of scholarships, which, in Capitalist society, tempered the arbitrariness of this classification, rendered a hypocritical hommage to equality, and allowed a few children of the people to jump into a bourgeois school, only more emphasized the hatefulness of this line of division. This partitioned off education was in accordance with an exploiting form of society, since it distributed knowledge in different doses, according to whether the children were destined to command or to obey, to make others work, or to drudge themselves, but it had no longer any reason for existing where liberty and equality existed.

The work of the Congress had two sides; to proceed to the remodelling of the teaching staff, and to clear up and define what the new education should be.

On this second point, the Congress, in which there took part, not only delegates from the Teachers' Unions, but also delegates from all educational associations, from the normal schools, as well as from the secondary and higher schools, and the Universities, had more the character of a thorough inquiry into education, than that of a Congress properly so called. All who had any idea on the subject to submit, or any project to propose, could make themselves heard there, could express their opinion, or throw light on the subject.

They concerned themselves, first of all, with the remodelling of the teaching staffs, in order to improve the wheels and mechanism; they eliminated what was useless and superfluous; and here, as everywhere, they substituted vivifying autonomy for stifling authority.

After this preliminary professional weeding out, which was also directly connected with the work of teaching, the main lines of the latter were defined.

The two classes of education, primary and secondary, were melted into one class, rational and integral. All children, whatever might be their turn of mind or their capacities, would draw from the common source of knowledge; their later development, however divergent it might be, would only be the result of a greater or less aptitude for learning, for assimilating human knowledge.

The corollary of these premises was absolute respect for the rights of the child,—the man of to-morrow. The child was considered as a being fundamentally free and independent, but in course of development; and the right to petrify his brain, to impress on him this way of looking at things and of thinking, rather than that, was not admitted in the case of any person, or any group of persons.

The right of parents over the brain of their child was denied, and proclaimed tyrannical and arbitrary. It was not admitted that they had any more right to petrify his brain in their way, than to bend his spinal column. Claims of the same kind that his teachers might wish to arrogate over the child were condemned with equal emphasis.

This idea, which laid down as a basis the sovereignty of the human being, and declared that the human being must be respected, alike in the germ and in the flower, was going to be the corner stone of an education given to all with equal liberality.

To make human beings, who should be harmoniously developed,—physically, intellectually, and morally,—and therefore able to turn their greatest activity in the direction they may choose. This was the aim.

Physical culture was the starting point of the method of instruction advocated; for it was admitted that intellectual development is related to physical activity. In elementary subjects, as well as in arithmetic, geometry, and the natural sciences, teaching was made as concrete and practical as possible. In these various branches of knowledge, no false direction was to be feared. The difficulty began with the study of history: it was advised that teachers should explain historical facts, with the aim, not to make their pupils share their opinions, but to put them in a position to appreciate, and judge, to form an opinion for themselves that should really be their own, and should not be a reflection of the master's personality. The latter should therefore aim at the awakening of the youthful intelligence, not by fatiguing

the memory, but by means of mental exercises, based
on experience, on facts and their explanation.

The best education would consist in giving the child
well-founded and exact ideas; and above all, in im-
planting within him so strongly the taste for knowledge,
that this passion should last all his life.

To the young man, whose individual development
was provided for by this education, which might be
called "primary," would be left the choice of what
"secondary" instruction he wished to receive. This theoretic instruction, wide, profound, only called to mind very
vaguely the instruction of the former Lyceums. Far
from being a "dead" education, it would, on the contrary,
be a very living one; science would there hold the first
place, and to general instruction would be added a professional instruction,—practical, technical, but not special-
ized. Social needs not being the same as they were during the Capitalist period, the schools no longer concerned
themselves with hatching magistrates, lawyers,—and other
specimens of the various mischievous species that had
disappeared,—but they tried to turn out men who should
be industrious, with an open mind, a well-selected knowledge, and capable of being useful to themselves and
their fellows.

After that, the young man could, if he wished, take
a course in one of the Technical Schools of Industry,
Trades or Agriculture; which had already existed, in
an embryonic state, in bourgeois society.

These Technical Colleges went beyond the limits
of education, properly so called. Their courses of study
included what was formerly called an apprenticeship.

These Colleges would be, in the future, the bond of
union between the schools and the productive life. Continuing the comparison with the old classification, they
might be compared to the schools for higher education.
For Industry, Agriculture, and Science, they were equiva-

lent to what were formerly the faculties of Law, Science, and Literature for the liberal professions; they were also equivalent to the new schools of Medicine, Surgery, and Pharmacy.

These Technical Colleges depended on the Trade Federations; the Colleges of Medicine, and Pharmacy, depended on the Medical or Pharmaceutical Societies; those of Agriculture on the Agricultural Federation; those of Weaving on the Textile Federation, and so on with the others.

No distinction was made between boys and girls; the two sexes were brought up together, on a footing of equality, in the same schools. Not that it was intended to drive women to the same work as men, but because co-education was held to be the best preparation for the general co-operation of the sexes.

When the girls became older, they could take a course in the special colleges where women's occupations were taught, and where they could prepare themselves for such social work as they wished to take up.

The integral education, of which we have just sketched the main lines, was the work of the Congress of Syndicates of teachers and professors, and its co-ordination depended on these societies, henceforth blended into one, unified. However, side by side with these, without injuring the autonomy of the teaching staff, School Associations were formed, which those parents joined who were interested in educational questions. In concert with the teachers, these Associations strove to beautify the schools, and to improve educational methods.

Whilst, with the help of all, they got this profoundly human education at work, around the chairs of the professors there crowded the new generation, glad to be alive, eager for knowledge. They had not the defects which formerly demoralised the young men; the harshness, the sharp hankering after success, the effort to elbow out some comrade, which in the old society, stifled generous feelings.

This young generation,—knowing nothing of fears for the morrow, not being worried by anxieties for the future, seeing no black clouds on the horizon,—were all vigorous and affectionate, healthy and strong.

CHAPTER XXV.

THE CREATION OF ABUNDANCE.

The fear of scarcity, which was such an obsession during the first days of the Revolution, had disappeared. The impetus given to production had been so intense that abundance grew, swelled into a flood, and with it grew delight. The joy of living flowed and extended everywhere. And they laughed at the anxieties of yesterday.

Nevertheless, however needless these anxieties might have been, it could be understood how it was that they should have occupied the minds of the best and most optimistic of the Revolutionists.

When the transition was made between the two systems, it was known how artificial were the crises of overproduction that threw Capitalist society into disorder: it was known that there had never been any real overproduction, but only crises of congestion, resulting from an unequal and insufficient distribution.

If peasants complained of having too much fruit, too much cider; if wine producers uttered jeremiads about the slowness of sales; if fishermen threw back into the water the fish that the fishmongers refused to buy from them; if the shops were encumbered with shoes and clothing;—this was not because there was too much fruit, cider, wine, fish, shoes, or clothes;—since whole populations lacked all these things!

Consequently, it was to be expected that, consumption becoming free, the so-called overproduction would not exist for long.

On the other hand, the theorists who supported

human exploitation had so often repeated that compulsion was indispensable to drive men to work, that, without the goad of hunger, without the passion for gain, men would give themselves up to laziness, that these absurd statements had given birth to apprehensions.

If it had come about as these bad augers had predicted; if the people, disheartened and weary of working for others, had refused to work for themselves, misery would not have been conquered!—And before long, reaction would have triumphed anew.

Was it not in this way that previous Revolutions had failed?

In 1848, the people shed their blood to win the Republic, and they put at its service three months of misery. But their lot, far from being improved, became worse. Then came the June fusillades. Then as business went badly, as work was not to be had, the loaf became more scarce than it was under Royalty. Disillusioned, therefore, the people allowed the Coup d'Etat of 1851 to be carried out.

Was not the same prospect to be feared, if, when the Capitalist reserves were exhausted, it became impossible to obtain fresh supplies? Was it not to be feared that discord would arise in the workers' ranks, and that the bourgeoisie would profit by it to re-establish their reign?

At the Confederal Congress this doubt weighed on the Syndicalist delegates. This was the reason why they dared not fix lower than at eight hours the daily maximum for the duration of work. Under the circumstances, they only interpreted the feeling of the working masses; for they also, still worried by the prejudices and errors in which they had been cradled, feared that they would not be able to assure the supply of all social needs.

Experience soon proved how little foundation there was for these fears. The passion for work had never been so strong, so unanimous, except perhaps in 1791,

when the peasant, who had just freed the land from
'feudal privileges,—had just seized it from the lord,—
felt his human dignity awake in him, and free, standing
on free land, set himself to work with all his heart and
with all his soul. One lived over again those splendid
days! And now, peasants and workmen had the same
delights, the same enthusiasm. With what energy they
threw themselves into their work!

Few were those who sulked at their work. So few,
that the Syndicates disdained to take with regard to them
any effective measures of boycott. They limited themselves to treating them with contempt, to keeping them
at arm's length. The idle were in as bad odour as were
formerly police spies and souteneurs. The latter had
occupations that fed their man well; but they were despised, regarded as debasing. Therefore individuals who
were sufficiently lacking in self respect, who had no desire for moral cleanness, and who, laughing at the contempt felt for them, could eat such bread, had been
exceptions.

The idlers were equally exceptions who preferred
to endure the contempt of those around them, rather
than take part in manual work, that had nothing about
it of irksome compulsion, and was a muscular exercise,
physical gymnastics, necessary to health.

The unoccupied and the idle had formerly been so
much glorified,—whilst labour was held in slight esteem,—that it was not surprising that the desire to live
as parasites had not disappeared of itself, amongst people
cankered by bourgeois surroundings. However, besides
the fact that this tendency to idleness was very restricted,
it was only momentary: it was a moral malaria, endemic to the Capitalist marsh, which persisted after its
disappearance, but which the new healthy atmosphere
would dissipate.

They worked therefore with a vigour that was unknown in the factories and workshops of the masters.
They were no longer slaves, wage slaves, bent under a

disagreeable task work, that weighed on them the more that it often had a useless or harmful result: they were free men, working on their own account, and therefore bringing to the work they had undertaken an unheard of eagerness.

The haunting fear that necessaries would be lacking made them accomplish prodigies. They toiled with a will. They made a colossal effort, that they would have refused to make as wage labourers. In some works, of their own free will, the comrades imposed on themselves an additional work, in order to increase the quantity of products at the disposal of all; elsewhere, men, having attained the age for retirement, declined to leave the workshop, not wishing to accept freedom from work so long as there was not an absolute certainty of abundance.

In the enormous human agglomerations,—Paris amongst others,—the fear of a lack of food products was the great obsession. In order to ward off this hypothetical peril, workers enrolled themselves by the thousand to cultivate the land, in the vast farms of the environs. The Syndicates of Agricultural Workers and of Market Gardeners, who swarmed in the district, and who, for a long time, had been associated with Confederal action, took possession of these estates without delay. Working gangs were organized, in which Parisians were incorporated, cheerfully allowing themselves to be guided by competent comrades. Their work was hard,—for they were not used to it,—but it was not so wearisome and tedious as was the agricultural labour of the year before. They had recourse to all the available machinery; motor ploughs and cultivators did marvels. They did so well that in a few months they were certain that they could produce regularly enough vegetables, potatoes, and wheat to satisfy the wants of the Parisian population.

As on the other hand, they had not neglected to enter into relations with the more remote country populations, they were fully re-assured from one end of the territory to the other,—nowhere,—was there any fear of famine.

With regard to industrial and manufactured products, the apprehension was less. They endeavoured to satisfy themselves with the home production,—at least as much as possible,—in order to have recourse to imported goods only to a restricted extent. Amongst other things they met the scarcity of raw materials,—like leather and wool,—by the considerable development of stock breeding, rationally organized, which at the same time satisfied the need for flesh food.

The transformation of raw material into industrial and manufactured products did not present any insurmountable difficulties. Machinery had already attained such a high degree of perfection that, even as bourgeois society had transmitted it, it enabled them to face all essential needs, without any grave anxieties.

On the industrial side, all efforts were concentrated on lessening, if not causing the complete disappearance of, the mischiefs due to dangerous industries, and unhealthy trades. In these circumstances, the reduction of the hours of work was an insufficient palliative; it was necessary that the work should not be a constant cause of suffering, a torture. This was necessary, in order that this work should not be deserted; and especially in order that there might be established a relative equality between all kinds of social work; for it was henceforth unacceptable and inadmissible that some work should be rather pleasant whilst other kinds should remain, as in the past, the work of a galley slave.

The Syndicates of these trades appealed to the initiative of all, to the knowledge of professionals and engineers. As there was no longer any question of placing human lives in the balance against the nett cost of a product, or of some indispensable work, satisfactory solutions were arrived at.

It mattered little, in fact, if in order to bring some product into consumption, it was necessary to spend double or treble the time taken before, provided that this work was not injurious to those who were in charge of it, and that it was carried out under suitable hygienic conditions.

In many cases, both in equipment and in methods of manufacture, the alterations necessary to be carried out were known; they only needed to be applied. If this had not been done previously, it was the fault of the employers, who had refused to do it so as not to increase their general expenses; and also the fault of the workmen, who through habit, lack of reflection,—and alas, under the goad of want!—submitted to doing work which they knew rapidly brought on grave organic disorders, if not death.

In this path of technical and hygienic betterment, they arrived at important results. Thus, by means of scientific arrangements, and various processes and methods, the work of sewage men no longer offered the dreaded dangers; in glass making, mechanical blowing, and the equally mechanical manufacture of window glass were made general, and with hygienic arrangements, this work was no longer an infernal toil; in the iron and steel industries, in chemical works, in the manufacture of woven goods,—everywhere,—changes of the same kind were carried out.

Laundry work was now modified from top to bottom: this work had remained most primitive, with little shops where the sorting out of linen spread the germs of infectious diseases, with the wash houses badly arranged, and inconvenient; when it had been attempted to industrialize this work, it had only been done to the detriment of the health of the workers, as it had then become for them still more murderous.

Breadmaking, which up to the twentieth century had remained prehistoric, was also turned upside down; the infected and badly ventilated bakehouses were suppressed; the worker no longer mixed his perspiration with the dough, a machine did the work of kneading.

Many other industries were equally transformed from top to bottom. No branch of human activity was left out of account; in all, inventive genius brought improvements which increased the output tenfold, and caused all trace of man's servitude to disappear; he was no longer the slave, but the master of the machine!

They applied a great number of discoveries that had remained dormant, that needed only to be taken from the Museum of Arts and Crafts. One saw a marvellous blossoming out of inventions that had not been able to break through before, stifled as they were by indifference, ill-will, routine or interest.

Great companies and large capitalists, in fact, were in the habit of buying up patents for improvements to their machinery or tools, for the purpose of preventing their use. There was an unmistakeable proof of this when possession was taken of the Paris works for generating electricity: in their lofts were discovered, amongst other things, a whole series of electric meters, each being an improvement on the preceding one. The Company had bought these patents from their inventors, not in order to use them, but to suppress them, so as to avoid a reconstruction of their outfit.

How many like examples could be cited! How many men of genius had suffered from obstacles placed in the way of the realization of their plans! How many had been unable to carry them out successfully for want of resources? How many had encountered the hatred of their contemporaries? How many had fallen by the way, and carried their ideas with them to the grave?

In the eighteenth century, Jacquard was hunted from place to place, and his loom broken up and burnt by the weavers of Lyons, who feared for their wages; at the end of the nineteenth century, the Northrop loom was as much cursed in the spinning mills as, half a century before, the mule jennys had been; when Lebon discovered lighting by gas, no one in France had the intelligence and boldness to put him in a position to apply his process; Achereau, a fruitful inventor, who enriched a pleiad of capitalists with the twentieth part of the discoveries he made in the course of his life, died of hunger in a garret at Ménilmontant; Martin, the inventor of the vacuum brake, which has prevented so many railway catastrophes, was ridiculed, and whilst he vegetated and died almost in want, his discovery was popularised, under the name of the Westinghouse brake, by Americans, who made millions by it, when they brought it into use; the genial inventor, the marvellous poet, Charles Cross, the inventor of colour photography and phonography,—which Edison turned to account,—lived in want all his life; Mimault, the inventor of the Baudot telegraph, died in prison for having fired a revolver at the man who was a guarantor for him, and who took the profit of his invention.......

And how many other names could be added to this martyrology!

Ah! Capitalist society was a rough stepmother for the men who left the old grooves! When it did not kill them, it ridiculed them: its official experts heaped condemnation on the forerunners, proving with great array of arguments that they were unbalanced, mad,—or ignorant.

Henceforth, it was so no longer. The man who had an idea in his head could, without hindrance, follow it out to its realization. No one having any interest in opposing the putting into practice of his projects, he received all the help possible. If it was an improvement to a machine, or a new process of whose application he dreamed, he found, amongst the comrades in his trade, not only support, but sometimes useful advice.

Labour was not lacking; nor yet raw material. All kinds of experiments were tried. They did not hold back even from uncertain experiments, under the vain pretext of avoiding a waste of work or material. They preferred to run the risk of a failure, rather than that of neglecting a valuable discovery.

This state of mind, born of the Revolution, was the

opposite of bourgeois mentality, which had been wholly that of conservatism and dislike of anything new.

The characteristic of the Capitalist system had been the fear of change, of any shock, of any modification : it delighted in never doing anything ; ankylosis and petrifaction might have been considered its ideals.

Now, it was just the opposite ; plasticity was the essence of the new order ; its equilibrium resulted from its extreme mobility ; by means of this perpetual becoming, society would be in constant transformation, in indefinite progress.

From this permeation of the new environment by the tendency to variation arose an ideal of life, higher than ever.

The equality of well-being had not given rise to carelessness and weakness, and far from having spoiled the sources of emulation, it had purified them. Those who had formerly laid it down that, if the passion for gain disappeared from society, the spirit of research, of enterprise, the taste for knowledge and discovery, would be injured, could see how mistaken were such assertions.

CHAPTER XXVI.

FOREIGN COMPLICATIONS.

The deep social disturbance that was so thoroughly transforming the face of France, had caused an echo throughout the whole of Europe. The peoples, roused by the example of the French working class, aspired to march in its footsteps.

Amongst the Latin nations, Royalty had been overthrown, and Spaniards and Italians tried to hasten their rate of progress, in order that their Revolution should not be restricted to a mere change of government, but that it should acquire an economic character, which alone could render it fruitful. In Saxon countries, belief in the General Strike not being so strong, the people hesitated to throw themselves into the adventure.

The Governments that were still standing, fearing that they would not be able indefinitely to repress the impulse towards emancipation, hated the Revolution all the more. Between them and the new régime which was established in France, diplomatic relations had been broken off, from the very first. Everywhere that was the case. There could be hardly any points of contact or relations between the economic institutions that arose from the Revolution,—which were the negation of all Government,—and such political excrescences as the various monarchical or democratic States.

There was indeed in France, at the head of the Syndical network, the Confederal Committee, formed by delegates from the federated organisations. But, even had it been wished, there could be no possible ambiguity here; this committee could not act like a Government.

It was, however, there that the question was raised of
diplomatic relations with foreign Governments. Should
they be maintained? It was decided in the negative.
On the contrary, it was agreed to strengthen and develope the relations already existing between the workers'
Federations and Confederations of all countries. These
decisions had received the unanimous approval of the
Confederal Congress.

This international solidarity between the peoples
was a need the more pressing because foreign Governments dreamed of intervening in the internal affairs of
France. It was easy to find a pretext; was it not their
duty to safeguard the interests of their citizens? In the
first place, of those established in France, whose commerce and industries were ruined, and then of those who
held French stocks and shares, (State Rentes, shares in
railways, mines, and other things), who were injured by
the financial failure of these undertakings.

The Governments were therefore moved by Capitalist solidarity, just as in 1792 their predecessors were
moved by Dynastic solidarity. Just as in 1792, the Revolution angered them, and they dreamed of drowning
it in blood, in order to end its proselytizing action.

The German Emperor, who was supported by a
powerful employing class, solidly organized and very
combative, became the head of the new coalition, with
the more eagerness that he felt the agitation gaining the
great Syndicates of German workmen. On the other
hand, he was incited to this attack against the French
Revolution by the emigrants who had taken Strasburg
as their rallying point, and who spent themselves in reactionary manoeuvres, begging the help of all Governments against their "Fatherland." It was, above all,
Germany and England that they tried to move and
mobilize against it; they dreamed of surrounding the
Revolution, and they arranged that an invasion by land
and an attack by sea should coincide with a new Vendée.

Thus history repeated itself: Strasburg repeated
Coblentz. The bourgeoisie of the twentieth century aped

the aristocrats of the eighteenth, and imitated the army of Condé.

Many were the capitalists who, at the first signs of Revolution, had taken refuge in the city of the Rhine; many also were the fugitives who, after the destruction of the camp at Châlons, took up their quarters there. There were there great financiers, who were connected with their fellow capitalists across the Rhine; there were the members of the Trust which controlled metallurgy, and the mines; they also being associated with their fellows in Germany; then there jostled one another the personnel of the Government and Parliament, as well as the Dynastic families of the Republic. Behind them, there were crowded a horde of adventurers, hooligans of various kinds, officers of fortune, refugees of every description, who preferred to continue living there as parasites to doing any useful work.

To all these, this city, severed from France, seemed to offer the best shelter: they felt at their ease there, under the folds of the German flag,—and henceforth, their best ally seemed to them to be the German Emperor.

In the same way as the refugees of 1792 had placed fidelity to their king above the nation, so, at the present time, for these new "emigrants," the idea of Fatherland was eliminated by the idea of Class; therefore the French capitalists found it quite natural to appeal to capitalist Germany against working class France.

At the first rumour of menaces of foreign intervention, the Confederal Committee, who had no authority for coming to a decision, appealed on the question to the people themselves, through their trade organisations: they convoked a General Congress of all the Unions.

This consultation of the people,—which was the second under the new order,—was rapidly carried out. In a few days the delegates were chosen, and they met in Paris. There were present delegates from all branches of human activity. All the professions were represented, all being henceforth grouped in Federations and Syndicates; and all being capable of discussing and deciding on questions affecting their general interests.

All the delegates abhorred war with intense passion. They hated it,—and also feared it. They dreaded it, not only for the frightful evils which were its attendants, but still more,—and above all,—for its baleful consequences. They saw in it a torrent of barbarism that threatened to ruin the fine harmony that was growing up.

Nevertheless, they could not let the Revolution be crushed out. They must defend it.

But how?

After anxious discussions, the Congress rejected the proposal for a military defence, which would have implied a return towards the former system. They considered that it would be buying victory at too high a price, if they had to owe it to a regular army, formed anew for the purpose. They did not wish in order to ward off an outside peril, to create a formidable peril at home.

It was therefore decided not to have recourse to the former system, which consisted in opposing armed masses, and hurling them one against the other. It was decided to face the foreign attacks by a war in scattered order, which would not be an ordinary guerilla war, but a struggle relentless and without pity. It was a question of taking advantage, for defence, of the latest scientific discoveries;—and of tearing to shreds, without hesitation, the rules of the game of war.

They started from the principle that, the more terrible were the expedients to which they had recourse, the more effective they would be, and the shorter would be the war.

Special committees composed of men with technical skill, energetic and bold, set to work. The greatest freedom of choice was left to them, and the Congress approved the means to which they intended to have recourse, the facts of which they explained.

After having guarded themselves against the menace of foreign reaction, by the necessary measures of public safety, the Congress affirmed its unshakeable confidence in the future by a decision which proved the fruitfulness of the Revolution. A precise inquiry having shown that, maintaining the necessary reserves, the level of production very largely surpassed the level of consumption, and that this could be satisfied with considerably reduced hours of work, the average duration of the day's work was reduced to six hours, instead of eight.

This decision, at such a time, proved how sure the Confederates felt of themselves; what faith was theirs, and how little they were affected by the preparations for invasion, which, in a few days, would perhaps imperil their work.

With an activity which was imposed on them by the uncertainty of events, the Committees of Defence began their work. They had, however, very little to alter. It was enough for them to prepare for the application of discoveries already known, even by the former Government, who had not dared to dream of using them, because they considered them too formidable.

One of these Committees concerned themselves with the utilization of Hertzian waves. In 1900, Gustave Lebon had already indicated the formidable help that could be obtained from their special properties: this expert then announced that, in a near future, it would be possible to direct, from a distance, on to battle ships, collections of electric rays, sufficiently powerful to bring about the spontaneous explosion of the shells and torpedoes piled up in their hulls; that it would be equally possible to obtain,—also from a distance,—the firing of the store of powder and shell contained in a fortress, of the parks of artillery of an army corps, and of the metal cartridges of soldiers in their cartridge boxes. Some years later, after the catastrophe to the ironclad "Iéna," an expert of La Seyne, M. Naudin, passed from theory to practice, and acting for the Government, he was the first to carry into effect the forecast of Gustave Lebon: in 1908, he succeeded in exploding a cask of powder at a distance.

They had arrived, on these lines, at results of a matchless power, stupefying; they succeeded in firing —with mathematical precision, and at a distance,—heaps of explosive materials, buried in the ground, or stowed away in the holds of ships. The Committee popularized this formidable discovery, and they constructed immediately, in sufficient quantity, the apparatus for radio-detonation, in order to be ready for whatever might happen.

Following out the same kind of ideas, the Committee applied to aerial torpedoes the methods of direction, by Hertzian waves, already applied to submarine torpedoes. They constructed a flotilla of aeroplanes, each one capable of carrying some hundreds of pounds of explosives, which, by a radio-automatic catch, would be dropped on to the ground at any desired point.

These aerial torpedoes were driven by a petrol motor, and directed in the air by the Gabet key; the operator, installed several miles away from the point to be attacked, launched the tele-mechanic aeroplane, and with his fingers on the keys of the radio-commutator, he made it manoeuvre, turn, advance, retreat. When the apparatus had arrived at a fixed point, the operator touched a special key on the keyboard, and the explosives on board the aerial torpedo were detached.

This machine had one formidable advantage; when it flew over a camp, the most imprudent action, for the army it menaced, was to seek to stop its course; this could only have one result, to hasten the catastrophe of the explosion.

A Committee for chemical and bacteriological study concerned itself with the work of protection in a different direction, but one from which still more terrifying results were possible: it was the question of infecting the invading armies, animals and people; inoculating them with plague, typhus, cholera, and this by contaminating them with powerful preparations, saturated with the pathogenic bacilli of these virulent epidemic diseases. All precautions were taken by means of the preventive and curative serums which they had at their disposal, to guard themselves against unpleasant reactions.

The practical use of this frightful means of extermination was arranged for in various ways; either by spreading in water, which the invading armies must necessarily drink, gelatinous or other products sown with bacilli, or by hurling on the enemy's army, from aeronefs, or by means of radio-directed aeroplanes, glass bombs, which, on exploding, violently scattered fine needles, whose prick inoculated them with infectious germs.

These methods of defence and extermination were, as we have said, already known. But Governments had always refused seriously to consider their use. They meant to keep, even on the field of battle, the outward show of civilization,—only the outward show. For there was more real barbarism in hurling thousands of men against one another, than in using these fearful methods.

By these means, war would become impossible. But Governments wanted to keep up war, for the fear of war was, for them, the best of the devices for maintaining domination. By means of the fear of war, cleverly maintained, they could make the country bristle with standing armies, which, under the pretext of protecting the frontier, only menaced in reality, the people, and only protected the governing class.

The day when it should become known that a handful of determined men could successfully oppose the armed crossing of a frontier,—that day, public opinion would insist upon the suppression of standing armies. In order to avoid being driven to this alternative, Governments kept secret, and stifled as much as they could, the inventions that would have enabled a people to protect its territorial independence by means of science, better than they could with an army.

What Governments had refused to consider, the Confederates were about to try: without an army, without fighting,—with nothing but the action of a very small minority,—they were going to make their frontiers inviolable.

The Confederates decided not to keep secret the methods of defence to which they were going to have recourse. By their making public these methods, the Governments would be informed of the reception that was being prepared for invaders. There was, besides, another advantage in this publicity; that of making known to the masses of the people in foreign countries who should consent to co-operate in the crime of invasion, the risks to which they would expose themselves.

Manifestos in all languages, were therefore issued, giving notice that, henceforth, there was constituted on the French frontier a danger zone, and that no armed band was allowed to cross it on pain of death.

CHAPTER XXVII.

THE LAST WAR.

Three army corps entered French territory at the same time: one crossed by the plains of Flanders, the second advanced on Nancy, and the third on Vesoul.

These army corps were formed of German, Austrian, and English soldiers, some Cossack hordes, and some battalions furnished by the Balkan and Northern kingdoms.

The allied Governments felt such a certainty of crushing out the Revolution without effort that they had not hurried to take action against it. They wished to give solemnity to the repression. They wished to make an example of it. They wanted the punishment inflicted on the working class of France to be such that it should freeze all the peoples with fear, and stifle in them, for ever, all desire for revolt. And it was in order to bring to the ruin of Revolutionary France a more doleful parade that the Coalition wanted it to be the collective work of the armies of Europe.

The concentration of troops had taken a long time. The military officials who had the direction of operations were not roused by this; they did not consider that time was valuable, they were so sure of success. They laughed loudly at the deliberations of the Confederal Congress; and the work of the score of experts, who claimed they could arrest the march of the most renowned warriors in Europe, gave them opportunities for constant jokes. They were not ignorant of the discoveries which gave confidence to the Confederates; but, proud of their profession, they considered that nothing was superior to a strong army.

When they should judge the hour propitious, they announced haughtily, they would give the signal for the invasion: in a few stages, they would enter Paris, and after having purged the capital of Revolutionists, they would re-establish the former régime.

The invasion began; the general staffs of the army of the coalition laughed at first. They had crossed the frontier. They were camping on the famous danger zone. And they were all right. They had not been struck by death.

This bravado soon gave place to surprise,—clouded with a shade of anxiety, which rapidly increased. Although they had received notice the generals were so pinned down to the usual methods of war, that they expected to meet with some resistance, — however feeble it might be. Now, there was nothing,—nothing whatever,—that rose up against them! No troops barred their passage. The forts which formerly guarded the frontier remained silent; the majority of them had been dismantled by the Revolutionists themselves.

On the other hand, the advance was thwarted and made difficult by various obstacles. They could not dream of utilizing the railways; besides the bridges being broken down and the tunnels obstructed, the defence had taken advantage of every change of level,—every cutting, every embankment,—to make them still more impracticable. The roads had not suffered less: at many points explosions had dug out trenches, or encumbered them either with rocks or shattered trunks of trees.

Water was lacking. The wells and springs were infected; the streams and rivers flowed with water charged with nauseaus and injurious chemical products.

The entire population had fallen back;—not without taking their cattle with them and destroying the provisions and crops they could not carry away.

It was worse than a desert! Before them, the invaders saw only ruins and devastation. It was not possible for them to plunge far into the country; before going far, or advancing quickly, it was necessary for them to assure their communications and provisions.

This war seemed to be a strange one.

So strange, that at the end of some days, without having seen an enemy, or fired a shot,—simply under the weight of uncertainty and anxiety,—the soldiers found themselves more demoralized than if they had stood the shock of a battle, heard the whistling of balls, and the bursting of shell and shrapnel.

Besides, the sanitary state of the camps began to decline. The horses had been the first to be attacked by epidemic diseases, which rapidly overcame them. As to the health of the men, it became worse and worse; in spite of the severe measures of hygiene prescribed, many cases of poisoning had been observed.

One morning, in the grey of the dawn, there flew above the camps some aeronefs; lit up by the first rays of the rising sun. The alarm was quickly given; cannons were pointed at them, and the dirigibles of the Coalition prepared to give them chase. Without concerning themselves with these dangers, the staffs of the aeros scattered thousands of manifestos, written in various languages. This was the Confederal ultimatum: a delay of twenty-four hours was accorded to the allied armies to strike their tents and retreat; then, it was intimated to the general staffs, that in case the Confederal conditions were accepted, they were to hoist the white flag at the next dawn. In the contrary case, the work of destruction would begin; by means which the ultimatum set forth.

During the whole day, the wireless telegraphic apparatus worked, between the invading armies and the Governments of the Coalition. These were indignant that anyone could dream of disarming and retreating before the Revolution, and they ordered that the advance should be pushed forward more actively.

When the troops knew that the invasion was to continue, the uneasiness that beset them was followed by a prostration of terror; they felt themselves doomed to death. Amongst many of the soldiers there was in-

dignation and anger. But as in their countries the Anti-
militarist propaganda had been very slight, these feelings
evaporated in curses, and did not condense into revolt.
Discipline carried the day, and the unfortunate men,
frightened and stupified, awaited events, which were not
slow in coming.

In the morning, the captive balloons, which were on
the watch over the camps, signalled the presence, some
miles away, of unusual installations, recalling those of the
wireless telegraph. This was reported to the superior
officers, but before it was possible to take measures for
reconnoitring or for protection, the destructive action
began.

Without any warning being given by atmospheric
disturbance, vast explosions tore up the soil. The earth
trembled, it was shaken, and burst open. One might
have said it was a volcano vomiting forth iron and
flames. It was the parks of artillery and the depôts
of ammunition which blew up spontaneously, almost at
the same time. With the detonation of the shells was
mixed the crackling of shrapnel and the snapping of
cartridges. At the same time they saw, coming in the
air, flexible and slender, the tele-mechanical aeroplanes;
they arrived, gracefully and with perfect ease. When
they had arrived above the troops, and at the instant
judged propitious by the operators installed at a distance,
the radio-automatic catch poured out over the plain
asphyxiating bombs, filled with prussic acid and subtle
poisons, as well as explosive bombs and shells of a
formidable shattering power.

A hurricane of iron and fire spread over the camp,
carrying everywhere fear and death. The victims were
innumerable. The killed and the wounded strewed the
ground, whence there arose the death rattle and cries
of pain. The soldiers who were still uninjured, mad
with fear, neither understanding nor hearing anything,—
neither the appeals to pity of the wounded, nor the rallying orders of the few officers who kept cool,—ran, dashed
straight on, one thought only surviving in their distracted

brains; to flee, to flee, to get quickly away from this scene of desolation.

It was a retreat,—a stampede,—a rout.

In a disordered pell-mell, what remained of the armies rolled towards the frontier. The instinct of self-preservation had drowned in these mobs all other feelings. There were only savage cries, outbursts of anger. Woe to him who should try to stem or dam up this flood.

The panic grew still more, reached a paroxysm of terror, when the fugitives perceived, flying above them, the aeronefs of the Confederates. Mad cries, shrieks of distress, arose; for the horrible thought came to them that these aerial ships were there to sow the frightful epidemics that the manifestos told of.

This would have been a useless cruelty and barbarism. The lesson was enough.

Whilst these dramatic catastrophes put an end to the war on land, the destruction of the fleets belonging to the Governments of the Coalition was brought about by the same means on the sea.

These fleets had taken as long to concentrate as the armies on the land. Therefore, when they arrived in view of the French ports, these were on the defensive,—provided with posts for radio-explosion.

The allied squadrons were, like the land armies, summoned to retire. Their admirals refused to yield to the Confederal ultimatum, with the more contempt that they knew they were powerfully equipped: they had at their disposal radio-automatic torpedoes, and the enormous guns of their ironclads had a long range.

Also it was necessary for them to have an enemy to attack. But neither ironclad, nor torpedo, nor submarine came to bar the assailants' way....

The allied fleets made the blocade closer. It was then that their destruction was pitilessly carried out.

One after the other,—without a ripple in the air to mark the passage of the exterminating waves,—the colossal ironclads, the cruisers, and the torpedo boats were struck by the invisible force. The formidable radioelectric discharges, concentrated on their powder magazines, fired the explosives that were stored there. With a crash of thunder, the sides of these ships cracked and opened, and colossal sheets of flame blazed out.

Then, after the luminous lightning of the explosion, all fell again to silence, and the débris of the ships, as well as their unfortunate crews, went to the bottom.

At the news of this gigantic destruction, which struck them on land and sea, the Governments were overwhelmed. They felt pass over them the cold shiver of death, whilst over the peoples, cheered and encouraged, blew a warm wind of revolt.

More than on the evening of Valmy were then befitting the prophetic words of Goethe; "Here begins for history a new era."

CHAPTER XXVIII.

LUXURIES.

The cares of resisting the assaults of reactionists within, as well as providing for the dangers coming from without, had not depressed the people, had not made them ignore or disdain things of an intellectual order.

In spite of the bitterness of the struggle, and in spite of all difficulties, the Revolution asserted itself as attractive, as in no way repulsive.

When the certainty was gained that necessaries would be abundant, that all would have enough to eat, they begin to think again about luxuries, which are the adornment of life. These had been neglected during the first days. Art workers had left their professions to devote themselves to work that was more immediately useful. The crisis passed, they returned to their occupations, in proportion to the orders that came in.

There was naturally in these trades, such as those of sculptors, goldsmiths, jewellers, decorators, a greater fluctuation in the amount of production than in those which had to respond to primary wants. In these, statistics estimated, nearly enough, what would be the amount of the demand; whilst, in the industries for the supply of luxuries there was a margin of the unforeseen, in consequence of the sudden great demands caused by fashion. The Syndical organizations in these various branches provided for these special conditions, either by having recourse to the sending of specimens to the distributive stores, or by drawing up catalogues. Then orders were executed, in proportion to their numbers.

Amongst these productions of secondary necessity, there were objects, such as watches, clocks, lamps, etc.,

entering into the list of free consumption, which, nevertheless, might be included in the list of rationed production, either because they were made of rare metals,
or because they would have taken so long to make that
it was not possible to produce them in abundance. In
this case, these objects acquired a value that was decided
upon, in accordance with the quantity of rare metals and
the labour time incorporated in them. It was only an
approximation, but it was considered satisfactory, as
no one was careful any longer to fix their exact value.
That was a problem belonging to older times, a problem
which had gone to join the search for the philosopher's
stone.

Besides these industries, which still kept a basis of
utility, art workers devoted themselves, according to the
demand, to works of luxury, working to delight the eyes,
and to satisfy the varied tastes of a population becoming
more and more refined.

Those who received the objects of rationed production, bought them, in exchange for consumers' " notes "
for luxuries, which, as we have indicated, had preserved
for mere convenience, the numerical division in francs,
although it no longer corresponded to anything.

This manufacture of rationed goods and objects of
luxury did not imply, for the workers who took part in
it, a different remuneration from that obtained by all
the others; they received, like other workers, their
free card and their book of "notes" for rationed consumption.

The relations between producer and consumer were
therefore,—here as everywhere,—relations of equality and
solidarity; there was between them, a simple exchange
of services. The "social cheque" only intervened to fix
the importance of the exchange effected, to note the
point of equilibrium; but it did not yield, as was formerly the case with money, a profit for the advantage of
one of the contracting parties, a profit which had on
the other side a loss endured by the other party to the
contract.

This mechanism of an organization, which measured out the using of things according to the possibilities of the moment,—and, by means of rationing, established a balance in the enjoyment of luxury,—was applied to various services; amongst others, to the working of the theatres.

Artistes and the entire staff who assisted in any way whatever in the life of the theatre, were united into Trade Unions and federated; and, as in every other branch of social work, the Trade Union organization took over the management of halls for amusements.

There, as in any other profession, no privileges were granted to talent; the remuneration for all was equal to what it was in the other Trade Unions. This equality of treatment, this social levelling, which raised the disinherited to ease, offended certain theatrical professionals, who would have accommodated themselves to any kind of régime, on condition that comedians should be at the top in large type and privileged; they were indignant, they cried out that the era of barbarism had begun; and, joining the party of those formerly rich, they left the country.

These strolling players, men and women, clothed in vanity, were more set upon gain than inspired by artistic passion. As to the true artistes, those who saw in the theatre, not a more or less profitable exhibition, but art, pure and simple, they remained with the people; they sacrificed gold, and adapted themselves to the new surroundings.

The former organization of theatres was, of course, completely modified. Directors, sleeping partners, shareholders, were products of the Capitalist régime; and they foundered with it. With Commercialism disappeared a class of piece which degraded the word art, and had no other end in view than to attain to financial success by methods that were little less than indecent. As soon as actors no longer played for money, and the public were not attracted to amusements by the schemes of advertisers, their taste, until then artificially misled, was purified.

Companies of artistes were formed, according to the class and the kind of pieces,—musicians, dramatists, singers,—recruiting by sympathies, and forming parties which lived a common life, and worked on a given scene. The theatres, as well as accessories, scenery and costumes, become public property, were placed freely at their disposal. When there was a question of renewing any material, or of staging a new play, the theatrical group,—either directly, or through their Syndicate,—communicated with the societies of the trades who were able to do this kind of work, and obtained what they required. At least, it was so when they were quite satisfied that the future was secure. Before that, during the period of uncertainty and transition, when there was a fear that necessaries might be lacking, superfluities were neglected, and the theatres had to be satisfied with the stocks in the shops.

Representations were subject to a tax, paid in "notes" for luxuries. These receipts were not for the payment of the Company; these notes being unilateral, they were never more than a means of consumption, not a means of exchange; in this case, they acted as theatre tickets, not as money. Nevertheless, this "payment" had some use; it marked the degree of pleasure that the public found in this or that play, and it was looked upon as a compensation to the community for the "payment" received by the staff of the theatre. It would indeed have been unreasonable, if this staff had worked in vacuum, and had devoted themselves to work the uselessness of which was shown by the indifference of the people.

By the side of these Theatrical Companies, which organized regular performances and made a profession of it, there developed what previously were called Amateur Theatres. Little by little, these became general, and perhaps they will end by replacing the professional theatre.

This was a consequence of the reduction in the hours of work due to society. With this duration, already reduced,—and which tended to become still more reduced,—each one had leisure, and employed it according to his tastes, his aspirations, and his abilities.

The lack of means, the lack of halls, and of scenery, which before had caused the inferiority of these groups of amateurs, no longer existed; they had the same facilities for staging a performance as the professional companies. Besides, there did not arise wretched rivalries between these various groups; the germ of conflicts, Commercialism, being radically extirpated, their relations were as cordial as artistic vanities, which still sometimes showed themselves, would allow; the professionals did not fear the competition of the amateurs, and mutually aiding each other, they lived as comrades.

Literary productions were arranged for by the same kind of procedure; Trade Unions of literary men, and of journalists, were formed; who also took part, on a footing of equality, in the new life.

During the fighting period, the newspapers had been an excellent means for popularising ideas, a means of which the Revolutionists had largely availed themselves. In their hands, the daily papers had been made wholesome, and they had frankly fulfilled the function for which they were intended; to retail news, to be the vehicle for information and for reports of events.

In Capitalist society, the journals had acquitted themselves of this function in a way almost always bad; some of them had even attained the height of evil-doing; created by Capital, they lived by it, and for it; the kings of finance used them for their speculations, and their least evil was that of leading people astray.

The period of transition having passed, the daily papers had no longer any reason for existing in their old form. Their multiplicity was an anomaly, since there were no more businesses to keep up, no more advertisements to spread; since it was only a question of loyally giving information to the people, of submitting for their appreciation and judgment a record of the events which unfolded themselves from day to day.

The mechanism of the daily papers was therefore revolutionized from top to bottom : the newspaper became one with the telegraphic and telephonic News Agencies which were united and amalgamated with it.

Owing to the installations of telegraphs and telephones, combined with processes of printing and photographing at a distance, the News Agency transmitted in all directions the news that it received.

In the waiting rooms of stations, in restaurants, in meeting places, in clubs, at crossways,—everywhere where it was thought it would be useful,—receiving apparatus was installed; and as they happened, events printed themselves, photographed themselves, wrote themselves down luminously, announced themselves by the voice of telephones. It was a journal whose publication was continuous.

In addition to this permanent gazette, which, at all hours and every minute, brought events under the eyes of all, printed editions appeared, which were delivered free to all the public institutions, the libraries, the clubs, and the public halls.

Individuals could, by an expenditure in "notes" for luxuries, subscribe either to the printed editions, or to the permanent gazette. In this last case, receiving apparatus was installed at their homes, and the printed and photographic transmission continued without stopping, whilst the oral transmission was cut off or established, at the wish of the subscriber, by means of commutators.

Besides this publication, numerous journals and reviews appeared; literary, philosophic, scientific, sociological and others; edited by individuals or groups. The question of the freedom of the press did not arise,— the field for criticism was unlimited.

The method of publication was simple; the founders obtained subscribers, who subscribed in "notes" for luxuries; or else, with their personal share of notes, they paid the first cost. If there flowed in a sufficient number of subscriptions to cover the cost of publication, it continued. It even happened that the editor or editors of this journal or that review devoted themselves entirely to the management of their publication, if the number of subscribers grew sufficiently. They then left their professional Syndicate, and joined the Syndicates of journalists or literary men. Their social remuneration did not alter with this change, nor even with the success of their publication; at most they could get the repayment of the "notes" for luxuries that they had personally advanced in order to guarantee the first numbers. The only thing that was possible to them, if the number of subscribers increased so far as to surpass the limit of "cost," was to improve the publication. But if the founders of these private publications did not receive a higher rate of payment than anyone else, they had the pleasure of spreading their ideas, of entertaining, of interesting, of arousing their contemporaries.

The publication of various works, novels, poetry, scientific and historic works, and others, was arranged for in nearly the same way: the Book Syndicates undertook the publication of these works, and besides a large free distribution amongst groups and libraries, they were placed on sale, in the stores and social depôts, as articles of luxury. The author often had to cover the cost of printing his work from his personal notes for luxuries, on the condition that he would receive repayment in case of success. On the other hand, it also happened that he could, during a time proportionate to the importance of this success, stay away from his ordinary public work, which allowed him to devote himself entirely to the preparation of a new work.

Owing to this organization for the production of literary works, of art, and of luxuries, new works appeared without their author's having to struggle against surrounding hostility; without their having to overcome custom and prejudice, without Calvary to climb. No barrier was raised between them and the public. There was amongst individuals and in the groups a flexibility and a largeness of view which made them open to original ideas, to new influences; to dissension succeeded comradeship, and on every side there arose a calm good-will.

It would be wrong to conclude from this that there was a great change for the better in the human being. This modification was a question of environment. Men were neither better, nor worse; they were, just as before, neither good nor bad. So long as they had evolved in a society where personal interest incited to bad actions, where the good of one was woven from the evil of his neighbour, life had been a bitter struggle, and all the badness of the human beast had come to the surface. Henceforth, this· was altered; the social environment was such that the interest of each found its satisfaction in the satisfaction of that of his fellows; the more all were happy, the more each one was happy. It was therefore natural that good acts should dominate, since they were the sole creators of well-being, of joys, of pleasures.

In this way more and more, each one spent himself without calculating, without concerning himself with the reward he got in return for his work.

This evolution was marked by the development of groups of amateurs, which, as we have shown with regard to the theatre, were formed by the side of professional groups, and outside the work of the Unions, from which work their members were not excused. They sprang up in great numbers, created for the most diverse ends. Some were connected with artistic or literary work; others devoted themselves to the most varied researches; scientific, linguistic, historic, archeological....

These societies increased so much that the time could be foreseen when, owing to the initiative, activity and effort of their members, the greater part of the work of art and of science would lose its professional character, and would be performed after the ordinary daily work was done, by associations of volunteers, who would find in it pleasure, recreation, and intellectual satisfaction.

This tendency was the more natural since the limit of age for work, about the fiftieth year, liberated the human being at a period when his faculties, far from being worn out, still kept their freshness, lucidity, and vigour.

A new life opened before those who had retired. Although freed from their trade work, they could not settle down to inactivity; their muscles and their brain cells needed, in order to avoid stiffness and to preserve the perfect equilibrium of the organism, to have exercise, both physical and intellectual. They were allowed to satisfy this need, either by taking part in the work of those groups of ·amateurs which best suited their temperaments and their inclinations, or by taking a greater part in the management of Trade Union affairs.

These were, in fact, carried on by free agreement, by Delegations elected by General Assemblies, and by various Syndical, Federal, and Confederal committees, without these Delegations implying any exemption from work. Any reconstitution of bureaucracy, was carefully avoided; this would have had the inconvenience of immobilising a certain number of persons, by isolating, them from productive activity, and would have risked the crystallization of the social organism, instead of its being kept in a permanent state of evolution and progress. Consequently, the work of the Trade Unions did not imply any special remuneration. Those devoted themselves to this work who had a very strong liking for it.

Each one could the better attend to the work of preparing statistics, of co-ordinating the data of production, of traffic and of consumption, because the ordinary daily work left him leisure. It was therefore possible, without creating a special class of officials, to provide for the work of public administration; and those who, disinterestedly, undertook this work, did it easily, and with the necessary continuity and regularity.

CHAPTER XXIX.

ART AND RELIGION.

The Revolution had brought about a marvel which, up to the time of its triumph, had appeared as fantastic as the search for the squaring of the circle,—the friendly blending of opinions.

The reconciliation was effected on the economic ground, and the foundering of the whole superstructure of the State had cemented this accord and made it lasting. Men came to laugh at their past folly. They were astonished that they could have hated each other so much, persecuted each other so bitterly, under the foolish pretext of discordant political ideas.

The same phenomena were observed in religious matters. Peace was made. The disagreement in individual beliefs no longer set men quarrelling. They ceased to hurl invectives at each other because of philosophical or metaphysical differences; they no longer cursed each other because their ideas about the universe and the problems of life and death were opposed.

Thus, still more distant than political quarrels, more profoundly buried in the limbo of history, seemed the epochs of barbarism in the course of which men killed each other in the name of religion.

This harmony in the region of ideas, this intellectual pacification, flowed from the social whole and not from individual wills. The Revolution after having broken up formulas and dogmas, had not imposed any others. It had limited itself to clearing the ground and uprooting the weeds, in order that the good seed might grow. And it had pushed through strongly. The principle of respect for the individual and of purified egoism, which was the spirit and attractive force of the Revolution, at the same time that it had created well-being, had brought about this serene calm in the intellectual and moral domain; a calm which did not exclude the blossoming out of varied doctrines.

The Revolution, as we have seen, above all attacked institutions. In that way it differed from previous Revolutions; and it was that which gave it its social character.

It held privileged persons to be inoffensive, as soon as they were deprived of their privileges,—no more dangerous than rattlesnakes who have been deprived of their poison fangs.

It had struck at the State through its institutions; and it had forgotten the evil part played by its personel, when they had agreed to enter the ranks, to regenerate themselves by work.

It struck equally at the Church through its living works, in the buildings where its work of evil and perversity was crystallized. They acted with regard to this as they did towards all the powers of the past: its wealth returned to the people, and its priests had to set to work, their parasitism being as incompatible as that of any others with the new organization.

Indeed, when the Revolution broke out, the power of the Church seemed to be decayed; its separation from the State seemed to have enfeebled it. The younger generation was very indifferent to religious matters. In spite of that, the people remembered that it was the original source of all servitude,—that the State was only its elder brother,—therefore they were not so unwise as to treat it with disdain.

Nevertheless, there were two currents amongst the Revolutionists, not with regard to the attitude that they should adopt towards the Church as a privileged caste, on this point the agreement was unanimous: but on what should be done with regard to religious buildings.

One side considered the churches and cathedrals

as places that could be utilized in various ways,—for example as public halls, or as museums; they recalled that in 1793, the sans-culottes transformed them into meeting places,—and even into barns for forage and into stables; they added that in the Middle Ages, although these were an epoch of religious fervour, the churches were put to many uses;—markets were held there, and they were also play-houses. Consequently, as much for utility as from artistic feeling, they were in favour of the preservation of religious buildings.

Against this position, others arose with vigour. They pronounced in favour of pulling down without pity all religious edifices. And those who advocated this destruction were far from being men of a barbarian spirit. On the contrary, they were among the most cultivated. In them was no hatred of the building,—nothing but hatred of the superstition of which it was the symbol. They maintained that criticism does not kill religions; that their absurdity can be demonstrated, from generation to generation, in vain;—that they continue to have faithful followers, as long as the magnetic centre of attraction, the Church, remains standing. And, in proof, they added that the first Christians knew this: that they acted as true Revolutionists, as soon as they triumphed, they took care to throw down the pagan temples,—when it would have been quite easy for them to have purified and used them. The Christians, they observed, understood that a new faith must have new buildings;—and in that was their strength.

This Revolutionary sense that the Christians of the fourth century had, the partizans of the demolition of the churches did not find amongst the Revolutionists of 1793-4. "Wretched revolutionists, who in order to dechristianize France, limited themselves to overthrowing, with great ceremony, the good fellows in stone at the doors of churches, and thought themselves to be outrageously bold in transforming these into barns or meeting places. How much better inspired they would have been if they had guillotined fewer priests and pulled down more churches!...Therefore, some years after, the consequence of this mistake was seen: when the first Napoleon wanted to restore the Christian religion, nothing was easier: he had only to re-open the churches and purify them." And they concluded, "Let us learn the lesson of the past. Let us not fall again into the mistakes of our grandfathers!"

Against these tactics the lovers of beautiful stonework were indignant; they pleaded for respect to the cathedrals, where there was crystallized the soul of our fathers,—who were not always very good Catholics.

Between these two contradictory arguments, after vigorous discussions, agreement was often arrived at by a compromise: it was agreed to respect the buildings that symbolised an epoch, and expressed its art; and to be without pity for the wretched constructions built by architects who were as much lacking in art as in faith.

In many centres de-christianization was thus prepared for. But in these circumstances, as in all others, the spirit of the Revolution was manifested: it set out to modify man by the transformation of the environment. And it was for that reason that, whilst detesting superstitions and whilst pulling down churches, the Revolutionists respected the faith of each individual.

This respect for beliefs gave rise, in the midst of Catholicism, to a modification of which the first symptoms were already shown during the Capitalist régime, on the morrow of the separation of the Churches and the State. A certain number of priests, principally in the country, strove to improve their incomes by devoting themselves to work. Some became bee keepers, others makers of preserved vegetables and fruits, or even cabinet makers and book binders. They had thus, more or less, ceased to be parasites, whilst remaining priests. They were therefore a little prepared for the life of the new society, from which parasitic beings were eliminated. Whilst the bishops and priests of the great centres, used to the artificial life which had been theirs until then, found themselves helpless, the village priests, who were already half workers, adapted themselves without much trouble to the new conditions; they continued between times to fulfil their religious functions. And this without anyone putting hindrances in their way. Whoever wanted sermons went to hear them.

Besides, religious indifference continued to increase. Before the Revolution, the spirit of examination had already shaken Catholicism from the inside: the priests who had set to work felt themselves more independent of episcopal authority, and becoming bold, they gave expression to their doubts; to the absurdities of Catholicism they opposed the words of the New Testament, and glided insensibly into a vague Christianity, with very little orthodoxy about it. This movement was hastened by the Revolution.

The important point was that all religious castes should be broken irrevocably; that no one arguing that he was a priest, protestant minister, or rabbi, should be able to claim an exemption from work, and live without doing anything, at the expense of his fellows. This was the chief point. This gained, everyone was free to believe or not to believe; to be Christian or Spiritualist, Buddhist or Theosophist. This was an individual matter, without any possible social reaction.

Besides, with the increase of well-being, still more than with education, the faith in creeds declined amongst the population. Formerly, many sought a consolation for the miseries of life in prostration at the feet of altars; as others hoped to find it at the bottom of a glass of alcohol. Religion and alcoholism played the same part as narcotics,—the one more intellectual, the other more material,—to which many desperate people had recourse, choosing one or the other, according to their moral condition, their degree of development.

Material security, henceforth assured, contributed to lessen these deplorable weaknesses. Alcoholism disappeared, and superstition lost ground.

Indeed, although life appeared more and more radiant, the road was not cleared of all briars and thorns. Beyond the comfort which now extended to all, the problem of happiness evaded social foresight, being a question entirely moral, entirely one of feeling.

In spite of that, in this psychological domain,—as everywhere else,—the effects of the transformation were felt ; moral suffering, emotional pain, intellectual anguish, were less sharp, less vivid : not being increased by misery and the difficulties of existence, they were in part tempered and blunted by the extension of well-being.

Manners and customs were rapidly modified. Their evolution, already outlined before the Revolution, was hastened.

During the Capitalist system, the struggle that the Trade Union organisations had carried on against alco-holism had been active, and effective. To give only one example, it will suffice to recall that before 1906, among navvies, until then very little organized, were counted a considerable percentage of heavy drinkers. Now a few years later, when the Syndicate of Parisian Navvies had organised the greater part of the members engaged in this occupation, alcoholism had considerably lessened; whilst, by the efforts of the Union, their wages had been raised by 25 per cent. The navvies drank less because they had gained well-being ; and because, at the same time, their sense of honour and self-respect was increased.

This development of temperance was not special to navvies. It was observed in other occupations. Thus, owing to the Syndicalist propaganda, drinking establish-ments had seen their number of customers decrease.

With the Revolution, the wine sellers, whose shops had been called the "poor man's drawing-room," had to disappear. And that the more quickly as they no longer supplied a need.

Whilst the workers had to drudge at intensive and excessive work, they demanded from alcohol the spur necessary to keep up overwork ; besides this after a long tiring day, or in order to return as late as possible to their often miserable homes, it was to the public house that they were too often accustomed to go in search of recreation. There, as a change from their daily occupation, they became absorbed in card-playing, or stretched their limbs with a game of billiards. Besides, the public house was for them a meeting place, the office of various societies and groups to which they belonged.

Since there were no longer any poor, it was natural that the establishments which had served them as "drawing-rooms" should disappear.

Habits were modified therefore, at the same time as the surroundings, and at least as much.

In the first place, they lived more the life of the family, which Capitalist Industrialism had rendered difficult,—and even abolished in some districts,—by subjecting to work not only the man, but the woman, and even the child. As there were no more unhealthy hovels, as all the houses were comfortable and pleasant, they tried the charm of living in their own homes.

As to the general places of assembly, which were substituted for the wine-shops, for the cafés, and for the bars, they had a distant likeness to the former clubs : one could get refreshments there, but they were centres for conversation, for reading, for meetings, more than for drinking. Many were installed in former cafés and similar establishments ; and, besides the fact that the libraries there had partly dethroned the cellar, they were distinguished by their artistic arrangement.

Some of these rooms were ornamented with furniture, pictures, sculptures, and articles of vertu of the most diverse ages, whilst others were expert reconstructions of special epochs : some evoking mediaeval periods ; others recalling the epoch of Moliére, or that of Diderot ; others according to the taste of 1793, or the style of 1830, or the Second Empire.

These reconstructions, which showed the good taste of the workers who presided over their arrangement, had been made at small cost, with the spoils of the collections made by the previously wealthy classes which had not been able to find a place in the museums. There were modern works there which some of the bourgeois, rich in money and poor in intellect, had bought at absurd prices, believing them to be ancient. The authenticity of these shams, which showed the cleverness and knowledge of the workers who had executed them, was traced, and the credit for them was, as far as possible, restored to their authors, and some of these works bore their name, or that of the workshop from which they came.

It was an ironic criticism of the fashions and vanities of Capitalist society; which, at the same time, underlined how much at this epoch of Commercialism, cheating, deceit, and falsehood were in honour.

It was a burlesque revision that the Revolutionists made when they took possession of special collections, heaped up by the privileged ones of Capitalist society for snobbery or ostentation, sometimes with some thought of speculation, and not through any real passion for art. Workmen and artists, qualified by their knowledge and ability, carefully sifted out these collections, and in the most noted, they found an abundance of shams. A judicious choice was made, and whilst some of these works went to enrich museums and libraries, the rest was used for the decoration of public halls, holiday retreats, and various places of meeting.

It is superfluous to add that museums ceased to be the incoherent piles of artistic riches, that they had been previously ; incomprehensible for the people, in general wretchedly educative and hardly more recreative for them. They were re-arranged, transformed, not by red-tape officials, but by men who were lovers of art and had good taste.

The care with which they proceeded to carry out this work showed the new impulse which artistic ideas were receiving : in becoming generalized they were refined, and gained in simplicity, truth and purity; and they were no longer altered by considerations of Commercialism, which had formerly led them astray, or even dominated them.

In this work of removing private collections, which was but the application of its principles of social expropriation, the Revolution made no innovation: it only imitated,—only followed the example of previous régimes.

How, indeed, during the nineteenth century, were the national museums enriched? In the first place, by the plundering which was shamelessly carried on by the generals of the Republic and First Empire in the course of their raids across Europe; they took by the right of conquest, without embarrassment, both what they found in museums and in private houses.

The museums were also enriched by expropriations from the clergy, and from the religious orders, and by those which took place after the separation of the Churches from the State.

Now, the action was of the same kind, but vaster; it was Capitalist property which was brought back to its collective source.

In the majority of cases, the sumptuous palaces of millionaires were transformed into hospitals or houses for the aged. Without stripping them of their furniture, it was nevertheless natural that the works of art which adorned them should be reserved for the museums. This was bringing them back to their true destination, for they had not been created in order to be hidden away, but to delight the eyes, to awake emotions, and to be admired.

Before the Revolution of 1789-93, art was essentially a Royal privilege. Later it became the monopoly of Capital. With the new Revolution, it was going to be universalized, humanized.

One after the other, the art of priests, the art of kings, the art of capitalists, had dominated. The hour had sounded for the art of humanity.

Art, with science, would fill up the void left in men's souls by the death of religions. These had cursed life, cursed beauty, condemned the senses and their joyous expansion, had exalted abasement and renunciation.

Life was going to take its revenge. The human being was no longer rivetted to the chain of wages; his aim in life passed beyond the mere struggle for a living. Industry was no longer his master, but his servant. Freed from all hindrances, he would be able to develop without constraint.

And there was no need to fear that the level of art would be lowered as it became universalized. Far from this, it would gain in extent and depth. Its domain would be unlimited! It would enter into all production. It would not restrict itself to painting large canvasses, to sculpturing marble, to moulding bronze. There would be art in everything. It would be in the water pitcher, as well as in the great decorations of a Puvis de Chavannes; in the smallest everyday things, as well as in a group by Constantin Meunier.

And we should no longer see great artists stifled by misery, lost in the quicksands of indifference; as was too often the case formerly.

Who could number the artists of high and rare value who,—like the inventors,—suffered from Capitalist society, died unrecognized, killed by hunger; or disappeared without leaving a trace, for want of favourable surroundings?

And how many amongst those who broke through, had to struggle terribly, enduring the worst sufferings, physical and mental? Still, were these not fortunate? . . . . How many others, after having struggled with anxieties and difficulties, after having endured troubles without end, died still suffering;—and only became very great artists after their death?

CHAPTER XXX.

THE FREEING OF WOMAN.

As a matter of fact, if hearts and minds had been sounded, very probably not a few of those who had formerly benefited by Capitalist society would have been found who, in their inmost hearts, cursed the Revolution; and who submitted to it, because they could not do anything else: carried away by the current, too weak to overcome social destinies, not being in the humour to revolt against them, they gave way, and did not endeavour to resist.

This is what had taken place during all previous Revolutions. The same thing happened now. There are, in the world, a number of passive beings who adapt themselves without resisting, who follow the pioneers, provided these are the winners.

This plasticity of the multitude, which, during epochs of exploitation and oppression, had assured the triumph of the ruling classes, was now placed at the service of the Revolution. Owing to it, the efforts of the Revolutionists had a more fortunate and easy end. With the least possible friction, habits, customs, and ways of living were profoundly transformed.

One of the characteristic signs of this transformation was the movement from the great cities. Swiftly, the congestion in these huge human agglomerations was removed, and the population swarmed towards the outskirts.

This tendency to decentralisation was already noticeable before the Revolution; the suburbs of tentacular cities,—of Paris chiefly,—were covered with houses and chalets, with which the working population were enamoured, glad to enjoy a little fresh air, and to acquire a home that would not be at the mercy of the owners of flats. The necessities of their work, the cost of travelling to and fro,—and also financial impossibilities, had hindered this decentralisation and lessened its scope. Now that these difficulties no longer existed; now that by the suppression of Commercialism, of stock jobbing, and all the complications of Capitalist society, life became simplified and lightened, the reason for the existence of city centralization largely disappeared. Therefore the exodus towards the country increased.

Parallel with this flight towards a life half like a country life, more individualized, more isolated, there were developed customs of living more in common, with a more and more pronounced industrialization of house- hold work.

The contradiction that seemed at first to exist between these two tendencies was superficial; in both cases there was a manifestation of the strong desire for independence, the need of which was felt by all. Only each one sought and found this independence in the conditions of living which suited him best.

In town centres, through the influence of woman, who wished to free herself from household drudgery, many industries developed, which formerly had remained embryonic for want of favourable conditions, either because these industries could not sufficiently remunerate the capital employed, or because the public had found their services too expensive.

These inconveniences no longer existed: the only thing that had to be taken into account was utility. Thus works were carried out and discoveries applied which would have been impossible under the Capitalist system, because they had been thought too expensive, in comparison with the return obtained.

In household matters, they endeavoured to industrialize the tedious work which, formerly, amongst the richer classes, was taken charge of by servants, and amongst the proletarians, was done by the wife.

For example, the cleaning of boots was done mechanically, by machines invented as a matter of fact long ago, and which now abounded in public places and large buildings. They could also do by machinery the drudgery of cleaning rooms, and this too had been known for a long time. In the same way, the work of washing up plates and dishes, and of cleaning clothes, was no longer laid on human labour. This work was industrialized, and laundry work also ; in each street, or each block of houses, there was installed an equipment for mechanical cleaning, and workers who undertook to take away and bring home again anything that needed cleaning. Besides this, in the food stores, a whole series of machines,—the use of which could not become general under the Capitalist system,—had come into ordinary use.

The preparation of meals no longer involved the unattractive smells of the former kitchen ; one could have sent home, from the public kitchens, the dishes that had been ordered; or better still, could have one's meals either in company, or alone, in the public restaurants, which were near at hand, and were very comfortably fitted up.

In this order of things, many conveniences and arrangements, which it is needless to enumerate, had been put into use, and many others were on the way to being tried.

Woman, therefore, was no longer compelled to be, according to Proud'hon's blunt saying, "a housekeeper or a courtizan"; neither had she to follow the childish hobby of the Suffragettes who saw no freedom for her except in the conquest of the vote. Woman could remain woman, in the most feminine and human sense of the word, without having to imitate man, without seeking to supplant him in his work.

Many occupations were undertaken by women, and this would remain the case for a long time. Only she was freed, more and more, from all the labours to which she had been subjected in bourgeois society, not because of her fitness, but because her work was paid for at a lower rate than that of men.

In the new organization it was thought useless to fix for women, in the same way as for men, the moral obligation to give a definite time to work. It was considered that her high function of possible maternity freed her from all other social duties. Woman was therefore entirely free to dispose of herself, to work or not, whether she consented to maternity or not. She no more misused this freedom than men abused it. She reserved for herself occupations in accordance with her abilities. In addition, she occupied herself with various works, such as the education of young children, and the care of the sick. Naturally, she worked for a shorter time and took more rest than men, and as a general rule, she quitted work at the first signs of maternity.

Woman had not, in the name of naturalness, renounced beautiful materials, adornments and ornaments. It did not displease her, after having adorned her mind, to beautify her body. But she was no longer the slave of fashion,—the disappearance of Commercialism had brought about its ruin,—to the benefit of good taste. Henceforth, she dressed herself with studied refinement, she thought out her adornments, and knew how to suit them to herself. In that she showed her greater grace, and no longer in the exhibition of expensive dress that displayed wealth, and not good taste.

Women, grouped, like men into Trade Unions, were on a footing of equality with them; and, like them, they shared in social administration.

This material and moral independence of women had as a first reaction the effect of purifying and ennobling sexual relationships. Henceforth, mutual attractions were the result of sympathy and love, and not of arrangements more or less revolting. The hateful marriage market, so common formerly, became unknown. Men no longer hunted for a dowry. The young girl no longer sought for someone to maintain her,—legally or otherwise. All the falsehoods, all the baseness, all the promiscuities and the foulness which the desire for wealth and the fear of poverty caused,—pestilential flowers of inequality,—had disappeared, now that well-being was the common lot.

Maternity was no longer feared. Woman, educated, understanding life, accepted it at the hour of her choice. The child could be born. The mother would be free to bring it up herself, or to confide it to the half-maternal care of her companions. She was certain that the little child would be welcomed,—there was a good place for him at the social banquet.

CONCLUSION.

We have come to the end of our task. We have recalled,—too imperfectly we know,—the great Revolutionary period which has transformed France, bringing to it peace, well-being, freedom!

Of course, this new society is not perfect. Many criticisms could be made. There are still difficulties and friction. There are still things to be desired in the system of production, as well as in the system of distribution....

Yes, the ideal has not yet been reached!—Will it ever be?

But, if there still exist shadows in the picture, at least the evil of the misery caused by poverty is vanquished; and the road of the future is cleared, is free from barriers.

No coercive force can set itself against this evolution.

As no one has any longer an interest in perpetuating the customs of the past; as no repressive institution can, —as the State did for centuries,—stifle new aspirations, crush progress in the bud, the advance will go on without hindrance.

In proportion as such improvements, such modes of living, are found preferable, their adoption will take place automatically,—without their supporters having to struggle against those who do not wish to have them, and without the latter being able to oppose the former.

THE BRIGHTER DAY.

In all domains, whether it be in the economic or in the moral field,—everywhere,—the Revolution has left its fruitful imprint.

A friendly human being,—a result of the new environment, of the new atmosphere,—is substituted for the human beast of the Capitalist period; man has become good, because he has no longer any interest in being bad!

Instead of struggle, rivalry, discord, rending, and war between human beings, are agreement, good feeling, mutual aid. Battle is only continued in the domain of nature; on this ground, working together, men overcome the adverse forces, so that they serve them.

And now that all misgivings have vanished; now that the Revolution is reverberating across the world, bringing equally to all peoples peace, freedom, well-being; now that no danger, either within or without, is to be feared,—now life is sweet and good to live!

Joy rises higher! Joy drawn from the certainty that the Revolution cannot be undone, that all reaction is impossible.

This certainty lights up the horizon.

And before man regenerated freed from all chains, from all servitudes, opens out, wide and straight, the road of the Future.

234

Freedom has to be won afresh every morning.

EDWARD CARPENTER.—"Towards Democracy."

O strange new wonderful justice! But for whom shall we gather the gain?
For ourselves and for each of our fellows, and no hand shall labour in vain.

Then all mine and all thine shall be ours, and no more shall any man crave
For riches that serve for nothing but to fetter a friend for a slave.

And what wealth then shall be left us when none shall gather gold
To buy his friend in the market, and pinch and pine the sold?

Nay, what save the lovely city, and the little house on the hill,
And the wastes and the woodland beauty, and the happy fields we till.

And the homes of ancient stories, the tombs of the mighty dead;
And the wise men seeking out marvels, and the poets teeming head;

And the painter's hand of wonder; and the marvellous fiddle-bow,
And the banded choirs of music:—all those that do and know.

For all these shall be ours and all men's, nor shall any lack a share
Of the toil and the gain of living in the days when the world grows fair.

WILLIAM MORRIS.—"The Day is Coming."

Forsooth, brothers, fellowship is heaven, and lack of fellowship is hell: fellowship is life, and lack of fellowship is death: and the deeds that ye do upon the earth, it is for fellowship's sake that ye do them, and the life that is in it, that shall live on and on for ever, and each one of you part of it, while many a man's life upon the earth from the earth shall wane.

Therefore, I bid you not dwell in hell but in heaven, or while ye must, upon earth, which is a part of heaven, and forsooth no foul part.

WILLIAM MORRIS.—"A Dream of John Ball."

Ἵνα Πάντες ἓν ὦσι. . . .

Jesus of Nazareth.

BIBLIOGRAPHY.

This book by Emile Pataud and Emile Pouget contains a clear statement of the Revolutionary Syndicalist position, by two of the best known, and most active men in the European Syndicalist movement.

None of the various works on Syndicalism which have been published in England, including those by Ramsay Macdonald, Sydney and Beatrice Webb, and H. G. Wells, gives a complete statement of Revolutionary Syndicalist aims and methods ; on many fundamental points there has been much misunderstanding of Syndicalist views.

There is a considerable literature in all countries which advocates the ideas of the Non-Governmental school of Socialist thought, such as in English the various works by Edward Carpenter, Peter Kropotkin, William Morris, and many other writers.

"The Conquest of Bread," by Peter Kropotkin, is published by Chapman & Hall, 10/6. An American Edition, 5/-, can be obtained from the Freedom Press, 127 Ossulston St., London, N.W.

"News from Nowhere," by William Morris, is published by Reeves & Turner, 2/- and 1/-.

Those wishing to study further the progress and development of the Syndicalist section of this school should consult, amongst other publications, the books and pamphlets by Tom Mann and a book by A. D. Lewis.

"From Single Tax to Syndicalism," by Tom Mann, is published by Guy Bowman, 4 Maude Terrace, Walthamstow, London, E., 2/6 and 1/-.

"Syndicalism and the General Strike," by Arthur D. Lewis, is published by T. Fisher Unwin, 7/6.

PERIODICALS.

"The Daily Herald," London, ½d., "the fighting Labour Daily," gives all progressive schools a fair platform, and takes a wide view of the Labour movement, so as to include all the elements that make for a higher civilisation.

"Wilshire's Magazine," 1 Cheapside, Golder's Green, London, N.W., 1d. or 2 cents. monthly, gives well written expositions of the Syndicalist point of view.

"The Syndicalist and Amalgamation News," 4 Maude Terrace, Walthamstow, London, E., 1d. monthly, the organ of the Industrial Syndicalist Education League, contains articles by Tom Mann, Guy Bowman, and other well known English Syndicalists.

"The Syndicalist," 1000 S. Paulina Street, Chicago, Ill., 2 cts., fortnightly, is a powerful advocate of the movement in America.

"Freedom," 127 Ossulston St., London, N.W., 1d. monthly, contains well thought out articles on various theoretical points connected with the Non-Governmental school of Socialism.

"The Irish Homestead," 34 Lower Abbey Street, Dublin, 1d. weekly, has excellently written articles on Co-operation as applied to Rural Reconstruction.

"The Co-operative News," Long Millgate, Manchester, 1d. weekly, and "The Scottish Co-operator," Glasgow, 1d. weekly, represent the ideals of English and Scottish Co-operators, and the progress made in applying these ideals to Distribution and Production.

The above is of course not a complete list, but contains some of the best known Papers.

We have translated this book for English speaking people, not because we are in complete agreement on all points with our comrades, Emile Pataud and Emile Pouget ; on a few incidental points we strongly differ, for instance, the description of the Suffragettes does not apply to the majority of those brave women who are striving to obtain the vote in England, as most of them only regard the vote as a symbol of sex equality ; in other parts of the book the authors fully accept this status for women who join equally with men in the administration of public affairs, and are freed from all economic slavery.

We think also they too readily accept the latest medical fad of serum treatment, overlooking also the cruelty to sentient beings which it involves ; but we feel the book is too valuable an addition to the Syndicalist's library to wish to overload it with notes on controversial points. These may be dealt with elsewhere.

We wish to thank Madame Marie D. Korchoff for her valuable help in getting this MS. ready for the press.

C. & F. C.